055870-2

THE
BEATLES

ALBUM FILE AND
DISCOGRAPHY
REVISED EDITION

THE
BEATLES
ALBUM FILE AND
COMPLETE DISCOGRAPHY

REVISED EDITION

JEFF RUSSELL

BLANDFORD

Blandford Press
An imprint of Cassell
Villiers House, 41–47 Strand, London WC2N 5TE

Original editions published in Great Britain 1982 by Blandford Press, Poole
Reprinted 1983
This revised edition first published 1989
Reprinted 1989, 1990

This revised edition only distributed in the United States by
Sterling Publishing Co. Inc.
387 Park Avenue South, New York, NY 10016–8810

Distributed in Australia by
Capricorn Link (Australia) Pty Ltd
PO Box 665, Lane Cove, NSW 2066

ISBN 0–7137–2065–4

British Library Cataloguing in Publication Data
Russell, Jeff
    The Beatles album file and complete
    discography — Rev. ed.
    1. Pop music. Beatles — Discographies
    I. Title
    016.7899′1245′00922

Typeset by Fakenham Photosetting Ltd
Printed in England by Clays Ltd, St Ives plc

Contents

Acknowledgements

I should like to thank Polydor International GmbH for their courteous permission to reproduce the sleeve of The Early Tapes Of The Beatles; Charley Records for their courteous permission to reproduce the sleeve of The Decca Sessions 1.1.62; A.F.E.(UK) Ltd, for their courteous permission to reproduce the sleeve of The Beatles Historic Sessions; EMI Records Ltd, for their courteous permission to reproduce all EMI, Parlophone, Capitol and Apple record sleeves; Omnibus Press, London and Quick Fox, New York for their courteous permission to reproduce the quotes on pages 17, 56, 68, 69, 83 and 87 which are from *The Beatles In Their Own Words* compiled by Miles.

I should like to thank the following people for the help and information they supplied during the updating of this book: Fiona Weaver (UK); Kevin Howlett of BBC Radio One (UK); Leslie Wood (UK); Charles Wooley (UK); Chris Michie (UK/USA); Donald Leighty (USA); Rick Fitzgerald (USA); Phillip Dyke (Australia); Manoel dos Santos Dantas (Rio de Janeiro, Brazil) and Aldo Jiménez of Radio Alvorado (Rio de Janeiro, Brazil).

I should also like to thank Mike Heatley of EMI Records' International Division for his assistance and information.

J.P.R.
Liverpool.

1 The Beatles on Record

The Beatles were the biggest phenomenon the world of music has ever known. Their music brings joy and excitement to millions of people world-wide, and never before or since has so much been said or written about any recording artists. They captured the hearts and affection of the world's youth and created a mystique that fascinates fans even now, nearly twenty years after they split up and went their different ways.

In those twenty years many books have been published, giving various accounts of their success. Their history has been well documented in a number of those books, particularly in Hunter Davies's excellently researched *The Beatles : The Authorised Biography*, and Mark Lewisohn's two books, *The Beatles Live!* and *The Beatles' Recording Sessions*. They are all excellent books within the realms of their content, but unfortunately for Beatles' fans world-wide those books, despite their excellence, can never be added to. The Beatles, as a group, no longer exist and with the death of John Lennon in 1980 can never exist as a group again. There is therefore very little that can be added to their history that hasn't already been written; they will never perform live again and there will never be another Beatles' recording session. So what's left? What's left is what the Beatles were all about — their music and, in particular, their records.

The Beatles had numerous recording sessions to produce those records; they performed the songs hundreds of times world-wide and if they hadn't made those records their history would have been extremely limited.

This book deals solely with those records. Not the records which were made individually by John, Paul, George or Ringo after they split up, but the records which the Beatles recorded as a group. During the sessions which produced those records the Beatles also recorded a wealth of material which, for various reasons, remains unreleased. However, the release of further Beatles' records will always remain a possibility.

Within the pages of this book you will find information relating to every song the Beatles officially issued on record, the titles of both albums and individual tracks, release dates, composer credits, timings and comments on each track with details of who plays and sings what, together with odd bits and pieces of information included here and there.

Some previous discussions of the Beatles' songs have fallen into the trap of losing sight of the original music while attempting highly technical explanations and over-analysis of the lyrics. In this book, there is a return to that original music — it's there and it will always be there, to *listen* to and enjoy, not to analyse.

Throughout the book, attempts have been made to identify the actual known writer of a song — John Lennon or Paul McCartney — even when the official and registered composing credit is Lennon and McCartney.

The first part of the book has been set out chronologically, with the albums in their basic order of release in Britain and internationally. The inevitable exceptions to this are The Beatles First, The Decca Sessions 1.1.62 and The Beatles' Historic Sessions.

Although not issued until 1964, 1987 and 1981, respectively, these albums were recorded prior to the Beatles' EMI/Parlophone signing, and have therefore been included before the Please Please Me album. Also, the Magical Mystery Tour and Hey Jude albums, although not issued in Britain until 1976 and 1979, respectively, have been placed in their international order of release, i.e. as the follow-up albums to Sgt. Pepper's Lonely Hearts Club Band and Abbey Road. Also included is The Beatles Box, which although not generally available in the stores, is obtainable through EMI's mail order division, World Records. Also covered for interest and completeness is The Songs Lennon and McCartney Gave Away, an album including songs, written by Lennon and McCartney and recorded by other artists, but never issued by the Beatles.

Following the chapters on British albums are chapters on the records released in the USA by Capitol Records. The albums discussed are those from Meet The Beatles to Revolver plus the American Rarities and 20 Greatest Hits — fourteen albums altogether. These are also in chronological order and each track is usefully cross-referenced to a British album. These fourteen albums are the only American albums listed separately, as all albums from Sgt. Pepper's Lonely Hearts Club Band onwards were issued in basically the same order world-wide.

After the album reviews, Chapter 50 *The Alternative Versions* discusses the alternative versions of recordings issued by the Beatles around the world. These have been a favourite topic amongst Beatles' fans for years. In Chapter 51 *The Unreleased Tracks* there are listed some 200 songs recorded by the Beatles in one form or another, but never released. Chapter 52, *The Non-Album Tracks*, covers those recordings issued (in one form or another) which are not yet available on album.

Lastly comes the Discography, giving a complete listing of all Beatles' records released in the UK, USA and Australia up to December 1988.

Also included, both in the main text and the Discography, are the compact discs released internationally by EMI during 1987/8. The contents of these, which are based on the British albums, are the same world-wide. So whether you are in London, New York, Sydney or indeed wherever you are, you can play your compact discs with the knowledge that everyone, for the first time ever, is able to listen to exactly the same compact disc.

Since the first edition of this book in 1982, in which was predicted the release of How Do You Do It? and Leave My Kitten Alone as a single (which didn't appear), EMI have tried on at least one other occasion (January 1985) to release both these and a further eleven unreleased tracks as an album entitled Sessions. This, together with a single featuring Leave My Kitten Alone and an alternative unreleased version of Ob La Di, Ob La Da, didn't make it to the stores either.

Like Beatles' fans everywhere my hopes of seeing the Beatles re-form were destroyed by the radio announcement which I heard at 7.00 a.m. GMT on Tuesday 9 December 1980. With the murder of John Lennon in New York, shortly after his return to the music scene after five years of self-imposed exile, a little bit died in all of us.

Ironically, his death led to Paul, George and Ringo getting together to record a George Harrison song, All Those Years Ago, as a tribute to John.

My tribute to John Lennon, and to the memory of the Beatles, is this book — written by a fan for other fans everywhere as a guide to Beatles records and, for the newer generation, as an introduction to the fabulous sound of the Beatles.

Jeff Russell
Liverpool.

THE BRITISH ALBUMS

UK Release : 10 December 1984
Polydor 823 701–2
US Release : 10 December 1984
Polydor 823 701–2
Intl CD No : 823 701–2
Producer : Bert Kaempfert
Running Time : 40:17

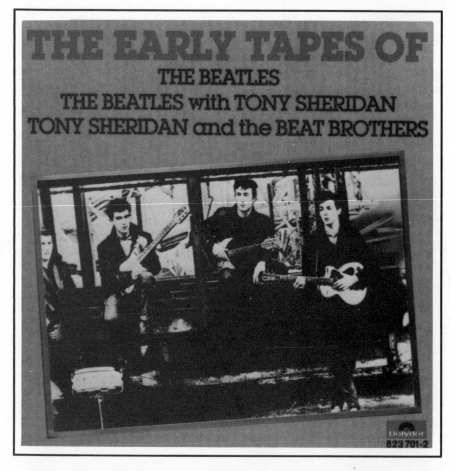

Ain't She Sweet; Cry For A Shadow; When The Saints Go Marching In; Why; If You Love Me,
Baby; (What'd I Say); Sweet Georgia Brown; (Let's Dance); (Ruby Baby); My Bonnie; Nobody's
Child; (Ready Teddy); (Ya Ya Parts 1+2); (Kansas City).

The Beatles' first album, recorded in Hamburg in 1961, features eight recordings made by the Beatles in their pre-Parlophone days. Of those eight, there are only two that could honestly be called Beatles' recordings. The remaining six feature the Beatles backing Tony Sheridan. To make the album worth while Polydor included a further four Tony Sheridan recordings backed by another group called The Beat Brothers, who were not, as many thought, the Beatles recording under a pseudonym.

The history behind this album is similar to the story of the meeting between the Beatles and Brian Epstein, only in this case it was Bert Kaempfert. Kaempfert, having heard reports of a group playing around the clubs in Hamburg's red light district who were attracting a great deal of interest, went to investigate. Arriving at the Top Ten Club in the notorious Reeperbahn, he witnessed an impressively enthusiastic group, Tony Sheridan and The Beatles. Kaempfert was aware of the effect they had on the audience. What he was not aware of at the time, however, was that Tony Sheridan and The Beatles were not all members of the same group. He approached them and finally persuaded them to sign a three-year recording contract with him.

The first recordings the Beatles made with Bert Kaempfert were My Bonnie, When The Saints Go Marching In, Why (Can't You Love Me Again) — (all featuring Tony Sheridan on lead vocal) and Cry For A Shadow (a Harrison-Lennon instrumental). The line-up for these recordings was John Lennon, Paul McCartney, George Harrison and Pete Best (Stuart Sutcliffe having left the group to study art), together with Tony Sheridan. The first release from this session was a single. My Bonnie/The Saints, which was released in Germany on Polydor 24 673 in June 1961. The record sold extremely well and the Beatles were soon in the German Top Ten.

A week after their first session the Beatles returned for a further recording session with Polydor at which they recorded Ain't She Sweet (featuring a lead vocal from John Lennon), If You Love Me, Baby, Nobody's Child and Sweet Georgia Brown (all of which have a lead vocal from Tony Sheridan). With the exception of Sweet Georgia Brown, which was included on the Ya Ya E.P. (Polydor H 21485) issued in Germany in October 1962, these new titles remained unissued until 1964. Then, after the success of the Beatles' first five singles and first two L.P.s on Parlophone, Polydor resurrected all eight tracks. Initially they issued Ain't She Sweet/Take Out Some Insurance On Me Baby (Polydor NH 52317) on 29 May 1964, but amidst a host of Parlophone No. 1s, this reached only No. 29 in the British charts. The remaining six Polydor tracks were also issued as singles but none reached the top fifty in Britain. Polydor, determined to have some success with their Beatles' recordings, took all eight tracks plus four recorded by Tony Sheridan and The Beat Brothers and subsequently compiled the album The Beatles First (Polydor 236 201) (US release : The Beatles — Circa 1960 — In The Beginning Polydor 24–4504) again without much luck. The album has been reissued a number of times, with an equal number of titles, the most recent being on compact disc as both The Beatles First and The Early Tapes Of The Beatles (Polydor 823 701-2) which also includes a further two Sheridan/Beat Brothers tracks, Ready Teddy and Kansas City and is the version of the album used here. Although the Beatles' recordings featured here hint at what was to come on future recordings, they are really only of interest to Beatles' collectors, mainly for their historical rather than musical value.

In addition to these eight recordings a further tape reputed to be from these sessions came to light in 1985. The contents have yet to be revealed and at present are open to speculation, but the tape is thought to contain at least two tracks which feature John Lennon on lead vocal : Some Other Guy and Rock and Roll Music.

Ain't She Sweet (Yellen–Ager)   2:12

Recorded : 22/23 June 1961, Hamburg-Harburg-Friedrich-Ebert-Halle, Hamburg, West Germany
The Beatles

John Lennon : Rhythm Guitar and Solo Vocal
Paul McCartney : Bass Guitar
George Harrison : Lead Guitar
Pete Best : Drums

This opening track features John Lennon's first officially recorded vocal performance. (This is the only recording on the album to feature any of the Beatles on lead vocal.) John gives the song the distinctive Lennon treatment; his raw nasal vocal almost jumps out of the speakers. The instrumental backing accentuates John's vocal without imposing on it. Overall the recording comes across well, although in places it sounds rather shallow. This was no doubt due to Bert Kaempfert's production techniques which, although flawless with his own orchestra, just do not seem to work with a beat group. Eighteen months later they were to meet George Martin, who was to bring out that distinctive 'Beatles' sound'.

Cry For A Shadow (Harrison–Lennon)   2:23

Recorded : 22/23 June 1961, Hamburg-Harburg-Friedrich-Ebert-Halle, Hamburg, West Germany
The Beatles

John Lennon : Rhythm Guitar
Paul McCartney : Bass Guitar
George Harrison : Lead Guitar
Pete Best : Drums

Co-written by George and John, this instrumental is the only published (or unpublished) Harrison–Lennon collaboration. The opening and main theme was thought up by George Harrison; John Lennon later added the rhythm sections. It is an interesting, although simple, piece of music consisting of opening and main theme, which is played through three times, with a few other bars added for the ending. George Harrison's lead guitar playing here is by far the best on the album (he is not given the opportunity on other tracks). The music is given more excitement by various screams and shouts from the four Beatles. The title was not chosen until after the recordings were finished. The toss of a coin decided that Cry For A Shadow and not Beatle Bop should be used. The Beatles had, in any case, felt that the latter title was rather coy so it was dismissed and Cry For A Shadow was agreed.

When The Saints Go Marching In (Trad. Arr. Sheridan)   3:18

Recorded : 22/23 June 1961, Hamburg-Harburg-Friedrich-Ebert-Halle,
   Hamburg, West Germany
The Beatles with Tony Sheridan

John Lennon : Rhythm Guitar
Paul McCartney : Bass Guitar
George Harrison : Lead Guitar
Pete Best : Drums
Tony Sheridan : Solo Vocal

The B-side of the now famous My Bonnie single features a solo vocal from
Tony Sheridan together with some very enthusiastic and exciting backing
music from the Beatles.

Why (Can't You Love Me Again) (Crompton–Sheridan)   2:58

Recorded : 22/23 June 1961, Hamburg-Harburg-Friedrich-Ebert-Halle,
   Hamburg, West Germany
The Beatles with Tony Sheridan

John Lennon : Rhythm Guitar and Backing Vocal
Paul McCartney : Bass Guitar and Backing Vocal
George Harrison : Lead Guitar and Backing Vocal
Pete Best : Drums
Tony Sheridan : Lead Vocal

Partly written by Tony Sheridan, this pleading song seems to suit his voice
perfectly. The Beatles provide an adequate musical backing, together with
harmony vocals and hand-clapping.

If You Love Me, Baby (aka : Take Out Some Insurance On Me Baby)
(Singleton–Hall)   2:53

Recorded : 24 June 1961, Studio Rahlstedt, Hamburg, West Germany
The Beatles with Tony Sheridan

John Lennon : Rhythm Guitar
Paul McCartney : Bass Guitar
George Harrison : Lead Guitar
Pete Best : Drums
Tony Sheridan : Solo Vocal

One of Tony Sheridan's favourite songs. Here the Beatles provide Sheridan
with an excellent backing for his solo vocal.

What'd I Say (Charles) 2:39

Recorded: 31 January 1963, Studio Rahlstedt, Hamburg, West Germany
Tony Sheridan and The Beat Brothers

Sweet Georgia Brown (Bernie–Pinkard–Casey) 2:05

Recorded: 21 December 1961, Musikhalle, Hamburg, West Germany
The Beatles with Tony Sheridan

John Lennon: Rhythm Guitar and Backing Vocal
Paul McCartney: Bass Guitar, Piano and Backing Vocal
George Harrison: Lead Guitar and Backing Vocal
Pete Best: Drums
Tony Sheridan: Lead Vocal

The Beatles, once again, provide a very enthusiastic backing to Tony
Sheridan's vocal talents. Incidentally, in 1963 Sheridan re-recorded the vocals
with specially adapted lyrics referring to the length of the Beatles' hair and the
then recently formed Beatles' Fan Club. This is the version here. The original
appears on the 1962 German E.P. Ya Ya (Polydor H 21485).

Let's Dance (Lee) 2:33

Recorded: 18 October 1962, Studio Rahlstedt, Hamburg, West Germany
Tony Sheridan and The Beat Brothers

Ruby Baby (Leiber–Stoller) 2:52

Recorded: 31 January 1963, Studio Rahlstedt, Hamburg, West Germany
Tony Sheridan and The Beat Brothers

My Bonnie (Pratt) 2:42

Recorded: 22/23 June 1961, Hamburg-Harburg-Friedrich-Ebert-Halle,
   Hamburg, West Germany
The Beatles with Tony Sheridan

John Lennon: Rhythm Guitar and Backing Vocal
Paul McCartney: Bass Guitar and Backing Vocal
George Harrison: Lead Guitar and Backing Vocal
Pete Best: Drums
Tony Sheridan: Lead Vocal

This must surely be the most famous track on the album, the A-side of the
single issued in Germany in 1961, and the cause of the meeting between Brian
Epstein and the Beatles. Tony Sheridan's lead vocal is given a rousing musical
and vocal backing by the Beatles, who also supply some enthusiastic hand-
clapping.

When this track was originally issued as a single in Germany (Polydor 24 673) it featured a slow introduction in German. When it was later issued in Britain (Polydor NH 66–833) the introduction was in English, and it is that version that is included here.

Nobody's Child (Foree–Coben)   3:55

Recorded : 22/23 June 1961, Hamburg-Harburg-Friedrich-Ebert-Halle,
   Hamburg, West Germany
The Beatles with Tony Sheridan

John Lennon : Rhythm Guitar
Paul McCartney : Bass Guitar
George Harrison : Lead Guitar
Pete Best : Drums
Tony Sheridan : Solo Vocal

The old country and western song is brought up to date here by Tony Sheridan, who is given an excellent backing by the Beatles.

Ready Teddy (Blackwell–Marascalco)   2:01

Recorded : 21 December 1961, Musikhalle, Hamburg, West Germany
Tony Sheridan and The Beat Brothers

Ya Ya (Parts 1 + 2) (Robinson–Dorsey–Lewis)   5:08

Recorded : 28 August 1962, Studio Rahlstedt, Hamburg, West Germany
Tony Sheridan and The Beat Brothers

Kansas City (Leiber–Stoller)   2:38

Recorded : Unknown
Tony Sheridan and The Beat Brothers

When the Beatles returned to Liverpool in October 1961 they brought a few copies of My Bonnie with them for their friends. One person to receive a copy was Bob Wooller, the DJ at the Cavern Club, who gave the record a considerable amount of play. Soon, several members of the club were asking for the record at the nearby music shop, NEMS (North End Music Stores).
   The manager, Brian Epstein, knew that the record was not in stock but wanted to know who the artists were so that he could obtain it. Brian was told that the record was by a German group called the Beatles. He made enquiries around Liverpool and found that the Beatles were not German but English and, above all, a local group who were currently playing at the Cavern Club just around the corner from his music shop. Intrigued, he went along to the Cavern Club to find out more about them and their record. He watched their performance and recognised the four scruffy lads who came into his shop on Saturday afternoons to listen to records, but who never bought anything. He

also could not fail to notice the enormous amount of excitement they generated within the audience. It seemed as though the moment they appeared on stage the atmosphere became electrically charged. Brian was fascinated. How could these four scruffs have so much effect on an audience? No wonder he was having so many requests for their record.

After their performance, Brian met the Beatles and found out that the record was on the Polydor label. He then began extensive enquiries amongst record importers, but drew a blank. Being the businessman that he was, he then contacted Polydor Records in Germany and imported 200 copies himself. Brian also made enquiries about how to go about managing a group. Receiving what he considered to be sufficient information, he invited the Beatles along to his office to discuss the possibility of becoming their manager.

The Beatles informed Brian that they were under a management contract to Allan Williams. Brian also learned that their recording contract with Polydor Records still had two years to run. He went along to see Allan Williams. Allan, glad to get rid of the Beatles, readily agreed that Brian could have them, adding that the Beatles had caused him nothing but trouble. It was a decision that he was soon to regret.

Brian then contacted Polydor Records who informed him that they were only interested in the Beatles as a backing group for Tony Sheridan, and that they had no plans whatsoever to record the Beatles on their own. After some discussion Polydor Records released the Beatles totally and unconditionally from their contract. Both situations now resolved, the Beatles, witnessed by Alistair Taylor (Brian's personal assistant), signed the contract which made Brian Epstein their new manager. (Brian himself never signed that contract but never revealed why.)

The first thing Brian did was to take over from Pete Best the responsibility for making bookings for the group. Next, he talked them into wearing suits on stage and told them to work out a regular stage performance in which they were to play only their best numbers. He also banned them from smoking, eating, drinking alcohol or chewing gum during their performances, and before every booking would issue each of the Beatles with typewritten instructions as to where the booking was and what time they were to be there (usually at least half an hour prior to the start of the performance).

Having organised the Beatles and given them a new appearance, the next task, Brian decided, was to get his newly signed Beatles a recording contract.

UK Release : 19 October 1987
Topline Top 181
US Release : Various
Intl CD No : Various
Producer : Mike Smith
Running Time : 32:02

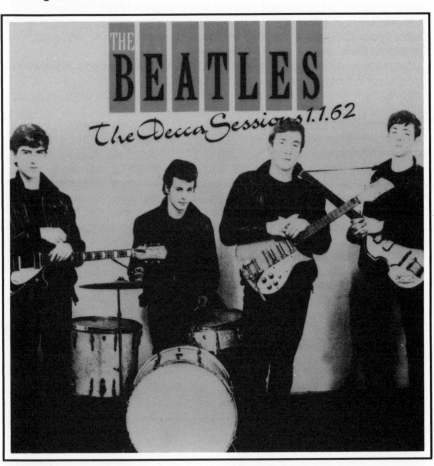

SIDE ONE : Three Cool Cats; Memphis, Tennessee; Besame Mucho; The Sheik Of Araby; Till There Was You; Searchin'.

SIDE TWO : Sure To Fall (In Love With You); Take Good Care Of My Baby; Money; To Know Her Is To Love Her; September In The Rain; Crying, Waiting, Hoping.

Brian Epstein, determined to get the Beatles a recording contract, managed (through his various contacts in the music business) to convince Mike Smith, an A & R manager from Decca Records, to come to the Cavern Club in Liverpool during December 1961 and see the group performing live. What he saw, unlike Bert Kaempfert, was a clean-cut, smartly dressed quartet who, no matter what they played, managed to drive the regulars at the Cavern wild. After seeing their performance, which impressed him immensely, Smith agreed to give the Beatles an audition, on 1 January 1962, at Decca's West Hampstead Studios. Both Brian Epstein and the Beatles were delighted. Brian told the Beatles to rehearse their best numbers for the audition and not to use any of their own compositions : a decision which (although open to a great deal of speculation) very possibly cost them their contract with Decca.

On New Year's Eve, 1961, the Beatles together with Neil Aspinall loaded their equipment into a van and drove down to London (Brian Epstein travelling by train). Arriving at about 10 p.m. they booked into their hotel, The Royal in Russell Square, and then went out on the town to, amongst other things, join the New Year revellers in Trafalgar Square.

The following morning the Beatles and Neil Aspinall arrived at Decca's studios to find Brian Epstein already there. Brian was quite annoyed that no one from Decca had arrived yet as the audition was set for 11 a.m., and it was rapidly approaching. Mike Smith eventually arrived at half past eleven and the Beatles began to unload their equipment and set it up, only to be told that their equipment wasn't required and that they were to use the guitars, etc., that were to be provided.

The Beatles, now in the relatively calm and controlled environment of the recording studio, ran through the songs they had selected from their repertoire, eventually recording (at least) fifteen songs, including three of their own which they had included despite Brian's instructions. The session finished at about 2 p.m. and Mike Smith, impressed with their recordings, informed them that there would not be an immediate decision, as that would come from higher above.

Twenty years after that audition, AFE Records became the first of many record companies to officially issue twelve of the fifteen recordings that, over the years, have become known as The Decca Tapes. AFE's release, The Complete Silver Beatles (UK : AFE AFELP 1047; US : AFE AR 2452) contained all but the three Lennon–McCartney originals : Like Dreamers Do, Love Of The Loved and Hello Little Girl. What were included, though, were early versions of both Money and Till There Was You, which the Beatles eventually re-recorded and included on the 1963 album With The Beatles. The remaining ten tracks include Beatles' versions of the Coasters' hits Three Cool Cats and Searchin', together with Chuck Berry's Memphis, Tennessee, along with seven other tracks that the Beatles were including in their stage act during 1960–61.

Over the years since The Decca Tapes made their first official appearance, the recordings seem to have been issued by as many different record companies as there are tracks (and in as many different running orders). The first company to issue these recordings on compact disc was Topline Records who issued them as The Decca Sessions 1.1.62 (Topline TOP CD 523). As the recordings will no doubt be issued by other record companies at some point, I have used that album as a sample release. Unfortunately, as previously mentioned, it doesn't contain Like Dreamers Do, Love Of The Loved or Hello Little Girl. This is apparently due to legalities over the copyright. To offer a complete commentary on the entire fifteen (although other sources claim there were more) original recordings, these three tracks have been included after the actual album.

SIDE ONE

Three Cool Cats (Leiber–Stoller)   2:41

Recorded : 1 January 1962, Decca Studios, West Hampstead, London

John Lennon : Rhythm Guitar and Backing Vocal
Paul McCartney : Bass Guitar and Backing Vocal
George Harrison : Lead Guitar and Lead Vocal
Pete Best : Drums

George is in excellent form on lead vocal in this complete send-up of the 1959 Coasters hit. John and Paul aid and abet with the various humorous interjections of 'I want that little chick' and 'Hey man, save one chick for me'. This comes across as a less than serious attempt to record the song.

Memphis, Tennessee (Berry)   2:40

Recorded : 1 January 1962, Decca Studios, West Hampstead, London

John Lennon : Rhythm Guitar and Solo Vocal
Paul McCartney : Bass Guitar
George Harrison : Lead Guitar
Pete Best : Drums

John's lead vocal on this late fifties Chuck Berry standard is by far one of his best performances on the album. It puts Chuck Berry's original version to shame although the Beatles do not stray far from his original arrangement. During their numerous BBC radio appearances in the early 1960s the Beatles featured this song on a number of occasions.

Besame Mucho (Velazquez–Skylar)   2:33

Recorded : 1 January 1962, Decca Studios, West Hampstead, London

John Lennon : Rhythm Guitar and Backing Vocal
Paul McCartney : Bass Guitar and Lead Vocal
George Harrison : Lead Guitar and Backing Vocal
Pete Best : Drums

This must be one of the Beatles' all-time favourite songs. Although not officially released until now, various versions by the Beatles had cropped up now and again on bootleg records. During the early sixties the Beatles recorded this song for a number of radio broadcasts. It also cropped up a few years later during the sessions for Let It Be as a much better, although never released version. Paul always sings the lead vocal, with backing from John and George.

They do an excellent job on this old 1930s song that was revived in 1959 by the Coasters.

The Sheik of Araby (Snyder–Wheeler–Smith)   1:37

Recorded : 1 January 1962, Decca Studios, West Hampstead, London

John Lennon : Rhythm Guitar
Paul McCartney : Bass Guitar
George Harrison : Lead Guitar and Solo Vocal
Pete Best : Drums

Although one of the best, this is unfortunately one of the shortest tracks on the album. George gives a rousing rendition of this ancient song and is given an equally rousing backing. John inserts some ad lib comments, which give the song a lighter feel than other recordings on the album and turn it into a send-up. This is a good recording, although the ending is sloppy.

Till There Was You (Willson)   2:55

Recorded : 1 January 1962, Decca Studios, West Hampstead, London

John Lennon : Rhythm Guitar
Paul McCartney : Bass Guitar and Solo Vocal
George Harrison : Lead Guitar
Pete Best : Drums

This is the first of two tracks on the album that were later re-recorded and released by the Beatles on the With The Beatles album. Paul's lead vocal is backed by his own bass guitar, George's lead guitar and Pete Best's drumming. The song is given a similar treatment to that of the later version, although the lead guitar and drums don't seem at ease.

Searchin' (Leiber–Stoller)   3:44

Recorded : 1 January 1962, Decca Studios, West Hampstead, London

John Lennon : Rhythm Guitar and Backing Vocal
Paul McCartney : Bass Guitar and Lead Vocal
George Harrison : Lead Guitar and Backing Vocal
Pete Best : Drums

The sixth track of the album is another song originally recorded by the Coasters; this one dates back to 1957. The Beatles featured it now and again in their stage act. Paul sings lead vocal, with John and George adding harmonies for the chorus. The two sections of falsetto that can be heard come from John Lennon, who nervously tries to inject some humour into the situation.

SIDE TWO

Sure To Fall (In Love With You)
Perkins–Cantrell–Claunch) 2:48

Recorded : 1 January 1962, Decca Studios, West Hampstead, London

John Lennon : Rhythm Guitar and Harmony Vocal
Paul McCartney : Bass Guitar and Lead Vocal
George Harrison : Lead Guitar and Harmony Vocal
Pete Best : Drums

The old Carl Perkins number is given the Beatles' treatment, with lead vocal from Paul and harmonies from John and George here and there. This is either a very straight-faced send-up or Paul has stage fright. Nevertheless it is still an enjoyable track.

Take Good Care Of My Baby (Goffin–King) 2:51

Recorded : 1 January 1962, Decca Studios, West Hampstead, London

John Lennon : Rhythm Guitar and Harmony Vocal
Paul McCartney : Bass Guitar and Harmony Vocal
George Harrison : Lead Guitar and Lead Vocal
Pete Best : Drums

Lead vocals are from George with harmonies in places from John and Paul. The Beatles stick closely to the original Bobby Vee recording.

Money (Bradford–Gordy) 2:57

Recorded : 1 January 1962, Decca Studios, West Hampstead, London

John Lennon : Rhythm Guitar and Lead Vocal
Paul McCartney : Bass Guitar and Backing Vocal
George Harrison : Lead Guitar and Backing Vocal
Pete Best : Drums

This track was also re-recorded and later issued by the Beatles on the album With The Beatles. This is much faster than the later version, and instead of piano it starts with John Lennon's rhythm guitar. The lead vocal also comes from John. He sounds like he would during a live performance, and the echo given to his voice emphasises this effect. The backing vocals from Paul and George are sung in a similar way to the later released version, but musically it doesn't compare — the song on With The Beatles is far superior.

To Know Her Is To Love Her (Spector) 2:27

Recorded : 1 January 1962, Decca Studios, West Hampstead, London

John Lennon : Rhythm Guitar and Lead Vocal
Paul McCartney : Bass Guitar and Backing Vocal
George Harrison : Lead Guitar and Backing Vocal
Pete Best : Drums

This was originally recorded by the Teddy Bears in 1958 and produced by the now legendary Phil Spector. The Beatles stick closely to Phil Spector's original arrangement, but change the title and lyrics from a female to male point of view. John again sings lead vocal, with Paul and George supplying the da, da, da, backing. The Beatles used to feature this during their early stage act, and a live version can be heard on The Star Club Tapes.

September In The Rain (Dubin–Warren) 2:17

Recorded : 1 January 1962, Decca Studios, West Hampstead, London

John Lennon : Rhythm Guitar
Paul McCartney : Bass Guitar and Solo Vocal
George Harrison : Lead Guitar
Pete Best : Drums

Originally a hit for Dinah Washington in 1961, this must definitely be one of the strongest tracks on the album. Paul gives the song a true Beatles' feel in the mould of I Saw Her Standing There. This is probably the only track that sounds as though the Beatles are thoroughly enjoying themselves.

Crying, Waiting, Hoping (Holly) 1:58

Recorded : 1 January 1962, Decca Studios, West Hampstead, London

John Lennon : Rhythm Guitar and Backing Vocal
Paul McCartney : Bass Guitar and Backing Vocal
George Harrison : Lead Guitar and Lead Vocal
Pete Best : Drums

During their career the Beatles recorded quite a few Buddy Holly songs. Prior to the release of The Decca Tapes (in various forms) the only Holly song that had been issued was Words of Love on the Beatles For Sale album. The lead vocal on this song comes from George, with backing vocals from John and Paul.

Although the following three tracks do not appear on this album, they are included here for the sake of completeness. In 1982 Like Dreamers Do and Love Of The Loved appeared on an American album of dubious legality but, along with Hello Little Girl, they have yet to appear on a British album.

Love Of The Loved (Lennon–McCartney)   1:48

Recorded : 1 January 1962, Decca Studios, West Hampstead, London

John Lennon : Rhythm Guitar
Paul McCartney : Bass Guitar and Solo Vocal
George Harrison : Lead Guitar
Pete Best : Drums

This McCartney-written song was eventually given away to Cilla Black who recorded it in 1963 (Parlophone R 5065). Here Paul sings lead vocal backed by John and George playing an incessant riff that appears throughout the recording.

Like Dreamers Do (Lennon–McCartney)   2:30

Recorded : 1 January 1962, Decca Studios, West Hampstead, London

John Lennon : Rhythm Guitar
Paul McCartney : Bass Guitar and Solo Vocal
George Harrison : Lead Guitar
Pete Best : Drums

This song was eventually recorded in 1964 by the Applejacks (Decca F11916) and produced by Mike Smith who also produced this version. Paul sings lead vocal in a slightly toned-down Little Richard voice. The recording generates as much excitement as many later releases, although because this was an audition a certain amount of fear can be heard in Paul's voice. The backing sounds more enthusiastic than on the Polydor sessions, and Pete Best's performance is much improved from the monotonous drumming on those recordings.

Hello Little Girl (Lennon–McCartney)   1:36

Recorded : 1 January 1962, Decca Studios, West Hampstead, London

John Lennon : Rhythm Guitar and Lead Vocal
Paul McCartney : Bass Guitar and Lead Vocal
George Harrison : Lead Guitar and Harmony Vocal
Pete Best : Drums

This track was written by John, who once said of the song, 'This was one of the first songs I ever finished. I was then about eighteen and we gave it to the Fourmost. I think it was the first song of my own that I ever attempted to do with the group.'
   The Fourmost did record this song in 1963 with the Beatles' future producer, George Martin. In comparison to the Fourmost's recording (Parlophone R 5056), this leaves much to be desired. The lead vocal is a duet between John and Paul, with John singing solo in places. For the chorus they are joined by George.

Having completed their recording session the Beatles returned to Liverpool and awaited Decca's decision. Three months later, in March 1962, Brian Epstein received a reply from Decca — they had turned the Beatles down. Disappointed, but still hopeful, Brian took the audition tapes to every record label he could find, and in quick succession was turned down by Pye, Philips, Columbia, and just about every other record label in London. A rather despondent Brian, determined that somebody was going to like the Beatles, decided to have one final try before giving up.

Deciding that the best way to present the Beatles was by having records made from the tapes, he ended up in the HMV shop in London's Oxford Street. Here, for approximately £1.50, you could get an album made from tapes; Brian subsequently did just that. The cutting engineer, impressed with what he was hearing, recommended that Brian take his records upstairs to the offices of Ardmore and Beechwood, whose offices were located above the HMV shop. There, Brian met Syd Coleman, who, after hearing the records, recommended that he go to see a friend of his called George Martin at Parlophone. The following day Brian went along to see George Martin and played him the tapes. George was not very impressed after hearing the tapes, but decided to take a chance and agreed to give the Beatles a recording test on Wednesday 6 June 1962.

On that date, the Beatles gave their first performance for their future producer, George Martin. Although again not too impressed, he had a feeling that there was something there — a certain something that he knew needed to be brought out. After the audition, George told Brian and the Beatles that he would give them a decision within a month. Having been disappointed by Decca's decision, the Beatles didn't pay much attention to George Martin's comment and, rather dejected, returned to Liverpool and subsequently to Hamburg to play an engagement at the Star Club. Meanwhile, George Martin was listening to the audition tapes over and over again. He could hear the Beatles' potential, but there was something not quite right with the drumming which was not regular enough and, in his opinion, did not give the right sort of sound. George informed Brian Epstein that he was prepared to sign the Beatles to a recording contract, but they would have to find a new drummer — he was not prepared to sign Pete Best.

The Beatles, still in Hamburg, received the following telegram from Brian : CONGRATULATIONS BOYS, EMI REQUEST RECORDING SESSION, PLEASE REHEARSE NEW MATERIAL. This was what they had waited months for. Upon their return from Hamburg, Brian found out that John, Paul and George had decided independently that they wanted Pete Best out and Ringo Starr in. He was now faced with the unenviable task of sacking Pete Best.

With Ringo Starr as the new drummer, George Martin offered them a recording contract in which he agreed to record two singles in the first year. The date set for the first recording session, when they were to record two tracks for release as a single, was Tuesday 4 September 1962. The two tracks selected for that first single were Love Me Do/P.S. I Love You and the single was issued on 5 October 1962. Within a few weeks it had reached No. 17 in the charts (the lowest position that any Beatles record issued on Parlophone was to reach during their entire recording career).

The Beatles were delighted, and so was George Martin — so delighted that he set up a second session for the follow-up. That second session was set for Monday 26 November 1962 and produced Please Please Me/Ask Me Why, although George Martin wanted the Beatles to record How Do You Do It?

(later a hit for another Liverpool group, Gerry and The Pacemakers). The Beatles, although not enthusiastic about How Do You Do It?, made a recording of it to please George Martin. After the second session the Beatles set off for Hamburg again to fulfil a two-week Christmas residency at the Star Club, which was to last from 18 to 31 December 1962. During that two-week period, Adrian Barber (formerly with The Big Three) made some recordings on a domestic tape recorder with a single microphone, amongst which were recordings of the Beatles.

UK Release : 25 September 1981
AFE AFELD 1018
US Release : Various
Intl CD No : Various
Producer : None
Running Time : 73:50

The Beatles Historic Sessions

JOHN LENNON
PAUL McCARTNEY
GEORGE HARRISON
RINGO STARR
STUART SUTCLIFFE

SIDE ONE : I'm Gonna Sit Right Down And Cry (Over You); I Saw Her Standing There; Roll Over Beethoven; Hippy Hippy Shake; Sweet Little Sixteen; Lend Me Your Comb; Your Feets Too Big.
SIDE TWO : Twist And Shout; Mr. Moonlight; A Taste Of Honey; Besame Mucho; Reminiscing; Kansas City/Hey Hey Hey Hey; Where Have You Been All My Life.

SIDE THREE : Till There Was You; Nothin' Shakin' (But The Leaves On The Trees); To Know Her Is To Love Her; Little Queenie; Falling In Love Again; Ask Me Why; Be Bop A Lula; Hallelujah, I Love Her So.
SIDE FOUR : Sheila; Red Sails In The Sunset; Everybody's Trying To Be My Baby; Matchbox; (I'm) Talking About You; Shimmy Shake; Long Tall Sally; I Remember You.

The recordings as available on this album were originally made in the Star Club in Hamburg, Germany, sometime between 18 and 31 December 1962. Adrian Barber (formerly of The Big Three) set up a domestic tape recorder and, over that two-week period, made some twenty hours of recordings of various Liverpool groups including the Beatles. The recordings were then given to Ted Taylor (of Kingsize Taylor and The Dominoes) who offered the recordings to the Beatles' manager Brian Epstein in 1964, after the Beatles had become famous. After listening to them, Epstein turned Taylor down, but nevertheless offered him £20 for the recordings, which Taylor refused. During the 1960s Taylor gave the tapes to a recording engineer in Liverpool with the hope of eventually getting them released, but to no avail. The tapes were then put aside until the early 1970s when Allan Williams, the Beatles' first manager, whilst talking to the engineer, discovered that the tapes still existed. Williams then attempted to sell the tapes around various record companies, trying unsuccessfully to have them released. Eventually, after threatening to destroy the tapes, he found a buyer.

It was reported at the time that $50,000 was spent transferring the original 3¾ inches per second mono recordings on to professional sixteen-track tape. With the aid of various filters, equalisers and compressers they set about cleaning up the recordings. Whilst these cannot be regarded as high quality — the original mono recording was scarcely that anyway — the overall sound is quite acceptable considering the way they were recorded.

From the recordings by the Beatles 30 tracks were selected for release (amongst those tracks which apparently remain unreleased, reported to be mostly alternative versions of those issued, is reputed to be a Beatles rendition of My Girl Is Red Hot featuring a lead vocal from John Lennon).

Of those 30 available, 26 recordings were then issued as a double album by Bellaphon Records in West Germany on 8 April 1977 as The Beatles Live! At the Star Club in Hamburg; Germany, 1962 (Bellaphon 5560). Then Lingasong Records, using the same title, issued the album in Britain (LNL 1) (on which four of the tracks differed) on 25 May 1977 and in America (LS-2-7001) on 13 June 1977.

In 1981, AFE Records (using all 30 tracks) issued this double album. As the recordings featured here have been/are/will be available from various record companies, this album has been used as a sample release.

On the whole, the album makes for interesting listening and contains some pre-Parlophone recordings of I Saw Her Standing There; Ask Me Why and Twist and Shout which were included on the first Parlophone album Please Please Me some three months after these recordings were made. Another eight songs can also be compared with the later studio versions which were issued on the With The Beatles and Beatles For Sale albums and Long Tall Sally E.P.

Finally, two of the recordings included here, Hallelujah, I Love Her So and Be Bop A Lula, feature vocals by Horst Obber (a waiter at the Star Club, who had joined the Beatles on stage).

SIDE ONE 17:41

I'm Gonna Sit Right Down and Cry (Over You)
(Thomas–Biggs)   2:30

Recorded : 18–31 December 1962, The Star Club, Grosse Freiheit 39, Hamburg, West Germany

John Lennon : Rhythm Guitar and Lead Vocal
Paul McCartney : Bass Guitar and Backing Vocal
George Harrison : Lead Guitar and Backing Vocal
Ringo Starr : Drums

I Saw Her Standing There (Lennon–McCartney)   2:25

Recorded : 18–31 December 1962, The Star Club, Grosse Freiheit 39, Hamburg, West Germany

John Lennon : Rhythm Guitar and Harmony Vocal
Paul McCartney : Bass Guitar and Lead Vocal
George Harrison : Lead Guitar
Ringo Starr : Drums

Roll Over Beethoven (Berry)   2:17

Recorded : 18–31 December 1962, The Star Club, Grosse Freiheit 39, Hamburg, West Germany

John Lennon : Rhythm Guitar
Paul McCartney : Bass Guitar
George Harrison : Lead Guitar and Solo Vocal
Ringo Starr : Drums

Hippy Hippy Shake (Romero)   1:42

Recorded : 18–31 December 1962, The Star Club, Grosse Freiheit 39, Hamburg, West Germany

John Lennon : Rhythm Guitar
Paul McCartney : Bass Guitar and Solo Vocal
George Harrison : Lead Guitar
Ringo Starr : Drums

Sweet Little Sixteen (Berry)   2:50

Recorded : 18–31 December 1962, The Star Club, Grosse Freiheit 39,
Hamburg, West Germany

John Lennon : Rhythm Guitar and Solo Vocal
Paul McCartney : Bass Guitar
George Harrison : Lead Guitar
Ringo Starr : Drums

Lend Me Your Comb (Wise–Weisman–Twomey)   1:45

Recorded : 18–31 December 1962, The Star Club, Grosse Freiheit 39,
Hamburg, West Germany

John Lennon : Rhythm Guitar and Lead Vocal
Paul McCartney : Bass Guitar and Lead Vocal
George Harrison : Lead Guitar
Ringo Starr : Drums

Your Feets Too Big (Benson–Fisher)   2:21

Recorded : 18–31 December 1962, The Star Club, Grosse Freiheit 39,
Hamburg, West Germany

John Lennon : Rhythm Guitar and Harmony Vocal
Paul McCartney : Bass Guitar and Lead Vocal
George Harrison : Lead Guitar
Ringo Starr : Drums

SIDE TWO 16:57

Twist and Shout (Medley–Russell)   2:12

Recorded : 18–31 December 1962, The Star Club, Grosse Freiheit 39,
Hamburg, West Germany

John Lennon : Rhythm Guitar and Lead Vocal
Paul McCartney : Bass Guitar and Backing Vocal
George Harrison : Lead Guitar and Backing Vocal
Ringo Starr : Drums

Mr. Moonlight (Johnson)   2:10

Recorded : 18–31 December 1962, The Star Club, Grosse Freiheit 39,
Hamburg, West Germany

John Lennon : Rhythm Guitar and Lead Vocal
Paul McCartney : Bass Guitar and Harmony Vocal
George Harrison : Lead Guitar
Ringo Starr : Drums

A Taste Of Honey (Marlow–Scott) 1:55

Recorded : 18–31 December 1962, The Star Club, Grosse Freiheit 39, Hamburg, West Germany

John Lennon : Rhythm Guitar and Backing Vocal
Paul McCartney : Bass Guitar and Lead Vocal
George Harrison : Lead Guitar and Backing Vocal
Ringo Starr : Drums

Besame Mucho (Velazquez–Skylar) 2:40

Recorded : 18–31 December 1962, The Star Club, Grosse Freiheit 39, Hamburg, West Germany

John Lennon : Rhythm Guitar and Backing Vocal
Paul McCartney : Bass Guitar and Lead Vocal
George Harrison : Lead Guitar and Backing Vocal
Ringo Starr : Drums

Reminiscing (Curtis) 1:41

Recorded : 18–31 December 1962, The Star Club, Grosse Freiheit 39, Hamburg, West Germany

John Lennon : Rhythm Guitar
Paul McCartney : Bass Guitar
George Harrison : Lead Guitar and Solo Vocal
Ringo Starr : Drums

Kansas City (Leiber–Stoller)/Hey Hey Hey Hey (Penniman) 2:10

Recorded : 18–31 December 1962, The Star Club, Grosse Freiheit 39, Hamburg, West Germany

John Lennon : Rhythm Guitar and Backing Vocal
Paul McCartney : Bass Guitar and Lead Vocal
George Harrison : Lead Guitar and Backing Vocal
Ringo Starr : Drums

Where Have You Been All My Life (Mann–Weill) 1:45

Recorded : 18–31 December 1962, The Star Club, Grosse Freiheit 39, Hamburg, West Germany

John Lennon : Rhythm Guitar and Lead Vocal
Paul McCartney : Bass Guitar and Backing Vocal
George Harrison : Lead Guitar and Backing Vocal
Ringo Starr : Drums

SIDE THREE 20:43

Till There Was You (Willson)   1:55

Recorded : 18–31 December 1962, The Star Club, Grosse Freiheit 39,
   Hamburg, West Germany

John Lennon : Rhythm Guitar
Paul McCartney : Bass Guitar and Solo Vocal
George Harrison : Lead Guitar
Ringo Starr : Drums

Nothin' Shakin' (But The Leaves On The Trees)
(Colacrai–Fontaine–Lampert–Cleveland)   1:15

Recorded : 18–31 December 1962, The Star Club, Grosse Freiheit 39,
   Hamburg, West Germany

John Lennon : Rhythm Guitar
Paul McCartney : Bass Guitar
George Harrison : Lead Guitar and Solo Vocal
Ringo Starr : Drums

To Know Her Is To Love Her (Spector)   3:05

Recorded : 18–31 December 1962, The Star Club, Grosse Freiheit 39,
   Hamburg, West Germany

John Lennon : Rhythm Guitar and Harmony Vocal
Paul McCartney : Bass Guitar and Harmony Vocal
George Harrison : Lead Guitar and Lead Vocal
Ringo Starr : Drums

Little Queenie (Berry)   3:57

Recorded : 18–31 December 1962, The Star Club, Grosse Freiheit 39,
   Hamburg, West Germany

John Lennon : Rhythm Guitar
Paul McCartney : Bass Guitar and Solo Vocal
George Harrison : Lead Guitar
Ringo Starr : Drums

Falling In Love Again (Hollander–Lerner)   1:58

Recorded : 18–31 December 1962, The Star Club, Grosse Freiheit 39,
   Hamburg, West Germany

John Lennon : Rhythm Guitar
Paul McCartney : Bass Guitar and Solo Vocal
George Harrison : Lead Guitar
Ringo Starr : Drums

Ask Me Why (Lennon–McCartney)   2:30

Recorded : 18–31 December 1962, The Star Club, Grosse Freiheit 39,
   Hamburg, West Germany

John Lennon : Rhythm Guitar and Lead Vocal
Paul McCartney : Bass Guitar and Backing Vocal
George Harrison : Lead Guitar and Backing Vocal
Ringo Starr : Drums

Be Bop A Lula (Vincent–Davis)   2:28

Recorded : 18–31 December 1962, The Star Club, Grosse Freiheit 39,
   Hamburg, West Germany

John Lennon : Rhythm Guitar
Paul McCartney : Bass Guitar
George Harrison : Lead Guitar
Ringo Starr : Drums
Horst Obber : Solo Vocal

Hallelujah, I Love Her So (Charles)   2:07

Recorded : 18–31 December 1962, The Star Club, Grosse Freiheit 39,
   Hamburg, West Germany

John Lennon : Rhythm Guitar
Paul McCartney : Bass Guitar
George Harrison : Lead Guitar
Ringo Starr : Drums
Horst Obber : Solo Vocal

Sheila (Roe)   1:55

Recorded : 18–31 December 1962, The Star Club, Grosse Freiheit 39,
   Hamburg, West Germany

John Lennon : Rhythm Guitar
Paul McCartney : Bass Guitar
George Harrison : Lead Guitar and Solo Vocal
Ringo Starr : Drums

Red Sails In The Sunset (Kennedy–Williams)   2:00

Recorded : 18–31 December 1962, The Star Club, Grosse Freiheit 39,
   Hamburg, West Germany

John Lennon : Rhythm Guitar
Paul McCartney : Bass Guitar and Solo Vocal
George Harrison : Lead Guitar
Ringo Starr : Drums

Everybody's Trying To Be My Baby (Perkins)   2:25

Recorded : 18–31 December 1962, The Star Club, Grosse Freiheit 39,
   Hamburg, West Germany

John Lennon : Rhythm Guitar
Paul McCartney : Bass Guitar
George Harrison : Lead Guitar and Solo Vocal
Ringo Starr : Drums

Matchbox (Perkins)   2:35

Recorded : 18–31 December 1962, The Star Club, Grosse Freiheit 39,
   Hamburg, West Germany

John Lennon : Rhythm Guitar and Solo Vocal
Paul McCartney : Bass Guitar
George Harrison : Lead Guitar
Ringo Starr : Drums

(I'm) Talking About You (Berry) 1:50

Recorded : 18–31 December 1962, The Star Club, Grosse Freiheit 39, Hamburg, West Germany

John Lennon : Rhythm Guitar and Solo Vocal
Paul McCartney : Bass Guitar
George Harrison : Lead Guitar
Ringo Starr : Drums

Shimmy Shake (South–Land) 2:18

Recorded : 18–31 December 1962, The Star Club, Grosse Freiheit 39, Hamburg, West Germany

John Lennon : Rhythm Guitar and Lead Vocal
Paul McCartney : Bass Guitar and Lead Vocal
George Harrison : Lead Guitar
Ringo Starr : Drums

Long Tall Sally (Johnson–Penniman–Blackwell) 1:50

Recorded : 18–31 December 1962, The Star Club, Grosse Freiheit 39, Hamburg, West Germany

John Lennon : Rhythm Guitar
Paul McCartney : Bass Guitar and Solo Vocal
George Harrison : Lead Guitar
Ringo Starr : Drums

I Remember You (Mercer–Schertzinger) 1:51

Recorded : 18–31 December 1962, The Star Club, Grosse Freiheit 39, Hamburg, West Germany

John Lennon : Rhythm Guitar and Harmonica
Paul McCartney : Bass Guitar and Solo Vocal
George Harrison : Lead Guitar
Ringo Starr : Drums

UK Release : 22 March 1963
Parlophone PMC 1202 : PCS 3042
US Release : February 1987
Capitol CLJ 46435
Intl CD No : CDP 7 46435 2
Producer : George Martin
Running Time : 31:48

SIDE ONE : I Saw Her Standing There; Misery; Anna (Go To Him); Chains; Boys; Ask Me Why; Please Please Me.

SIDE TWO : Love Me Do; P.S. I Love You; Baby It's You; Do You Want To Know A Secret; A Taste Of Honey; There's A Place; Twist And Shout.

The Beatles' first album for Parlophone combines their two previously issued singles Love Me Do/P.S. I Love You and Please Please Me/Ask Me Why with ten newly recorded songs. Four of the new songs are Lennon–McCartney originals, while the remaining six are Beatles' versions of some of their favourite songs, which they had been including in their live performances at the Cavern Club in Liverpool and the Star Club in Hamburg for quite some time prior to gaining a recording contract with EMI.

Despite the success of the two singles — Please Please Me had just reached No. 1 — EMI were still not convinced that the Beatles were going to last. However, wanting to cater to the overwhelming demand for their records EMI requested that the Beatles make an album as soon as possible, and preferably call it Please Please Me so that it would be instantly recognisable to the buyers of the single.

George Martin initially planned to record a live album capturing all the excitement of a Beatles performance at the Cavern Club in Liverpool, but the idea proved to be impractical and was quickly dismissed. He then decided that the Beatles should make the album in a recording studio although it would still consist of songs that they would have performed on a live album.

On 11 February 1963 the Beatles, with George Martin, entered EMI's Abbey Road studios to record the remaining tracks on this album in one long exhaustive recording session, from 10 a.m. to 11 p.m. As he had not decided upon the content of this album, George Martin asked the Beatles to run quickly through some of their favourite songs. From these he selected nine of the final ten album titles. The tenth was Twist and Shout. With the contents now decided, and with the knowledge that the Beatles had been playing these songs for years, Martin started the recording session.

Thirteen hours, ten songs and £400 later the album was finished. To record an album, mix it and have it ready to go into production in one day is no mean feat but they managed it. Incidentally it is interesting to note that at the time of recording Lennon and McCartney had written nearly 100 songs, and were heavily criticised for not including more of their own songs on this album. However, EMI were delighted with the recordings. A decision was made that upon release of the album, two tracks from it should also be issued as a single.

To combat EMI's plan, and with the knowledge that four of the tracks had already been issued as singles, the Beatles had a further recording session on 5 March 1963, which produced From Me To You and Thank You Girl. These were released as a single, on 12 April 1963, two weeks after the release of the album. Like its predecessor, Please Please Me, this single went to No. 1.

The release of the album changed the British music scene. Previously the British album chart had been filled with film sound-track albums, recordings of London and Broadway musicals and, with the exception of Elvis Presley and two or three other American artists, very little else. The only British pop music artists before the Beatles who had had any sort of success in the British album charts were Cliff Richard and The Shadows.

SIDE ONE

I Saw Her Standing There (Lennon–McCartney) 2:50

John Lennon : Rhythm Guitar and Harmony Vocal
Paul McCartney : Bass Guitar and Lead Vocal
George Harrison : Lead Guitar
Ringo Starr : Drums

A great opener to the album, this was initial proof that Lennon and McCartney could and would write good old rock and roll. It is hard to imagine a better start to the Beatles' first album than Paul counting in 'one–two–three–four'. Paul's lead vocal with harmonies from John is backed by some excellent 'Shadows'-style lead guitar from George. The recording features some of the Beatles' early 'trademarks' — handclapping, used to add more excitement to an already exciting recording, and 'oooo' which was to be put to good use on future recordings. Overall, this is a good chunk of pounding rock and roll that featured in Beatles' live performances and was a huge favourite amongst members at both the Cavern and Star clubs.

On 28 November 1974 John Lennon recorded this song with Elton John. After a concert given by Elton John at Madison Square Garden, Lennon joined him on stage and announced this song 'we thought we'd do a number of an old estranged fiancé of mine, called Paul'.

Misery (Lennon–McCartney)   1:43

John Lennon : Rhythm Guitar and Lead Vocal
Paul McCartney : Bass Guitar and Lead Vocal
George Harrison : Lead Guitar
Ringo Starr : Drums

The lead vocal on this up-tempo ballad sounds double-tracked; it is, in fact, a close-harmony duet between John and Paul, and is a fine example of how they blended their two voices to sound like one. It is fine proof that not only could Lennon and McCartney write songs, but they could also sing.

Anna (Go To Him) (Alexander)   2:56

John Lennon : Rhythm Guitar and Lead Vocal
Paul McCartney : Bass Guitar and Backing Vocal
George Harrison : Lead Guitar and Backing Vocal
Ringo Starr : Drums

John's powerful pleading lead vocals do justice to this Arthur Alexander song, which Arthur had recorded a year earlier for the Dot label. Arthur Alexander, as John Lennon later revealed, was a big influence on his early writing. This song and the equally mournful You Better Move On, recorded by the Rolling Stones, are two of Arthur's songs made internationally famous for him.

Chains (Goffin–King)   2:21

John Lennon : Rhythm Guitar, Harmonica and Harmony Vocal
Paul McCartney : Bass Guitar and Harmony Vocal
George Harrison : Lead Guitar and Lead Vocal
Ringo Starr : Drums

The musical introduction to this Goffin–King song, originally recorded by the American girl group The Cookies, heralds the first appearance on the album of John's harmonica. The vocals are a three-part harmony between John, Paul and George, with George singing solo between the chanting chorus line that dominates the song.

Boys (Dixon–Farrell) 2:24

John Lennon : Rhythm Guitar and Backing Vocal
Paul McCartney : Bass Guitar and Backing Vocal
George Harrison : Lead Guitar and Backing Vocal
Ringo Starr : Drums and Lead Vocal

This song, originally recorded by the Shirelles, gives Ringo his first appearance on the album as vocalist. He belts out the lyrics in fine form, sounding like any good rock and roller should. John, Paul and George supply the 'bop-shoo-wop' backing as Ringo hurtles his way through his beloved Shirelles song. Luther Dixon and Wes Farrell must have found this to be a good rendition of their song.

Ask Me Why (Lennon–McCartney) 2:24

John Lennon : Rhythm Guitar and Lead Vocal
Paul McCartney : Bass Guitar and Harmony Vocal
George Harrison : Lead Guitar and Harmony Vocal
Ringo Starr : Drums

Released as the B-side to the Beatles' second single for Parlophone, Please Please Me, this is the first song on the album not to have been recorded at the 11 February session. One of John's early attempts at ballad writing, it features him on lead vocal with some very pleasant harmonies from Paul and George. Another of the Beatles' early trademarks, falsetto, can be heard on this song.

Please Please Me (Lennon–McCartney) 2:00

John Lennon : Rhythm Guitar, Harmonica and Lead Vocal
Paul McCartney : Bass Guitar and Harmony Vocal
George Harrison : Lead Guitar and Harmony Vocal
Ringo Starr : Drums

Two minutes of sheer excellence. This highly commercial recording was the title track of the album and also the title of the Beatles' second single for Parlophone, which shot to No. 1 within weeks of being released. John's lead vocal is given some fine close harmony backing from Paul and George. The track is interspersed with some interesting harmonica from John. This recording is quite amazing because it manages to condense so much into such a short space of time. Paul has since given George Martin credit for improving the tempo of this track, which was the main reason for its success.

SIDE TWO

Love Me Do (Lennon–McCartney) 2:19

John Lennon : Harmonica and Lead Vocal
Paul McCartney : Bass Guitar and Lead Vocal
George Harrison : Acoustic Guitar and Harmony Vocal
Ringo Starr : Tambourine
Andy White : Drums

This recording was the A-side of the Beatles' first single for Parlophone. (The next track, P.S. I Love You was the B-side.) Released on 5 October 1962, it hovered around the lower half of the Top Twenty at No. 17. It was on the chart for six weeks — which by later standards was short. The recording is dominated by John's harmonica. The main lead vocals are a duet from John and Paul, with John singing solo at various times. The lyrics are sparse but with the dominant harmonica and John's asthmatic Liverpudlian 'scouse' vocals it was definitely an 'ear catcher' in 1962.

There are two recordings of Love Me Do; one features Ringo on drums and the other features a session musician, Andy White. This version is the 'Andy White' version (with Ringo on tambourine). The single featured Ringo on drums.

The reason for the two recordings was that after Ringo replaced Pete Best, George Martin, who had not heard him play, had brought in Andy White just in case Ringo's drumming didn't match up to expectations. Martin insisted that the Beatles use Andy White as the drummer, but the Beatles wanted Ringo. As a compromise, two recordings were made. None of the Beatles were particularly pleased either about a session musician being used on their records, or about the fact that Ringo had been given a tambourine, and they all insisted that the version featuring Ringo on drums be released as the single. The version featuring Ringo is included on Record 1 of the Beatles Box.

P.S. I Love You (Lennon–McCartney) 2:02

John Lennon : Acoustic Guitar and Lead Vocal
Paul McCartney : Bass Guitar and Lead Vocal
George Harrison : Lead Guitar
Ringo Starr : Maracas
Andy White : Drums

Previously released as the B-side to Love Me Do, this sounds rather like a Paul McCartney re-write of John Lennon's Ask Me Why, although it is still a very pleasant song.

Baby It's You (David–Williams–Bacharach) 2:36

John Lennon : Rhythm Guitar and Lead Vocal
Paul McCartney : Bass Guitar and Backing Vocal
George Harrison : Lead Guitar and Backing Vocal
Ringo Starr : Drums
George Martin : Piano

This easygoing ballad was previously recorded by one of the Beatles' favourite groups, The Shirelles. John's lead vocals are backed by Paul and George who supply the 'sha, la, la, la, la' backing. John Lennon's ability to change the tone, pitch and feeling in his voice is finely displayed on this recording.

Do You Want To Know A Secret (Lennon–McCartney) 1:55

John Lennon : Rhythm Guitar and Backing Vocal
Paul McCartney : Bass Guitar and Backing Vocal
George Harrison : Lead Guitar and Lead Vocal
Ringo Starr : Drums

George Harrison's first appearance on the album as a vocalist is on this song, of which John Lennon was once quoted as saying 'I wrote this one for George.' Unfortunately for George the whole recording is badly mixed, with George's lead guitar mixed into oblivion somewhere down the right channel, and John and Paul's backing vocals given far too much echo, producing an out-of-keeping, almost ethereal atmosphere. The song was later recorded by Billy J. Kramer and The Dakotas and reached No. 1 in the British charts.

A Taste Of Honey (Marlow–Scott) 2:02

John Lennon : Rhythm Guitar and Harmony Vocal
Paul McCartney : Bass Guitar and Lead Vocal
George Harrison : Lead Guitar and Harmony Vocal
Ringo Starr : Drums

Taken from the theme music of the film of the same name, A Taste Of Honey has been recorded by many musicians, from blues singers to classical orchestras. This song featured in the Beatles' early stage performances, was very popular in the early sixties, and was a good vehicle for Paul McCartney's voice. John and George supply harmonies.

There's A Place (Lennon–McCartney) 1:44

John Lennon : Rhythm Guitar, Harmonica and Lead Vocal
Paul McCartney : Bass Guitar and Harmony Vocal
George Harrison : Lead Guitar
Ringo Starr : Drums

The tight harmony of John and Paul, with John singing solo at times, combine perfectly with the wailing soulful harmonica on this fine example of John's early ballad writing. This is an extremely pleasant, well-recorded song.

Twist And Shout (Medley–Russell)   2:32

John Lennon : Rhythm Guitar and Lead Vocal
Paul McCartney : Bass Guitar and Backing Vocal
George Harrison : Lead Guitar and Backing Vocal
Ringo Starr : Drums.

This is the strongest track on the album, and one of the few songs that Lennon and McCartney must have wished they had written themselves. Originally recorded by the Isley Brothers in 1962, this Phil Medley and Bert Russell song was a Beatles' show-stopper at early concerts, the song that most people would remember after the show was over. John's rasping, leathery vocals turn the invitation to twist and shout into a demand. The chunky combination of the lead and rhythm guitar, coupled with Paul's chugging bass guitar and Ringo's tight drum beat makes this a truly magnificent recording. According to legend, when the Beatles had finished the recordings for the Please Please Me album they still had some studio time left. So, in one take, they recorded Twist and Shout. Every time I listen to the track I wonder how long it took John Lennon to recover from the sore throat he must have suffered after the recording.

UK Release : 22 November 1963
Parlophone PMC 1206 : PCS 3045
US Release : February 1987
Capitol CLJ 46436
Intl CD No : CDP 7 46436 2
Producer : George Martin
Running Time : 32:44

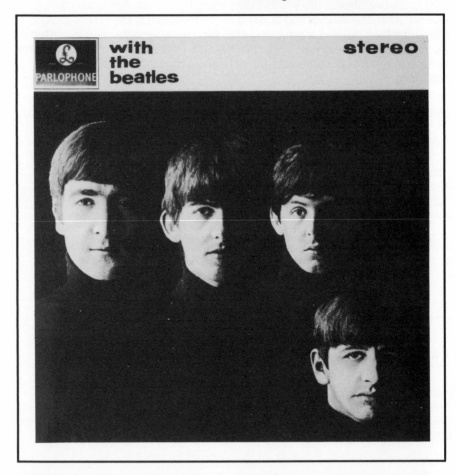

SIDE ONE : It Won't Be Long; All I've Got To Do; All My Loving; Don't Bother Me; Little Child; Till There Was You; Please Mister Postman.

SIDE TWO : Roll Over Beethoven; Hold Me Tight; You Really Got A Hold On Me; I Wanna Be Your Man; Devil In Her Heart; Not A Second Time; Money.

The Beatles' second album for Parlophone features 14 newly recorded songs. Seven were written by Lennon–McCartney, one by George Harrison and the remaining six being a further selection of the Beatles' personal favourites.

After the huge success of the Please Please Me album it was important to follow it with another equally good, if not better, album. This the Beatles managed to do. On three of the tracks the Beatles are joined by their producer, George Martin, on piano — You Really Got a Hold On Me (the old Miracles number), Lennon and McCartney's Not A Second Time and finally John's powerful rendition of the Janie Bradford and Berry Gordy song, Money.

Unlike Please Please Me, this album is not dependent on earlier single releases. To ensure that none of the tracks were extracted for release as a single, the Beatles recorded, on 19 October 1963, I Want To Hold Your Hand and This Boy. These were issued as a single on 29 November 1963, exactly one week after the release of the album.

SIDE ONE

It Won't Be Long (Lennon–McCartney)   2:11

John Lennon : Rhythm Guitar and Lead Vocal
Paul McCartney : Bass Guitar and Backing Vocal
George Harrison : Lead Guitar and Backing Vocal
Ringo Starr : Drums

John's double-tracked lead vocal on this song is given some neat close-harmony backing from Paul and George. The song is structured in a similar way to Money, the album's closing track, inasmuch as John sings the statement-style lyrics and Paul and George reply with 'yeah-yeah'. The recording also makes use of a repetitive, although not over-obvious or annoying, riff.

All I've Got To Do (Lennon–McCartney)   2:05

John Lennon : Rhythm Guitar and Lead Vocal
Paul McCartney : Bass Guitar and Harmony Vocal
George Harrison : Lead Guitar
Ringo Starr : Drums

This recording starts with an unusual semi-blues/country beat. It then moves at a much faster pace before reverting to the earlier beat. John handles the lyrics perfectly, with Paul supplying harmonies. The combination works extremely well.

All My Loving (Lennon–McCartney)   2:04

John Lennon : Rhythm Guitar and Harmony Vocal
Paul McCartney : Bass Guitar and Lead Vocal
·George Harrison : Lead Guitar and Harmony Vocal
Ringo Starr : Drums

Paul's first lead vocal performance on the album in All My Loving has become one of the Beatles' standards, recorded by many artists in many styles. Paul's voice is double-tracked on this powerful song which tears along at a furious pace. The song starts and stops, but unobtrusively, and makes effective use of a second or so of silence — an effect to be used often on future recordings. Listen to George's country and western guitar playing during the instrumental break; it fits in with the rest of the track perfectly to make this one of Paul McCartney's most likeable songs.

Don't Bother Me (Harrison)   2:28

John Lennon : Rhythm Guitar and Tambourine
Paul McCartney : Bass Guitar and Claves
George Harrison : Lead Guitar and Solo Vocal
Ringo Starr : Drums, Bongos and Loose-Skinned Arabian Bongo

This was the first George Harrison song to appear on a Beatles' album, although not his first composition as he had written, with John, the instrumental Cry For A Shadow which was included on the Polydor album The Beatles First.

This song would probably never have been written had it not been for Bill Harry, editor/owner in the early sixties of the Merseyside newspaper *Merseybeat*. He repeatedly teased George, asking him when he was going to start writing songs like John and Paul. Giving in finally, George came up with Don't Bother Me in reply to Bill Harry's persistent questioning. It was a good first song from George. It is structured like All My Loving, starting and stopping in a similar manner. In addition to the normal instrumentation, George's double-tracked lead vocals are backed by Paul beating out the rhythm on claves, John joining in on tambourine, and Ringo on loose-skinned Arabian bongo.

Little Child (Lennon–McCartney)   1:46

John Lennon : Rhythm Guitar, Harmonica and Lead Vocal
Paul McCartney : Bass Guitar, Piano and Lead Vocal
George Harrison : Lead Guitar
Ringo Starr : Drums

John's harmonica leads into this rhythm and blues song, one of few such to be recorded by the Beatles. The lead vocal is a duet between John and Paul, although John predominates. His superb blues harmonica contribution is very derivative of Cyril Davies, the exponent of some fine harmonica playing on many British rhythm and blues records during the late fifties and early sixties when he worked with Alexis Korner's Blues Incorporated.

Because of the influence of Cyril Davies on John, and that of Nicky Hopkins (another early British exponent of rhythm and blues) on Paul, who plays piano on the track, the call and answer of the vocals versus the harmonica and piano gives the song a strong Rolling Stones feel.

Till There Was You (Willson)   2:12

John Lennon : Acoustic Guitar
Paul McCartney : Bass Guitar and Solo Vocal
George Harrison : Acoustic Guitar
Ringo Starr : Bongos

Taken from the stage show/film *The Music Man*, this song had been used for a long time by the Beatles in their stage performances. It always went down extremely well with members of both the Cavern and Star clubs and was used as a slow melodic 'breather' in between the up-tempo dance beat songs. With almost magical control the Beatles would always bring an audience to near silence whenever they performed this number. For proof of this listen to the album The Beatles' Historic Sessions. The lead vocal is a solo from Paul with John and George playing acoustic guitars and Ringo tapping out a gentle beat on a set of bongos. The only electrically operated instrument on this track is Paul's bass guitar.

Please Mister Postman (Holland)   2:34

John Lennon : Rhythm Guitar and Lead Vocal
Paul McCartney : Bass Guitar and Harmony Vocal
George Harrison : Lead Guitar and Harmony Vocal
Ringo Starr : Drums

Another early favourite of the Beatles, this one-time American chart-topper for the American girl group the Marvelettes features John Lennon on lead vocal with Paul and George adding harmonies and some interesting backing vocals. What sounds like a duet between John and Paul is actually John's voice double–tracked. This is another song that the Beatles probably wished they had written themselves.

SIDE TWO

Roll Over Beethoven (Berry)   2:44

John Lennon : Rhythm Guitar
Paul McCartney : Bass Guitar
George Harrison : Lead Guitar and Solo Vocal
Ringo Starr : Drums

With John's rhythm guitar chugging away, George double-tracks the lead vocals for this rendition of the Chuck Berry classic. The Beatles performed this song quite often during their early days at the Cavern and Star clubs, and it was a popular request number. An early live recording of the song can be heard on The Star Club Tapes.

Hold Me Tight (Lennon–McCartney)   2:30

John Lennon : Rhythm Guitar and Backing Vocal
Paul McCartney : Bass Guitar and Lead Vocal
George Harrison : Lead Guitar and Backing Vocal
Ringo Starr : Drums.

Paul is on lead vocal for this one with John and George adding energetic backing vocals and joining on chorus. Paul sings with a slightly Little Richard sound similar to I Saw Her Standing There on the first album. Both songs show Paul's increasing interest in writing his own rock and roll songs.

You Really Got A Hold On Me (Robinson)   2:58

John Lennon : Rhythm Guitar and Lead Vocal
Paul McCartney : Bass Guitar and Backing Vocal
George Harrison : Lead Guitar and Lead Vocal
Ringo Starr : Drums
George Martin : Piano

The lead vocal for this song, originally recorded by the American group the Miracles, is brilliantly handled by John. It is not the easiest of songs to sing, but he does it well. George duets with John and alternates with him on the main line of the song. Paul joins them both for the chorus, while George Martin adds a dramatic piano.

In the late fifties and early sixties, American soul was virtually unknown in Britain, and almost nobody had heard of the Miracles or Smokey Robinson. It was not until the Beatles and other Liverpudlian groups started to put out their versions of American records such as You Really Got a Hold On Me that interest in the originals began to grow. Smokey Robinson later went on to write such classics as The Tracks Of My Tears and The Tears Of A Clown.

I Wanna Be Your Man (Lennon–McCartney)   1:59

John Lennon : Rhythm Guitar, Hammond Organ and Harmony Vocal
Paul McCartney : Bass Guitar and Harmony Vocal
George Harrison : Lead Guitar
Ringo Starr : Drums, Maracas and Lead Vocal

After the public response to Ringo's performance of the Shirelles' number Boys on Please Please Me, John and Paul came up with I Wanna Be Your Man for him. Ringo handles the lyrics professionally, with a helping hand from John and Paul on chorus. The instrumentation for this track is supplemented by a Hammond organ played by John and maracas added by Ringo.

After failing to reach the Top Twenty with their first single Come On, the Rolling Stones recorded I Wanna Be Your Man as their follow-up and the song took them to No. 12 in the British charts.

Devil In Her Heart (Drapkin)   2:23

John Lennon : Rhythm Guitar and Harmony Vocal
Paul McCartney : Bass Guitar and Harmony Vocal
George Harrison : Lead Guitar and Lead Vocal
Ringo Starr : Drums and Maracas

When the Beatles got hold of this song (originally recorded by the American girl group the Donays) they changed the lyrics slightly for George to sing. He handles the song skilfully, and John and Paul add harmonies and backing vocals. During their career the Beatles were to record in many styles; on this track they play a samba beat, and the final chord could almost have been replaced with a vocal 'cha, cha, cha'.

Not A Second Time (Lennon–McCartney)   2:03

John Lennon : Acoustic Guitar and Solo Vocal
Paul McCartney : Not Present
George Harrison : Not Present
Ringo Starr : Drums
George Martin : Piano

The last Lennon and McCartney song on the album features a double-tracked vocal from John with George Martin on piano. This is one of their few early songs without backing vocals. The track is backed by Martin, John on acoustic guitar and Ringo on drums.

This is the song that William Mann of *The Times* described so graphically in 1963. After writing about Lennon and McCartney at great length as '. . . the outstanding English composers of 1963 . . .' Mann then gave a review of This Boy and continued with the following '. . . but harmonic interest is typical of their quicker songs too, and one gets the impression that they think simultaneously of harmony and melody, so firmly are the major tonic sevenths and ninths built into their tunes, and the flat submediant key switches, so natural in the Aeolian cadence at the end of Not A Second Time (the chord progression that ends Mahler's Song of the Earth) . . .' to which John Lennon replied 'Really it was chords just like any other chords.'

Money (Bradford–Gordy)   2:47

John Lennon : Rhythm Guitar and Lead Vocal
Paul McCartney : Bass Guitar and Backing Vocal
George Harrison : Lead Guitar and Backing Vocal
Ringo Starr : Drums
George Martin : Piano

John shouts out his demands for 'money' with the full force of his raw leathery voice. Paul and George add the backing answers to his demands, and Ringo adds an almost hypnotic 'jungle' beat on drums. George Martin is again featured on piano, which is one of the predominant instruments on this powerful rendition. The song was partly written by the boss of Motown Records, Berry Gordy, and originally recorded by the American artist Barratt Strong for the American Anna record label in 1959; it was then re-issued on the Motown label in 1960.

UK Release : 10 July 1964
Parlophone PMC 1230 : PCS 3058
US Release : February 1987
Capitol CLJ 46437
Intl CD No : CDP 7 46437 2
Producer : George Martin
Running Time : 29:53

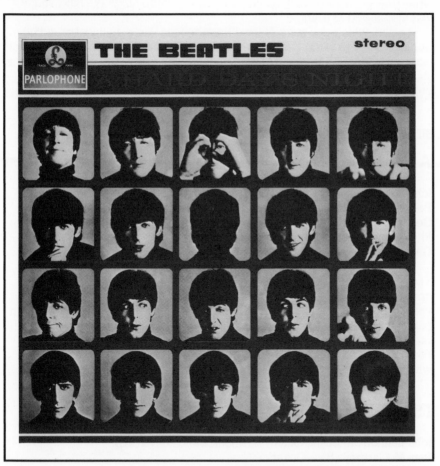

SIDE ONE : A Hard Day's Night; I Should Have Known Better; If I Fell; I'm Happy Just To Dance With You; And I Love Her; Tell Me Why; Can't Buy Me Love.

SIDE TWO : Any Time At All; I'll Cry Instead; Things We Said Today; When I Get Home; You Can't Do That; I'll Be Back.

The soundtrack album from the Beatles' first film features 13 new Lennon and McCartney songs; this was to be the only Beatles' album to consist entirely of Lennon and McCartney compositions. Future albums always contained at least one track written by George Harrison and in two cases tracks written by Ringo Starr.

The first side features seven new songs used in the film, from the powerful opening title track to the slow melodic And I Love Her. The soundtrack also used some of the Beatles' older songs such as I Wanna Be Your Man, Don't Bother Me, All My Loving and She Loves You but these are not included on the album. The second side has a further selection of Lennon and McCartney originals including I'll Cry Instead, which, although written for the film, was not considered strong enough for inclusion by the film's director, Dick Lester. Amongst the remaining five tracks is You Can't Do That, issued with Can't Buy Me Love as a single some three months prior to the release of this album. Upon release of the album the title track along with Things We Said Today was also issued as a single.

The film, which also stars Wilfred Brambell (as Paul's mythical grandfather), depicts two days in the lives of the Beatles from boarding a train in Liverpool (shot at Paddington Station, London) on their way to give the concert which is shown at the end of the film. It has some hilarious moments and is highly enjoyable.

SIDE ONE

A Hard Day's Night (Lennon–McCartney) 2:32

John Lennon : Rhythm Guitar and Lead Vocal
Paul McCartney : Bass Guitar and Harmony Vocal
George Harrison : Lead Guitar
Ringo Starr : Drums
George Martin : Piano

The opening chord of this strong opening track shows typical Beatles' originality and sounds more like the end of a record than the beginning. As the chord fades, John double-tracks the lead vocals with Paul harmonising in part and sometimes also singing lead vocals. In the excellent instrumental break in the middle George's guitar sounds like a harpsichord and Ringo's backing beat rounds the whole thing off. A good strong solid opening track which in the film is played over the opening titles.

I Should Have Known Better (Lennon–McCartney) 2:42

John Lennon : Acoustic Guitar, Harmonica and Solo Vocal
Paul McCartney : Bass Guitar
George Harrison : Lead Guitar
Ringo Starr : Drums

John's wailing harmonica introduces this song which also features him on lead vocals in a double-tracked solo with an extremely energetic backing. The song makes an early appearance in the film, where the Beatles are seen playing cards in the train.

If I Fell (Lennon–McCartney)   2:16

John Lennon : Acoustic Guitar and Lead Vocal
Paul McCartney : Bass Guitar and Lead Vocal
George Harrison : Lead Guitar
Ringo Starr : Drums

This pleasant up-tempo ballad opens with a solo vocal from John on the first verse before he is joined by Paul in a duet for the rest of the song. In the film the Beatles are seen performing this during rehearsals for a television show.

I'm Happy Just To Dance With You (Lennon–McCartney)   1:59

John Lennon : Rhythm Guitar and Backing Vocal
Paul McCartney : Bass Guitar and Backing Vocal
George Harrison : Lead Guitar and Lead Vocal
Ringo Starr : Drums and Loose-Skinned Arabian Bongo

George is on lead vocals for this song, written for him by John. The 'Oh-oh' backing comes from John and Paul, and Ringo's loose-skinned Arabian bongo producing a hollow thumping sound makes its second appearance on a Beatles' record (its first was in Don't Bother Me on With The Beatles).

And I Love Her (Lennon–McCartney)   2:27

John Lennon : Acoustic Guitar
Paul McCartney : Acoustic Guitar and Solo Vocal
George Harrison : Claves and Acoustic Guitar Solo
Ringo Starr : Bongos

Paul McCartney's earliest ballad has become an international standard recorded by scores of artists each with a different treatment. George Martin's orchestral version is included on the American album; here, the song features Paul on lead vocals, first double-tracked then triple-tracked to add his own harmonies. It also features a striking and memorable acoustic guitar riff accompanied by claves, two further acoustic guitars and bongos.

Tell Me Why (Lennon–McCartney)   2:04

John Lennon : Rhythm Guitar and Lead Vocal
Paul McCartney : Bass Guitar and Harmony Vocal
George Harrison : Lead Guitar
Ringo Starr : Drums

The vocals on this track are an interesting and unusual three-part harmony between John and Paul, with John's vocals double-tracked and Paul harmonising. The recording also features an effective use of falsetto, by John and Paul, who manage to sound like a crowd of children.

Can't Buy Me Love (Lennon–McCartney)   2:15

John Lennon : Rhythm Guitar
Paul McCartney : Bass Guitar and Solo Vocal
George Harrison : Lead Guitar
Ringo Starr : Drums

Previously issued as a single, three months before this album, the song features a double-tracked vocal from Paul and sounds rather like a re-write of A Hard Day's Night, minus the opening chord. The recording also features an interesting double-tracked guitar during the instrumental break. The Beatles first recorded Can't Buy Me Love in a theatre dressing room. The recording started with the verses instead of the chorus as it does here. Only three of the Beatles were on that recording, John and Paul singing and playing guitar and Ringo adding the backing beat, courtesy of a suitcase. George had gone to the toilet, and at the end of the song there is the sound of the toilet being flushed. The Beatles wanted to issue that version as a single but George Martin was not amused so this recording was made instead.

SIDE TWO

Any Time At All (Lennon–McCartney)   2:10

John Lennon : Acoustic Guitar and Solo Vocal
Paul McCartney : Bass Guitar and Piano
George Harrison : Lead Guitar
Ringo Starr : Drums

A lively song featuring a solo vocal from John and enthusiastic backing that includes a guitar/piano duet between George and Paul during the instrumental break. Neither this nor the remaining five tracks on this side of the album are featured in the film *A Hard Day's Night*.

I'll Cry Instead (Lennon–McCartney)   1:44

John Lennon : Acoustic Guitar, Tambourine and Lead Vocal
Paul McCartney : Bass Guitar and Lead Vocal
George Harrison : Lead Guitar
Ringo Starr : Drums

This country and western influenced song written by John for inclusion in the film features a lead vocal duet between John and Paul with George playing some neat country and western/rockabilly guitar.

Things We Said Today (Lennon–McCartney)   2:35

John Lennon : Acoustic Guitar, Tambourine and Harmony Vocal
Paul McCartney : Bass Guitar and Lead Vocal
George Harrison : Lead Guitar
Ringo Starr : Drums

The opening riff is reminiscent of the Shadows' Guitar Tango, although it was uncharacteristic for the Beatles to borrow from other artists' material. Paul double-tracks the lead vocal with John harmonising in places. The song is a pleasant up-beat ballad written by Paul.

When I Get Home (Lennon–McCartney)   2:14

John Lennon : Rhythm Guitar and Lead Vocal
Paul McCartney : Bass Guitar and Harmony Vocal
George Harrison : Lead Guitar
Ringo Starr : Drums

Lead vocals are from John on this one with Paul harmonising in parts. Unfortunately the overemphatic use of the line 'whoa-ho-I' overshadows the rest of the song.

You Can't Do That (Lennon–McCartney)   2:33

John Lennon : Rhythm Guitar and Lead Vocal
Paul McCartney : Bass Guitar and Harmony Vocal
George Harrison : Twelve String Lead Guitar and Harmony Vocal
Ringo Starr : Drums, Cowbell and Bongos

This was previously issued as the B-side to Can't Buy Me Love. John's gravelly lead vocal shouts out the lyrics in an attempt at being Wilson Pickett (as he admitted later) and Paul and George harmonise on the chorus. Ringo bangs out a metallic beat on a cowbell and for good measure bongos are added.

I'll Be Back (Lennon–McCartney)   2:22

John Lennon : Acoustic Guitar and Lead Vocal
Paul McCartney : Bass Guitar, Acoustic Guitar and Harmony Vocal
George Harrison : Acoustic Guitar
Ringo Starr : Drums

The closing track is a pleasant up-tempo ballad featuring a double-tracked lead vocal from John, with Paul harmonising in places. The sentiment of the title was a nice way to finish the album.

UK Release : 4 December 1964
Parlophone PMC 1240 : PCS 3062
US Release : February 1987
Capitol CLJ 46438
Intl CD No : CDP 7 46438 2
Producer : George Martin
Running Time : 36:58

SIDE ONE : No Reply; I'm A Loser; Baby's In Black; Rock And Roll Music; I'll Follow The Sun; Mr. Moonlight; Kansas City/Hey Hey Hey Hey.

SIDE TWO : Eight Days A Week; Words Of Love; Honey Don't; Every Little Thing; I Don't Want To Spoil The Party; What You're Doing; Everybody's Trying To Be My Baby.

For this album Lennon and McCartney wrote eight new songs, and added a further six from the vast repertoire of other material which they had been performing for some time. Three of the new songs, Eight Days A Week, No Reply and I'm A Loser, were all considered as possible singles; the Beatles once again did not want to issue a single from the album. Instead, John came up with I Feel Fine and Paul with She's A Woman, which were issued as a single on 27 November 1964, one week prior to the release of this album.

The Beatles had just completed their second major tour of the USA when they began work on this album during mid to late August 1964 and their obvious exhaustion can be heard in some of the tracks. On Every Little Thing and I Don't Want To Spoil The Party, for example, the vocals sound rather weary and slightly strained. But, as they had issued an album in time for the Christmas market of 1963 they had planned to do the same for Christmas 1964 and so recording continued. (Each year they were to repeat this, and issued Christmas singles until 1969.)

In spite of the strain which shows through on a couple of tracks, this album contains some of the Beatles' classic early recordings, such as John's powerful rendition of the old Chuck Berry standard Rock and Roll Music, and Roy Lee Johnson's classic Mr. Moonlight and Paul's new song I'll Follow The Sun.

As with the previous three albums, both George and Ringo feature on one track each. Ringo sings the old Carl Perkins standard Honey Don't and George takes lead vocal on another Carl Perkins track, Everybody's Trying To Be My Baby.

The sleeve photographs for this album also reveal the strain in the form of four unsmiling Beatles. The inner photograph shows the Beatles standing against a background of photographs of various music hall and film stars, pieced together to form a collage. This is an obvious forerunner to the sleeve of the 1967 Sgt. Pepper album.

SIDE ONE

No Reply (Lennon–McCartney)   2:15

John Lennon : Acoustic Guitar and Lead Vocal
Paul McCartney : Bass Guitar and Harmony Vocal
George Harrison : Lead Guitar and Harmony Vocal
Ringo Starr : Drums
George Martin : Piano

This strong opening track features a double-tracked lead vocal from John, with Paul helping here and there and George joining them for the chorus. They go straight into the lyrics without musical introduction or opening chorus. This was a style of writing used by John and Paul for quite some time. It was often George Martin who would add a chorus as an introduction before the main lyrics.

I'm A Loser (Lennon–McCartney)   2:31

John Lennon : Acoustic Guitar, Harmonica and Lead Vocal
Paul McCartney : Bass Guitar and Harmony Vocal
George Harrison : Lead Guitar
Ringo Starr : Drums and Tambourine

Lead vocals again are from John with Paul harmonising in parts and joining John for the chorus. At the time of writing, John had become influenced by Bob Dylan. Here he uses many of Dylan's expressions and nuances.

Baby's In Black (Lennon–McCartney)   2:02

John Lennon : Acoustic Guitar and Lead Vocal
Paul McCartney : Bass Guitar and Lead Vocal
George Harrison : Lead Guitar
Ringo Starr : Drums and Tambourine

Lead vocals on this track are a duet between John and Paul. Some 18 months after this recording, the Rolling Stones and a group called Los Bravos had hit records with Paint It Black and Black Is Black, respectively, both of which were probably inspired by this song. All three tracks convey the black feeling of lost love.

Rock And Roll Music (Berry)   2:02

John Lennon : Rhythm Guitar, Piano and Solo Vocal
Paul McCartney : Bass Guitar and Piano
George Harrison : Acoustic Guitar
Ringo Starr : Drums
George Martin : Piano (with John and Paul)

John's leathery vocals make a far better job of this Chuck Berry classic than Berry ever did, and do the song justice. It tears along at neck-breaking speed. John, as well as singing, joins George Martin *and* Paul McCartney to add the piano for the backing. Yes, they are all on the same piano, and all at the same time.

I'll Follow The Sun (Lennon–McCartney)   1:46

John Lennon : Acoustic Guitar and Harmony Vocal
Paul McCartney : Acoustic Guitar and Lead Vocal
George Harrison : Lead Guitar
Ringo Starr : Bongos

Paul's lead vocal on this song is mostly double-tracked with John harmonising in places. Ringo adds some gentle taps on a set of bongos and George's lead guitar puts in a brief appearance during the instrumental break of this very pleasant, relaxing song.

Mr. Moonlight (Johnson)   2:35

John Lennon : Acoustic Guitar and Lead Vocal
Paul McCartney : Bass Guitar, Hammond Organ and Harmony Vocal
George Harrison : Lead Guitar and African Drum
Ringo Starr : Bongos

John screams out the opening of Mr. Moonlight with all the power and expression that the Lennon larynx can supply. As can be guessed, he is the lead vocalist on this track with Paul harmonising in parts. Paul also plays a dramatic Hammond organ sounding like a cross between the phantom of the opera and Reginald Dixon. Ringo adds the backing beat on a set of bongos, while George supplies that hollow 'thump' on an ancient African drum.

Kansas City (Leiber–Stoller)/**Hey Hey Hey Hey** (Penniman)   2:30

John Lennon : Rhythm Guitar and Backing Vocal
Paul McCartney : Bass Guitar and Lead Vocal
George Harrison : Lead Guitar and Backing Vocal
Ringo Starr : Drums and Backing Vocal
George Martin : Piano

Originally, it was Little Richard's idea to join Kansas City together with his own Hey Hey Hey Hey in 1955. Paul, being a big fan of Little Richard, then used this medley during the Beatles' early stage performances. It was recorded here exactly as they had always performed it, with Paul on lead vocal using his best Little Richard voice and John, George and Ringo supplying the 'hey hey hey hey' backing for the second song. There was an error on the album cover, listing this track as Kansas City. This was corrected on the actual record label, by adding the Hey Hey Hey Hey credit, and on later covers of albums which included the track.

SIDE TWO

Eight Days A Week (Lennon–McCartney)   2:43

John Lennon : Rhythm Guitar, Acoustic Guitar and Lead Vocal
Paul McCartney : Bass Guitar and Harmony Vocal
George Harrison : Lead Guitar
Ringo Starr : Drums

The fade-in, build-up of guitars at the beginning of this track, thought to be innovative at the time, has since been copied many times. John's lead vocal is double-tracked, and he also supplies his own harmonies for this song. Many people considered this to be dedicated to Brian Epstein, because of his problems at that time — trying to divide his management attentions between too many groups and solo artists, and literally trying to live 'eight days a week'.

However, the song was written by John when the Beatles were approached to make a second film, tentatively called *Eight Arms To Hold You*. John set about writing a song with the same title, but it turned out as Eight Days A Week; then John came up with Help!, after which the title of the film was changed.

Words Of Love (Holly) 2:10

John Lennon : Rhythm Guitar and Lead Vocal
Paul McCartney : Bass Guitar and Lead Vocal
George Harrison : Lead Guitar
Ringo Starr : Drums and Packing Case

John and Paul's close harmony on this, the only Buddy Holly song that the
Beatles released on record, is the best example of how John and Paul blended
their voices. Buddy Holly was one of Paul McCartney's favourite American
artists, so much so that he has since bought all publishing rights to every
Buddy Holly song.
    That hand-clapping sound on the backing is Ringo playing a packing case!

Honey Don't (Perkins) 2:56

John Lennon : Acoustic Guitar and Tambourine
Paul McCartney : Bass Guitar
George Harrison : Lead Guitar
Ringo Starr : Drums and Solo Vocal

On Ringo's usual one track per album opportunity, he eases his way through
the words of this old Carl Perkins song, producing his own sing-a-long style
that suited his voice so well, and that he was to use on many future recordings.
    Carl Perkins was present at the session when this and some of his other
songs were recorded by the Beatles. He was reported to have thoroughly
enjoyed watching the session, although he did not take part. (In 1982, Perkins
joined Paul McCartney for a song on McCartney's album Tug of War.)

Every Little Thing (Lennon–McCartney) 2:01

John Lennon : Acoustic Guitar and Lead Vocal
Paul McCartney : Bass Guitar, Piano and Lead Vocal
George Harrison : Lead Guitar
Ringo Starr : Drums and Timpani

More close harmonies from John and Paul on this track, which has the interesting inclusion of a timpani drum, played by Ringo, to accentuate sections of
the song; George adds some very pleasant country and western style guitar.

I Don't Want To Spoil The Party (Lennon–McCartney) 2:33

John Lennon : Acoustic Guitar and Lead Vocal
Paul McCartney : Bass Guitar and Lead Vocal
George Harrison : Lead Guitar
Ringo Starr : Drums and Tambourine

John and Paul again harmonise on lead vocals, sounding very much as they do
on Words of Love. This interesting track has a 'square-dance' style backing,
although John and Paul's vocals sound rather tired.

What You're Doing (Lennon–McCartney)   2:30

John Lennon : Acoustic Guitar and Backing Vocal
Paul McCartney : Bass Guitar and Lead Vocal
George Harrison : Lead Guitar
Ringo Starr : Drums
George Martin : Piano

On many Beatles' early recordings, they paid homage to various artists. Here, they pay tribute to Phil Spector.
The drum intro is a straight lift from the Spector-produced Be My Baby by the Ronettes. It is even used again at the end, exactly as it is on the Ronettes' record. The vocals on this track come from Paul.

Everybody's Trying To Be My Baby (Perkins)   2:24

John Lennon : Acoustic Guitar and Tambourine
Paul McCartney : Bass Guitar
George Harrison : Lead Guitar and Solo Vocal
Ringo Starr : Drums

The second Carl Perkins song to be included on this album, recorded a week earlier than Honey Don't, features George on lead vocals (although he is swamped somewhat by echo) and country and western guitar.

UK Release : 6 August 1965
Parlophone PMC 1255 : PCS 3071
US Release : April 1987
Capitol CLJ 46439
Intl CD No : CDP 7 46439 2
Producer : George Martin
Running Time : 33:06

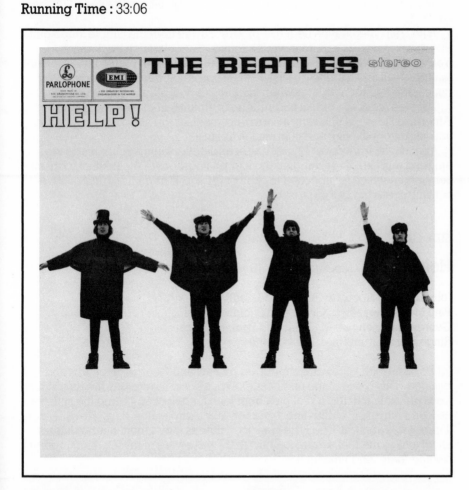

SIDE ONE : Help!; The Night Before; You've Got To Hide Your Love Away; I Need You; Another Girl; You're Going To Lose That Girl; Ticket To Ride.

SIDE TWO : Act Naturally; It's Only Love; You Like Me Too Much; Tell Me What You See; I've Just Seen A Face; Yesterday; Dizzy Miss Lizzy.

The Beatles' fifth album for Parlophone was also the sound track from their second film. The first side contains seven of the eight Beatles' songs featured in the film (the eighth, She's A Woman, is not included on this album). Amongst the seven tracks, Another Girl and Ticket To Ride feature Paul McCartney playing lead guitar for the first time on record. The second side has four Lennon and McCartney originals; It's Only Love, with an unusual quavering guitar sound, Tell Me What You See, I've Just Seen A Face and the brilliant Yesterday.

Of the other three tracks featured on the second side, You Like Me Too Much is written by George Harrison and Act Naturally and Dizzy Miss Lizzy are two of the last non-Beatle written songs that they recorded. Bad Boy, although recorded at the same time, was unavailable in Britain for 18 months, when it was included on the compilation album A Collection of Beatles Oldies. Previously the track was available on the American album Beatles VI (Capitol ST 2358).

With Help! the Beatles began to progress away from the simple 'three guitar and drums' towards a more complex sound, particularly on tracks such as You've Got To Hide Your Love Away, It's Only Love and Yesterday. The latter features Paul and a string quartet. (The progression was particularly noticeable four months later when the Rubber Soul album was issued.)

The sleeves of the British and American albums differ greatly. The American sleeve is basically an advertisement for the film, being a gatefold with stills from the film and information about it.

Also, on the front cover of the American sleeve, someone has made the amusing mistake of rearranging the four photographs of the Beatles so that the semaphore which is supposed to spell out H-E-L-P! as on the British sleeve actually spells out H-P-E-L!

SIDE ONE

Help! (Lennon–McCartney)   2:16

John Lennon : Acoustic Guitar and Lead Vocal
Paul McCartney : Bass Guitar and Backing Vocal
George Harrison : Lead Guitar and Backing Vocal
Ringo Starr : Drums and Tambourine

John's nasal lead vocals are supported by Paul and George on chorus and backing. This is one of the first Beatles' lyrics not to have a boy meets girl/boy loses girl situation. It is a real plea from John for help, comparing the situation he found himself in at the time to earlier, less complicated days. He said later 'I meant it — it's real. The lyric is as good now as it was then. It is no different, and it makes me feel secure to know that I was aware of myself then. I was just singing "help" and I meant it.'

The Night Before (Lennon–McCartney)   2:33

John Lennon : Electric Piano and Backing Vocal
Paul McCartney : Bass Guitar and Lead Vocal
George Harrison : Lead Guitar and Backing Vocal
Ringo Starr : Drums

Double-tracked lead vocals are from Paul with backing vocals from John and George effectively mixed into the song like fragments of a half-remembered dream. The electric piano is played by John.

You've Got To Hide Your Love Away
(Lennon–McCartney)   2:08

John Lennon : Acoustic Guitar and Solo Vocal
Paul McCartney : Acoustic Guitar
George Harrison : Acoustic Guitar
Ringo Starr : Tambourine
Session Musicians : Flutes

John Lennon's most intriguing lyrics show the influence of Dylan. The vocal is a solo from John; just near the end he is joined by flutes.

I Need You (Harrison)   2:28

John Lennon : Acoustic Guitar and Backing Vocal
Paul McCartney : Bass Guitar and Backing Vocal
George Harrison : Lead Guitar and Lead Vocal
Ringo Starr : Drums

A double-tracked lead vocal from George on this, his own song, proves that he could write songs as good as John and Paul's.
    The backing vocals and pleasant harmony are added by John and Paul. The eerie guitar sound played by George is achieved with the volume/tone control pedal which he was to use on a number of other tracks during 1965. At the end of the song it sounds as if he will play a guitar solo, but not having mastered the pedal he decided against it.

Another Girl (Lennon–McCartney)   2:02

John Lennon : Acoustic Guitar and Backing Vocal
Paul McCartney : Bass Guitar, Lead Guitar and Lead Vocal
George Harrison : Lead Guitar and Backing Vocal
Ringo Starr : Drums

Lead vocals are from Paul on this track, with John and George harmonising on the main line and chorus. The song has the same syncopated beat used in She's A Woman. The lead guitar is played by Paul for the first time on a Beatles' album and his solo at the end is really worth listening to.

You're Going To Lose That Girl (Lennon–McCartney)   2:18

John Lennon : Acoustic Guitar and Lead Vocal
Paul McCartney : Bass Guitar, Piano and Backing Vocal
George Harrison : Lead Guitar and Backing Vocal
Ringo Starr : Drums and Bongos

John's nasal lead vocal again works perfectly on this song, with Paul and George adding the backing vocals, plus some vocal support on chorus. Lead guitar comes from George, and Ringo adds bongos.

Ticket To Ride (Lennon–McCartney)   3:03

John Lennon : Rhythm Guitar, Tambourine and Lead Vocal
Paul McCartney : Bass Guitar, Lead Guitar and Harmony Vocal
George Harrison : Lead Guitar
Ringo Starr : Drums

Previously issued as a single, this song features John mainly on lead vocal with Paul harmonising in parts and making his second appearance on lead guitar.

SIDE TWO

Act Naturally (Morrison–Russell)   2:27

John Lennon : Acoustic Guitar
Paul McCartney : Bass Guitar and Harmony Vocal
George Harrison : Lead Guitar
Ringo Starr : Drums and Lead Vocal

Lead vocals are from Ringo, his only appearance as a vocalist on the album. Paul helps out with some harmony vocals, while John and George play the country and western/rockabilly guitars in the backing.

It's Only Love (Lennon–McCartney)   1:53

John Lennon : Acoustic Guitar, Tambourine and Solo Vocal
Paul McCartney : Bass Guitar
George Harrison : Lead Guitar
Ringo Starr : Drums

This started life with the intriguing title of That's A Nice Hat, before John wrote the lyrics. George Martin recorded an orchestral interpretation of the original instrumental, and included it on his orchestral version of the Help! album. This must be John's first inoffensive wandering into expanded consciousness lyrics as the song starts with the words 'I get high'. The quavering lead guitar is more experiments by George on the volume/tone control pedal, use of which he did not perfect until Yes It Is.

You Like Me Too Much (Harrison) 2:34

John Lennon : Acoustic Guitar and Electric Piano
Paul McCartney : Steinway Piano and Harmony Vocal
George Harrison : Lead Guitar and Lead Vocal
Ringo Starr : Drums and Tambourine
George Martin : Steinway Piano (with Paul)

George provides lead vocals, with harmonies from Paul on the chorus. The piano introduction features Paul and George Martin on the same Steinway. John plays electric piano in the backing and on the call and answer style instrumental break, which also features lead guitar from George. George's talent as a song writer is seen in this song as well as in I Need You featured on the first side of this album.

Tell Me What You See (Lennon–McCartney) 2:35

John Lennon : Washboard and Lead Vocal
Paul McCartney : Bass Guitar, Electric Piano and Lead Vocal
George Harrison : Lead Guitar and Tambourine
Ringo Starr : Drums and Claves

The vocal structure for this song is unusual with John and Paul duetting on the statement style lyrics and Paul singing solo on the 'answers'. Paul also plays the electric piano in the backing.

I've Just Seen A Face (Lennon–McCartney) 2:04

John Lennon : Acoustic Guitar
Paul McCartney : Acoustic Guitar and Solo Vocal
George Harrison : Acoustic Guitar
Ringo Starr : Drums and Maracas

This track started life as an instrumental entitled Aunty Gin's Theme; it was also recorded by George Martin under that title. Paul's lyrics show slight Dylan influence although the song is more like an up-tempo Rocky Racoon.

Yesterday (Lennon–McCartney) 2:04

John Lennon : Not Present
Paul McCartney : Acoustic Guitar and Solo Vocal
George Harrison : Not Present
Ringo Starr : Not Present
Session Musicians : String Quartet

Paul McCartney's most famous song to date started life as an instrumental entitled Scrambled Eggs and has the same history as both It's Only Love and I've Just Seen A Face. For the first time, none of the other Beatles appear on this recording, and it can be classified as a Paul McCartney solo song. It features a solo vocal from Paul, who also plays an acoustic guitar backed by a string quartet.

Dizzy Miss Lizzy (Williams)   2:51

John Lennon : Hammond Organ and Solo Vocal
Paul McCartney : Bass Guitar
George Harrison : Lead Guitar
Ringo Starr : Drums

John Lennon's leathery lead vocals are once again put to effective use on this Larry Williams song which was another of the Beatles' Cavern Club standards. They stick closely to the original arrangement of the song, but include some 'oooo's' and 'ows' to give it more of a live sound.

UK Release : 3 December 1965
Parlophone PMC 1267 : PCS 3075
US Release : April 1987
Capitol CLJ 46440
Intl CD No : CDP 7 46440 2
Producer : George Martin
Running Time : 34:50

SIDE ONE : Drive My Car; Norwegian Wood (This Bird Has Flown); You Won't See Me; Nowhere Man; Think For Yourself; The Word; Michelle.

SIDE TWO : What Goes On; Girl; I'm Looking Through You; In My Life; Wait; If I Needed Someone; Run For Your Life.

This sixth album from the Beatles showed a new musical direction. Here they move even further away from the instant pop product of their first five albums towards the second stage of their recording career. The album contains some of the Beatles most classic mid-sixties songs, like Norwegian Wood and Girl, which sound as fresh now as they did in 1965. It was after the release of this album, and the realisation that its contents could not be reproduced live, that the Beatles decided to give up live performances and concentrate solely on making records.

On this album John gives a foretaste of the events of 1967 with the mysterious lyrics of The Word and a glimpse into his past with In My Life. Paul dabbles with the French language for the lyrics of Michelle. George, as on Help!, has two songs included, Think For Yourself and If I Needed Someone, and Ringo joins forces with John and Paul to come up with the country and western flavoured What Goes On. On two of these tracks, the Beatles try out new instruments. George tries out the sitar on John's Norwegian Wood and Paul tries out the newly invented fuzz bass guitar on George's Think For Yourself.

The sleeve of this album shows, like the Beatles For Sale, four unsmiling faces. Beatles' fans complained at the time that the photograph made the Beatles look rather anaemic. However, the music is far from being anaemic.

SIDE ONE

Drive My Car (Lennon–McCartney)   2:25

John Lennon : Tambourine and Lead Vocal
Paul McCartney : Bass Guitar, Piano and Lead Vocal
George Harrison : Lead Guitar and Backing Vocal
Ringo Starr : Drums

Paul uses his Little Richard voice once again for a duet with John on lead vocals, and George joins them here and there throughout the song for the chorus. George also plays some nice blues-sounding guitar on the intro and during the instrumental break. Paul plays piano during this blues/Motown influenced song.

Norwegian Wood (This Bird Has Flown)
(Lennon–McCartney)   2:00

John Lennon : Acoustic Guitar and Lead Vocal
Paul McCartney : Bass Guitar and Harmony Vocal
George Harrison : Sitar
Ringo Starr : Tambourine

The first classic track on the album reveals, in the introduction, George playing a sitar for the first time. The sitar was featured in the incidental music for the Beatles' second film *Help!* George was fascinated by its sound and acquired one. He achieved his effect by tuning his new 'weird' instrument to western notes. As usual this led the way for other artists to copy the Beatles' innovation and many records featuring the sitar, some good and some bad, were soon on the market. The song, which is really an account of a love affair set to music, has John on lead with additional vocals in places from Paul.

You Won't See Me (Lennon–McCartney)   3:19

John Lennon : Tambourine and Backing Vocal
Paul McCartney : Bass Guitar, Piano and Lead Vocal
George Harrison : Lead Guitar and Backing Vocal
Ringo Starr : Drums
Mal Evans : Hammond Organ

Here, Paul is on lead vocals with John and George supplying harmony for chorus and backing. Mal Evans, one of the Beatles' roadies, is heard for the first time playing the Hammond organ. The piano is played by Paul.

Nowhere Man (Lennon–McCartney)   2:40

John Lennon : Acoustic Guitar and Lead Vocal
Paul McCartney : Bass Guitar and Lead Vocal
George Harrison : Lead Guitar and Lead Vocal
Ringo Starr : Drums

John initially brought this surrealistic character to life as a self-description. Later, after his admission of drug taking, the character became one of the focal points for analysts who decided that the 'Nowhere Man' was anything from a drug pusher to the captain of the Yellow Submarine.

John, Paul and George harmonise for the a cappella intro, then John sings lead vocals, with Paul and George adding backing harmonies and joining John for the chorus.

Think For Yourself (Harrison)   2:16

John Lennon : Tambourine and Backing Vocal
Paul McCartney : Fuzz Bass Guitar and Backing Vocal
George Harrison : Lead Guitar and Lead Vocal
Ringo Starr : Drums and Maracas

The first of two tracks on the album written by George features him on lead vocal with John and Paul harmonising in places. Paul can also be heard trying out the then newly invented fuzz bass guitar. Obviously he cannot have been impressed by it because it was four years before he was to use it again on a Beatles' record.

The Word (Lennon–McCartney)   2:42

John Lennon : Rhythm Guitar and Lead Vocal
Paul McCartney : Bass Guitar, Piano and Lead Vocal
George Harrison : Lead Guitar and Lead Vocal
Ringo Starr : Drums and Maracas
George Martin : Harmonium

A foretaste of what was to come later with All You Need Is Love. The phrase 'the word is love' and the 'love one another' theme were both to be adopted by the hippy movement.

John, Paul and George harmonise with John mainly singing lead. George Martin plays harmonium and Paul joins in on piano. The recording seems to fade out rather early, giving the impression of an incomplete ending.

Michelle (Lennon–McCartney)   2:42

John Lennon : Acoustic Guitar and Backing Vocal
Paul McCartney : Bass Guitar and Lead Vocal
George Harrison : Acoustic Guitar and Backing Vocal
Ringo Starr : Drums

Written by Paul for the daughter of an American millionaire, Michelle features Paul on lead vocals with John and George adding the close harmony backing. This was another of the Beatles' songs to become an all-time standard. The song lapses into French now and again as with the phrase 'Ma belle' ('My beautiful') and 'Sont les mots qui vont très bien ensemble' ('These are words that go together very well'). When Michelle was issued in France as the title track of an E.P. (the French did not then release singles, all 45 rpm records were E.P.s), it shot to the No. 1 spot.

SIDE TWO

What Goes On (Lennon–McCartney–Starkey)   2:44

John Lennon : Rhythm Guitar and Backing Vocal
Paul McCartney : Bass Guitar and Backing Vocal
George Harrison : Lead Guitar
Ringo Starr : Drums and Lead Vocal

Co-written by John, Paul and Ringo, this song provided Ringo with another of the sing-a-long, rockabilly numbers that always seemed to suit his voice. John and Paul provide the harmony vocals for the chorus and George adds some nice country and western style guitar.

Girl (Lennon–McCartney)   2:26

John Lennon : Acoustic Guitar and Lead Vocal
Paul McCartney : Bass Guitar and Backing Vocal
George Harrison : Sitar and Backing Vocal
Ringo Starr : Drums

Lead vocals are from John with Paul and George adding a wordless and the 'tit-tit' backing vocal and also joining John for the chorus. There is an interesting section when the backing vocals build up and dissolve along with John's voice into the chorus.

I'm Looking Through You (Lennon–McCartney)   2:20

John Lennon : Acoustic Guitar and Harmony Vocal
Paul McCartney : Bass Guitar and Lead Vocal
George Harrison : Lead Guitar and Tambourine
Ringo Starr : Drums and Hammond Organ

Paul on lead vocals on this semi-rock and roll song reveals the influences of both Little Richard and Buddy Holly. It sounds rather like a re-written version of Buddy Holly's Everyday sung with a Little Richard voice but curiously enough it works. The recording also features Ringo on a Hammond organ mixed so far into the backing it might just as well not be there.

The American stereo version of this track includes two false starts but is then identical to this version.

In My Life (Lennon–McCartney)   2:23

John Lennon : Lead Vocal
Paul McCartney : Bass Guitar and Harmony Vocal
George Harrison : Lead Guitar
Ringo Starr : Drums
George Martin : Piano

Nostalgically John recalls people and places who played an important part in his younger days. The song is beautifully set to unobtrusive music, and is reminiscent of Penny Lane or Strawberry Fields Forever.

Wait (Lennon–McCartney)   2:13

John Lennon : Tambourine and Lead Vocal
Paul McCartney : Bass Guitar and Lead Vocal
George Harrison : Lead Guitar
Ringo Starr : Drums and Maracas

A lively track, featuring a lead vocal duet between John and Paul that for some reason does not seem to fit in with the previous tracks. It sounds almost as if it was left over from either Beatles For Sale or Help!

If I Needed Someone (Harrison) 2:19

John Lennon : Tambourine and Backing Vocal
Paul McCartney : Bass Guitar and Backing Vocal
George Harrison : Lead Guitar and Lead Vocal
Ringo Starr : Drums
George Martin : Harmonium

A George Harrison composition which shows how he improved with each new song he wrote. This can be compared with a few Lennon and McCartney songs of the same period.

The Beatles make use of an extremely pleasant guitar riff that crops up every now and then and accentuates both the lyrics, and style of George Harrison's singing.

Run For Your Life (Lennon–McCartney) 2:21

John Lennon : Acoustic Guitar and Lead Vocal
Paul McCartney : Bass Guitar and Backing Vocal
George Harrison : Lead Guitar and Backing Vocal
Ringo Starr : Drums
George Martin : Tambourine

This is not one of John and Paul's best compositions. It sounds rather like a mixture of their previous Little Child from the album With The Beatles, and the Larry Williams song Bad Boy. Even John Lennon, who wrote it, went on record as not liking it.

UK Release : 5 August 1966
Parlophone PMC 7009: PCS 7009
US Release : April 1987
Capitol CLJ 46441
Intl CD No : CDP 7 46441 2
Producer : George Martin
Running Time : 35:01

SIDE ONE : Taxman; Eleanor Rigby; I'm Only Sleeping; Love You To; Here, There And Everywhere; Yellow Submarine; She Said, She Said.

SIDE TWO : Good Day Sunshine; And Your Bird Can Sing; For No One; Dr. Robert; I Want To Tell You; Got To Get You Into My Life; Tomorrow Never Knows.

The musical direction the Beatles appeared to be taking with 'Rubber Soul' changed quickly with Revolver. Released eight months after Rubber Soul, this album contains brilliant, diverse music and moves further into the realms of fantasy. Revolver contains some rather interesting social statements from the Beatles in the form of George Harrison's sarcastic comments on Taxman and Paul McCartney's sad tale of loneliness on Eleanor Rigby. Various flights of fantasy and strange lyrics feature on a range of titles from the sing-along Yellow Submarine to the weird and frightening Tomorrow Never Knows.

The sleeve shows a collage of drawings (by Klaus Voormann) and photographs of the Beatles (including two of the photographs previously used on the back of Rubber Soul). A collection of faces, as on the inner photograph of the Beatles For Sale album, is again used just as it would be used again even more effectively on the sleeve of the Sgt. Pepper's Lonely Hearts Club Band album.

Although fans did not realise at the time, the Beatles were to give their last full concert three weeks after the release of this album. Their music had progressed to such a point that with Rubber Soul and Revolver it had become almost impossible to reproduce live.

SIDE ONE

Taxman (Harrison)   2:36

John Lennon : Tambourine and Backing Vocal
Paul McCartney : Bass Guitar and Backing Vocal
George Harrison : Lead Guitar and Lead Vocal
Ringo Starr : Drums

George's first song to make a social comment takes a swipe at the taxman. Lead vocal is from George with backing and harmony vocals from John and Paul. The musical accompaniment is as harsh as the lyrics, with a very strong attacking lead guitar riff.

Eleanor Rigby (Lennon–McCartney)   2:11

John Lennon : Not Present
Paul McCartney : Solo Vocal
George Harrison : Not Present
Ringo Starr : Not Present
Session Musicians : Four Violins, two Violas, and two Cellos

This classic McCartney composition has become another of his 'standards'. Here it features a lead vocal from Paul who double-tracks in part to produce his own harmonies. Like Yesterday on the Help! album, this features only Paul McCartney — John, George and Ringo do not sing or play any instrument on this recording. All of the backing music is played by a string octet.

The lyrics make a valid social statement about the loneliness of Eleanor Rigby and Father McKenzie's empty church. It is generally thought that Paul wrote this song after John made his now famous comment 'Christianity will go.

It will vanish and shrink. I needn't argue about that. I'm right and I will be proved right. We're more popular than Jesus now. I don't know which will go first, rock and roll or Christianity....'

I'm Only Sleeping (Lennon–McCartney)   2:58

John Lennon : Acoustic Guitar and Lead Vocal
Paul McCartney : Bass Guitar and Backing Vocal
George Harrison : Lead Guitar and Backing Vocal
Ringo Starr : Drums

The song idles along at tick-over speed and with John's lethargic vocal interpretation creates a lazy, stay-in-bed atmosphere mirroring the lyrics about him lying in bed watching the world go by. The strange guitar sound is George's overdubbed, backwards lead guitar.

Love You To (Harrison)   3:00

John Lennon : Not Present
Paul McCartney : Not Present
George Harrison : Solo Vocal
Ringo Starr : Not Present
Anil Bhagwat : Tabla
Session Musicians : All Other Instruments

After George Harrison had become interested in the sitar and played it on Norwegian Wood he enlisted the help of Anil Bhagwat to play the tabla on this recording, the second of three on the album written by George Harrison, and also the first full-scale use of Indian instruments by George for a Beatles' recording. None of the other Beatles appeared on this track.

Here, There And Everywhere (Lennon–McCartney)   2:29

John Lennon : Backing Vocal
Paul McCartney : Acoustic Guitar and Lead Vocal
George Harrison : Lead Guitar and Backing Vocal
Ringo Starr : Drums

This is a gentle but slightly up-tempo ballad from Paul, featuring his lead vocal multi-tracked and spread across the stereo. The wordless backing vocals from John, Paul and George are mixed onto the left-hand channel and blend in with the lead vocal creating the pleasing impression of a single voice.

Yellow Submarine (Lennon–McCartney) 2:40

John Lennon : Acoustic Guitar and Backing Vocal
Paul McCartney : Acoustic Guitar and Backing Vocal
George Harrison : Tambourine and Backing Vocal
Ringo Starr : Drums and Lead Vocal
Chorus : Includes George Martin, Patti Harrison, Mal Evans, Neil Aspinall and Geoff Emerick
Session Musicians : Brass Band

Issued as a single with Eleanor Rigby, on the same day as the album, this is one of the Beatles' most famous sing-along records, with an extremely catchy chorus. The lead vocal comes from Ringo (the only track to feature him as vocalist) with John, Paul and George joining in on chorus. Some of the many sound effects included were John blowing bubbles through a straw into a bucket of water, George swirling water round in another bucket, 'cocktail party' sounds, a brass band, various engine-room noises and shouted orders. The final chorus makes use of all the people at the recording — the four Beatles, George Martin, Patti Harrison, roadies Mal Evans and Neil Aspinall, Geoff Emerick and presumably several more. The song was to inspire the cartoon film of the same name, which was released three years after this recording. (See the Yellow Submarine album.)

She Said She Said (Lennon–McCartney) 2:39

John Lennon : Acoustic Guitar and Solo Vocal
Paul McCartney : Bass Guitar
George Harrison : Lead Guitar
Ringo Starr : Drums

This is apparently John Lennon's account of a conversation with Peter Fonda during an LSD trip. If the backing to this track is anything to go by, the trip must have been a chaotic one.

SIDE TWO

Good Day Sunshine (Lennon–McCartney) 2:08

John Lennon : Harmony Vocal
Paul McCartney : Lead Vocal
George Harrison : Harmony Vocal
Ringo Starr : Drums
George Martin : Piano

The lead vocal on this track comes from Paul with harmonies from John, reflecting influences from the thirties with a honky-tonk New Orleans style piano break. This interesting and inventive recording features two separate drum beats, one on each channel of the stereo. With this track the Beatles began successfully experimenting with stereo. On the fade the title/chorus line comes out of each of the speakers alternately.

And Your Bird Can Sing (Lennon–McCartney)   2:02

John Lennon : Rhythm Guitar and Lead Vocal
Paul McCartney : Bass Guitar and Harmony Vocal
George Harrison : Lead Guitar and Harmony Vocal
Ringo Starr : Drums and Tambourine

Lead vocal is from John, with Paul harmonising here and there. The recording features a very prominent lead guitar riff mixed so far forward it becomes part of the main recording rather than part of the backing.

For No One (Lennon–McCartney)   2:03

John Lennon : Not Present
Paul McCartney : Bass Guitar, Piano and Solo Vocal
George Harrison : Not Present
Ringo Starr : Drums and Tambourine
Alan Civil : Horn

This is a very pleasant track featuring a solo vocal from Paul, who also plays a bouncy piano. An unobtrusive horn is played by Alan Civil.

Dr. Robert (Lennon–McCartney)   2:14

John Lennon : Maracas, Harmonium and Lead Vocal
Paul McCartney : Bass Guitar and Harmony Vocal
George Harrison : Lead Guitar
Ringo Starr : Drums

The lyrics of this song were apparently based on a real character in New York who supplied anyone and everyone with drugs of various kinds. The lead vocals are from John with harmonies in part from Paul.

I Want To Tell You (Harrison)   2:30

John Lennon : Tambourine and Harmony Vocal
Paul McCartney : Bass Guitar, Piano and Harmony Vocal
George Harrison : Lead Guitar and Lead Vocal
Ringo Starr : Drums

Lead vocals are from George, with John and Paul harmonising in places. This is not one of George Harrison's better compositions as it sounds slightly off-key with a rather erratic backing beat.

Got To Get You Into My Life (Lennon–McCartney) 2:31

John Lennon : Tambourine
Paul McCartney : Bass Guitar and Solo Vocal
George Harrison : Lead Guitar
Ringo Starr : Drums
George Martin : Organ
Eddy Thornton : Trumpet
Ian Hamer : Trumpet
Les Conlon : Trumpet
Alan Branscombe : Tenor Sax
Pete Coe : Tenor Sax

This track, heavily influenced by the Motown sound, features a solo vocal from Paul, with brass backing played by Eddy Thornton, Ian Hamer and Les Conlon on trumpets and Alan Branscombe and Peter Coe on tenor sax. A good strong solid track. Later to be recorded by Cliff Bennett and the Rebel Rousers, who had a British Top Ten hit with it.

Tomorrow Never Knows (Lennon–McCartney) 3:00

John Lennon : Tambourine and Solo Vocal
Paul McCartney : Bass Guitar
George Harrison : Sitar and Lead Guitar
Ringo Starr : Drums
George Martin : Piano
Sounds effects devised by John and Ringo and arranged by Paul.

Some of the lyrics of this song, which had the working title of Mark 1, come straight from the Tibetan *Book of the Dead*. They are set to an hypnotic drum beat with a collage of sound effects made up of backward-running tapes and tape loops, which sound, at times, rather like a herd of rampaging elephants. John's solo vocal, treated to various studio effects, filters through like a nightmare set to music. This was the Beatles' most experimental recording to date, and a very successful experiment at that, both musically and lyrically. Lyrics like 'listen to the colour of your dreams' herald the appearance of psychedelia. Curiously, nowhere in the lyrics do the words 'tomorrow never knows', a title invented by Ringo, appear.

UK Release : 10 December 1966
Parlophone PMC 7016 : PCS 7016
US Release : None
Intl CD No : None
Producer : George Martin
Running Time : 38:06

SIDE ONE : She Loves You; From Me To You; We Can Work It Out; Help!; Michelle; Yesterday; I Feel Fine; Yellow Submarine.

SIDE TWO : Can't Buy Me Love; Bad Boy; Day Tripper; A Hard Day's Night; Ticket To Ride; Paperback Writer; Eleanor Rigby; I Want To Hold Your Hand.

Following the recording of the Revolver album the Beatles embarked on what proved to be their final world tour which ended with a concert on 29 August 1966 at San Francisco's Candlestick Park (their final UK concert had been some months earlier on 1 May when they performed at The Empire Pool, Wembley, during the New Musical Express Poll Winner's Show). During 1966 they also became involved in various personal projects : John appeared in the film *How I Won The War*, shot in Germany and Spain; Paul wrote the soundtrack for the film *The Family Way*; and George became more involved with Indian music (at one point flying to India to take sitar lessons from Ravi Shankar).

During this period (June–December 1966), and because of their various activities, the Beatles were not involved in any recording sessions to produce material for release. So for their pre-Christmas release the Beatles compiled this album.

It is a rather makeshift release containing eight tracks not previously included on a British album together with a further eight tracks which had previously appeared on the A Hard Day's Night, Help!, Rubber Soul and Revolver albums. Amongst the 'new' material included here is Bad Boy which had previously only been available on the American album Beatles VI (Capitol ST 2358) released some eighteen months earlier. The remaining seven tracks included on a British album for the first time are She Loves You, From Me To You, We Can Work It Out, I Feel Fine, Day Tripper, Paperback Writer and I Want To Hold Your Hand. For the stereo version of the album George Martin (not having a stereo master available) tried to create a stereo version of She Loves You from the mono recording (although abandoned, the various 'stereo' mixes are still on file at EMI).

As a 'greatest hits' album this seemed to fit the bill at the time, but more recently all of the tracks not previously included on albums have been more sensibly repackaged on Past Masters — Volumes One and Two. Surprisingly, at the time of release of A Collection Of Beatles Oldies there were nineteen tracks available (plus the German-language versions of She Loves You and I Want To Hold Your Hand) which had not previously been included on any British album, from which the Beatles chose to use only eight.

SIDE ONE

She Loves You (Lennon–McCartney)   2:18

Recorded : 1 July 1963, EMI Studios, Abbey Road, London

John Lennon : Rhythm Guitar and Lead Vocal
Paul McCartney : Bass Guitar and Lead Vocal
George Harrison : Lead Guitar and Harmony Vocal
Ringo Starr : Drums

The A-side of the Beatles' fourth single, issued on Parlophone in Britain on 23 August 1963, features the usual lead vocal duet from John and Paul. The song includes the now famous catchy chorus line of 'yeah, yeah, yeah' and the equally famous 'oooo', which was previously used in I Saw Her Standing There on the Please Please Me album. If Love Me Do, Please Please Me and From Me To You had not convinced people that the Beatles had staying power the catchy chorus line and excitement generated by She Loves You must surely have done so.

From Me To You (Lennon–McCartney)   1:55

Recorded : 5 March 1963, EMI Studios, Abbey Road, London

John Lennon : Rhythm Guitar, Harmonica and Lead Vocal
Paul McCartney : Bass Guitar and Lead Vocal
George Harrison : Lead Guitar and Harmony Vocal
Ringo Starr : Drums

With this, the follow-up single to Please Please Me and the Beatles' second No. 1, they began to prove that they had both musical and song-writing ability. According to some charts Please Please Me only reached No. 2, and From Me to You was their first No. 1 single. If it was, it began a string of eleven consecutive No. 1 singles — a record that has never been equalled to date. Like so many of the Beatles' early recordings the lead vocal is shared by John and Paul with George joining in here and there, and on chorus. The recording also makes very effective use of John's harmonica.

From Me To You was reputed to have been written on 28 February 1963 after John and Paul had read the letters column, From You To Us, in the *New Musical Express* during a coach journey from York to Shrewsbury while they were on tour (as the support act!) with Helen Shapiro.

During the early sixties the Beatles had their own BBC radio show, some episodes of which were entitled From Us To You, which featured a reworded recording of From Me To You.

We Can Work It Out (Lennon–McCartney)   2:10

Recorded : 20 and 29 October 1965, EMI Studios, Abbey Road, London

John Lennon : Harmonium and Harmony Vocal
Paul McCartney : Bass Guitar and Lead Vocal
George Harrison : Acoustic Guitar and Tambourine
Ringo Starr : Drums

This could be classified as the Beatles' first ever peace song. It predated All You Need Is Love by two years and Give Peace A Chance by four years. Released as the follow-up to Help! in 1965 this is the Beatles' eleventh Parlophone single and their ninth No. 1. By 1965 the Beatles had progressed from the 'beat group' sound of some of their early 1963–4 singles to a more technically and musically proficient group of musicians. Lead vocal on this is by Paul, with John joining in for the chorus and also playing harmonium. At various times the recording lapses into a slow waltz but then picks up again for the verses. John later used the same style for the instrumental break in the middle of Being For The Benefit of Mr. Kite on Sgt. Pepper's Lonely Hearts Club Band. Paul's optimistic main lyrics are countered by John's realism with the verse beginning 'Life is very short ...'. John did a similar thing with Paul's Getting Better on Sgt. Pepper's. The main part of the track was recorded in two takes on 20 October and completed with an overdub on 29 October.

Help! (Lennon–McCartney)   2:16

John Lennon : Acoustic Guitar and Lead Vocal
Paul McCartney : Bass Guitar and Backing Vocal
George Harrison : Lead Guitar and Backing Vocal
Ringo Starr : Drums and Tambourine

Previously included on the album Help!

Michelle (Lennon–McCartney)   2:42

John Lennon : Acoustic Guitar and Backing Vocal
Paul McCartney : Bass Guitar and Lead Vocal
George Harrison : Acoustic Guitar and Backing Vocal
Ringo Starr : Drums

Previously included on the album Rubber Soul.

Yesterday (Lennon–McCartney)   2:04

John Lennon : Not Present
Paul McCartney : Acoustic Guitar and Solo Vocal
George Harrison : Not Present
Ringo Starr : Not Present
Session Musicians : String Quartet

Previously included on the album Help!.

I Feel Fine (Lennon–McCartney)   2:19

Recorded : 18 October 1964, EMI Studios, Abbey Road, London

John Lennon : Rhythm Guitar, Lead Guitar and Lead Vocal
Paul McCartney : Bass Guitar and Backing Vocal
George Harrison : Lead Guitar and Backing Vocal
Ringo Starr : Drums

With advance orders of three quarters of a million copies, this was issued as a single on 27 November 1964 as the follow-up to A Hard Day's Night. It was the Beatles' eighth single and sixth consecutive No. 1. The recording, which was completed in nine takes, opens with a single note of feedback, which then goes into the riff around which the song is constructed. This was the first time that feedback had been used on a record, and it gave ideas to many musicians like Jimi Hendrix, who later used feedback as a musical note and not just as a noise. Theories at the time about the sound at the beginning of the record included the idea of an amplified humming bee. In fact the Beatles did not use pre-recorded sound effects until 1966, two years later. The lead vocal is from John, with Paul and George joining him on the chorus. Paul and George also sing a wordless vocal backing.

Yellow Submarine (Lennon–McCartney)   2:40

John Lennon : Acoustic Guitar and Backing Vocal
Paul McCartney : Acoustic Guitar and Backing Vocal
George Harrison : Tambourine and Backing Vocal
Ringo Starr : Drums and Lead Vocal
Chorus : Includes George Martin, Patti Harrison, Mal Evans, Neil Aspinall and
  Geoff Emerick
Session Musicians : Brass Band

Previously included on the album Revolver.

SIDE TWO

Can't Buy Me Love (Lennon–McCartney)   2:15

John Lennon : Rhythm Guitar
Paul McCartney : Bass Guitar and Solo Vocal
George Harrison : Lead Guitar
Ringo Starr : Drums

Previously included on the album A Hard Day's Night.

Bad Boy (Williams)   2:17

Recorded : 10–11 May 1965, EMI Studios, Abbey Road, London

John Lennon : Rhythm Guitar, Hammond Organ and Solo Vocal
Paul McCartney : Bass Guitar and Electric Piano
George Harrison : Lead Guitar
Ringo Starr : Drums and Tambourine

This was originally issued as part of the American album Beatles VI on 14 June
1965 and later included on the British album A Collection Of Beatles Oldies
released on 9 December 1966. The recording, which was completed in four
takes, features a solo vocal from John and a very enthusiastic backing from the
rest of the Beatles. This and another Larry Williams song, Dizzy Miss Lizzy
(recorded during the same session), were the last two songs (leaving aside
the rather short rendition of Maggie Mae on Let It Be) issued by the Beatles
during their collective career that they did not write themselves.

Day Tripper (Lennon–McCartney) 2:37

Recorded : 16 October 1965, EMI Studios, Abbey Road, London

John Lennon : Rhythm Guitar, Tambourine and Lead Vocal
Paul McCartney : Bass Guitar and Lead Vocal
George Harrison : Lead Guitar and Harmony Vocal
Ringo Starr : Drums

This track was issued together with We Can Work It Out as a double A-sided single on 3 December 1965; the same day also saw the release of the Rubber Soul album. It was written mainly by John with Paul contributing some of the lyrics. The lyrics are reminiscent of the earlier Ticket To Ride (and the title is similar). It was recorded in three takes on 16 October 1965, and features a lead vocal duet between John and Paul with George joining them for the harmony sections. Upon its release it entered the British charts at No. 1 where it stayed for five weeks, selling over one million copies before the end of the month.

A Hard Day's Night (Lennon–McCartney) 2:32

John Lennon : Rhythm Guitar and Lead Vocal
Paul McCartney : Bass Guitar and Harmony Vocal
George Harrison : Lead Guitar
Ringo Starr : Drums
George Martin : Piano

Previously included on the album A Hard Day's Night.

Ticket To Ride (Lennon–McCartney) 3:03

John Lennon : Rhythm Guitar, Tambourine and Lead Vocal
Paul McCartney : Bass Guitar and Harmony Vocal
George Harrison : Lead Guitar
Ringo Starr : Drums

Previously included on the album Help!.

Paperback Writer (Lennon–McCartney) 2:25

John Lennon : Rhythm Guitar and Backing Vocal
Paul McCartney : Bass Guitar and Lead Vocal
George Harrison : Lead Guitar and Backing Vocal
Ringo Starr : Drums

As this is also included on the Hey Jude album, along with its B-side, Rain, it is discussed with that album.

Eleanor Rigby (Lennon–McCartney)   2:11

John Lennon : Not Present
Paul McCartney : Solo Vocal
George Harrison : Not Present
Ringo Starr : Not Present
Session Musicians : Four Violins, two Violas and two Cellos

Previously included on the album Revolver.

I Want To Hold Your Hand (Lennon–McCartney)   2:24

Recorded : 17 October 1963, EMI Studios, Abbey Road, London
John Lennon : Rhythm Guitar and Lead Vocal
Paul McCartney : Bass Guitar and Lead Vocal
George Harrison : Lead Guitar and Harmony Vocal
Ringo Starr : Drums

This record, as a single, sold over fifteen million copies world-wide. In fact, prior to its release in Britain on 19 November 1963, there were advance orders approaching one million copies. Needless to say, upon its release in Britain it entered the charts at No. 1, where it remained for six weeks. This was the record which in 1964 gave birth to Beatlemania in America, where it sold nearly five million copies and opened up the American market for other British artists.

The recording opens with John's rhythm guitar, a sound which builds up to an intense pitch and then virtually explodes as John and Paul begin their lead vocal duet. For the chorus line John and Paul are joined by George and all three add excited hand-clapping to make this one of their most powerful early recordings.

Recorded in seventeen takes on 17 October 1963, this was the Beatles' first four-track recording which enabled George Martin to, amongst other things, produce a rather better stereo image than the previous two-track recordings of earlier sessions.

SGT. PEPPER'S LONELY HEARTS CLUB BAND

UK Release : 1 June 1967
Parlophone PMC 7027 : PCS 7027
US Release : 2 June 1967
Capitol MAS 2653 : SMAS 2653
Intl CD No : CDP 7 46442 2
Producer : George Martin
Running Time : 39:02

SIDE ONE : Sgt. Pepper's Lonely Hearts Club Band; With A Little Help From My Friends; Lucy In The Sky With Diamonds; Getting Better; Fixing A Hole; She's Leaving Home; Being For the Benefit of Mr. Kite.

SIDE TWO : Within You, Without You; When I'm Sixty-Four; Lovely Rita; Good Morning, Good Morning; Sgt. Pepper's Lonely Hearts Club Band (Reprise); A Day In The Life.

Regarded by many as the Beatles' finest album, Sgt. Pepper has been copied, emulated and drawn from, but never equalled. The title has slipped into everyday language in the music world to describe any artists' new album as being their finest achievement — 'their Sgt. Pepper'.

The album took four months and £50,000 to make — staggering when compared with the Beatles' first Parlophone album, Please Please Me, which was recorded in one 13-hour session and cost £400.

This album's concept began to take shape during the late summer/early autumn of 1966 when Paul came up with the title song. Ideas were then exchanged and it was decided that Sgt. Pepper should be the theme for the album with the track opening the album and appearing again near the end. So the title was recorded twice and the second recording slotted in just before A Day In The Life, the album's final track. The album, in the words of the Beatles themselves, after this point 'generated its own togetherness' and as each new recording was made it seemed to fall into place.

Recording began in November 1966 with Strawberry Fields Forever, When I'm Sixty-Four and Penny Lane, but it was decided to issue Penny Lane/Strawberry Fields Forever as a single, and these tracks were extracted from the recordings already made. After a Christmas break, recording recommenced on 19 January 1967 when the Beatles began work on the album's closing track A Day In The Life. Recording continued through to 3 April 1967, when, with the exception of a few final overdubs of strings, the album was completed.

The first rock music album to be issued with a continual theme running through it, Sgt. Pepper was dubbed the first 'concept album'. As a result concept albums of varying degrees of quality by other artists soon began to appear.

Like its contents, the sleeve of this album is highly original. Designed by Peter Blake, from ideas by the Beatles, it shows a collection of faces of people they admired or who had influenced them in various ways. Amongst the fifty-odd faces are W.C. Fields, Aldous Huxley, Fred Astaire, Bob Dylan, Tony Curtis, Laurel and Hardy, Max Miller and a host of others. The only person missing from the collage of faces was Adolph Hitler (reputed to have been picked by John). His photograph had been selected and blown up to fit in with the rest, but at the last minute it was decided that the inclusion of Adolph Hitler would be in bad taste. The collage also includes wax models of the Beatles themselves, Sonny Liston and Diana Dors, all of which were loaned from Madame Tussaud's in Baker Street, London. Other features of the cover photograph include the Beatles dressed in bright satin uniforms as Sgt. Pepper's band, with their name painted on the bass drum of the kit. The foreground is set out as a garden with the word 'Beatles' spelt out in flowers and also a guitar shaped out of flowers. Across the top of the garden and foreground right are marijuana plants, included as a protest about the non-legalisation of the drug. Statues and ornaments included in the foreground were from various Beatles' homes. The Beatles are holding instruments they did not normally play — John has a French horn, Ringo a trumpet, Paul a cor anglais and George a flute. A line printed on the back of the sleeve sums up the intention of the album: 'a splendid time is guaranteed for all'.

SIDE ONE

Sgt. Pepper's Lonely Hearts Club Band
(Lennon–McCartney)   1:59

John Lennon : Lead Guitar and Backing Vocal
Paul McCartney : Bass Guitar and Lead Vocal
George Harrison : Lead Guitar and Backing Vocal
Ringo Starr : Drums
George Martin : Organ
Session Musicians : Four Horns

The album opens with the sound of an orchestra tuning up and an expectant audience. The 'Sgt. Pepper band' then strike up the first few chords on their guitars, and the album begins. The Beatles had introduced heavy guitar sounds on Rain issued as the B-side to Paperback Writer some 12 months earlier, but here is their first full use of guitars as a sound, as opposed to just backing instruments. The Beatles' instrumentation on this track is supplemented by George Martin on organ (just near the end) and a group of four studio musicians who add the horns, to make the 'Sgt. Pepper band' a semi-rock/brass outfit. Lead vocals are from Paul, who also joins John and George for the backing and the chorus.

With this album the Beatles started experimenting with stereo and discovered that it actually moved. On this track the chorus starts on the left-hand channel then begins to drift across to the centre of the stereo. When Paul sings again he starts on the right-hand channel.

With A Little Help From My Friends
(Lennon–McCartney)   2:46

John Lennon : Backing Vocal
Paul McCartney : Bass Guitar, Piano and Backing Vocal
George Harrison : Tambourine
Ringo Starr : Drums and Lead Vocal

Ringo is in the vocal spotlight with vocal support from John and Paul on both the backing and the chorus. His vocal performance on this song is rated by many to be one of his best. This is another Lennon and McCartney song that had a working title bearing no relation to the finished song. It started out as Bad Finger Boogie, and is said to have influenced one of the groups signed to the Apple label in their choice of name. They started out as The Ivies and then became Badfinger.

Lucy In The Sky With Diamonds (Lennon–McCartney)   3:25

John Lennon : Lead Guitar and Lead Vocal
Paul McCartney : Bass Guitar, Hammond Organ and Harmony Vocal
George Harrison : Sitar and Harmony Vocal
Ringo Starr : Drums

John Lennon went on record as saying that his most surrealistic lyrics were inspired, not by an LSD trip as many thought (and some still maintain) but by a painting that his son Julian had brought home from school. When John enquired as to what it was, Julian replied 'It's Lucy in the sky with diamonds'. Lucy, Julian's best friend at school, had inspired Julian to paint a girl on a black background surrounded by stars, which he insisted were not stars but diamonds.

Lead vocals are by John with Paul and George joining in on chorus and also supplying backing vocals. The track opens with what sounds like a string instrument, but this is a Hammond organ. Its in-built special effects were used to produce a harpsichord/celeste sound.

Getting Better (Lennon–McCartney)   2:47

John Lennon : Lead Guitar and Backing Vocal
Paul McCartney : Bass Guitar and Lead/Backing Vocal
George Harrison : Lead Guitar, Tamboura and Backing Vocal
Ringo Starr : Drums and Bongos
George Martin : Piano

It certainly is. Paul's lyrics are set to the same syncopated beat that he had used a few years earlier on tracks such as She's A Woman. Lead vocals are from Paul, who also joins John for the backing. George had experimented with the sitar on earlier Beatles' albums and here tries a new Indian instrument, a tamboura. This looks like an oversized sitar, but doesn't produce musical notes in terms of western music. Instead, it produces a droning resonant tone that in Indian music is used as it is here — more as a backing tone than as part of the instrumentation. Near the end of the track, George Martin joins in with a piano; interestingly he doesn't actually play the keyboard but strikes the strings instead.

Fixing A Hole (Lennon–McCartney)   2:33

John Lennon : Maracas and Backing Vocal
Paul McCartney : Harpsichord, Bass Guitar, Lead Guitar and Lead Vocal
George Harrison : Lead Guitar and Backing Vocal
Ringo Starr : Drums

Lead vocal on this one again comes from Paul, who also plays the harpsichord. The guitar solo in the middle is played by George. This is a good up-tempo song from Paul but its lyrics, like Lucy In The Sky With Diamonds have been misconstrued. Paul McCartney commented on this track. 'This song is just about the hole in the road where the rain gets in; a good old analogy — the hole in your make-up which lets the rain in and stops your mind from going where it will. It's you interfering with things . . . If you're a junkie sitting in a room *fixing* a hole then that's what it will mean to you, but when I wrote it I meant if there's a crack or the room is uncolourful, then I'll paint it.'

She's Leaving Home (Lennon–McCartney)   3:24

John Lennon : Lead/Backing Vocal
Paul McCartney : Lead/Backing Vocal
George Harrison : Not Present
Ringo Starr : Not Present
Session Musicians : Harp and Strings

This is another classic McCartney ballad, and a sad social statement about a girl running away from home and 'everything that money could buy', because love and attention were missing from her life. Paul had said he was inspired to write the song by a newspaper article which reminded him of the same loneliness he had conveyed in Eleanor Rigby. The vocals are interestingly interwoven. Paul sings a double-tracked lead vocal with John singing here and there. This is the only track on the album where the Beatles do not play any of the backing; they are accompanied by a harp and some sweet-sounding violins which were scored by Mike Leander.

Being For The Benefit of Mr. Kite (Lennon–McCartney)   2:36

John Lennon : Hammond Organ and Solo Vocal
Paul McCartney : Bass Guitar and Lead Guitar
George Harrison : Harmonica
Ringo Starr : Harmonica
George Martin : Wurlitzer Organ and Piano
Mal Evans : Harmonica
Neil Aspinall : Harmonica

John was inspired to write this song by a Victorian circus poster announcing 'being for the benefit of Mr. Kite, a grand circus, The Hendersons, Pablo Fanques Fair ...'. Amongst the acts appearing in the circus was 'Henry The Horse'. John's vivid imagination helped him to collect these characters together and create the lyrics for the track. After reading them and those for Lucy In The Sky With Diamonds, George Martin described John as 'an oral Salvador Dali'. John sings the solo lead vocal on the track and plays Hammond organ. Paul plays a guitar solo and Ringo, George, Neil Aspinall and Mal Evans (the Beatles' roadies) each play a different type of harmonica. George Martin adds a few touches with a Wurlitzer organ, and the whole thing is rounded off with recorded snippets of a Victorian steam organ. To achieve the required random effect with the recording of the fairground organ, it was cut into 12-inch long strips, hurled into the air, then edited back together again, parts being played backwards and parts forward.

SIDE TWO

Within You, Without You (Harrison)   5:03

John Lennon : Not Present
Paul McCartney : Not Present
George Harrison : Tamboura and Solo Vocal
Ringo Starr : Not Present
Neil Aspinall : Tamboura
Session Musicians : Dilruba, Tamboura, Tabla and Swordmandel
Session Musicians : Eight Violins and three Cellos

Having previously tried his hand at recording Indian music with Love You To on Revolver, George Harrison's dabblings go one step further on this track. He merges an assortment of Indian instruments including a dilruba, tabla, a swordmandel and three tambouras (of which two are played by George and Neil Aspinall) with eight violins and three cellos. This is more of an event than a recording and at five minutes and three seconds it either sends you into a trance or to sleep; depending on your point of view, you either love it or hate it. George is the only member of the Beatles featured and in addition to playing one of the three tambouras he has a solo vocal. The sound of raucous laughter breaks the atmosphere and closes the track.

When I'm Sixty-Four (Lennon–McCartney)   2:38

John Lennon : Lead Guitar and Backing Vocal
Paul McCartney : Bass Guitar, Piano and Lead/Backing Vocal
George Harrison : Backing Vocal
Ringo Starr : Drums
Session Musicians : Two Clarinets and one Bass Clarinet

The track opens with the sound of two clarinets plus a bass clarinet (played by session musicians). Paul wrote the song for his father who had at the time recently turned 64. Its inoffensive lyrics and its equally inoffensive accompaniment jog along at a pleasant pace and divert us from the Indian temple and the raga-rock of George's extravaganza on the previous track. Lead vocal is from Paul with a three-part harmony backing from John, Paul and George. The piano is played by Paul.

Lovely Rita (Lennon–McCartney)   2:43

John Lennon : Acoustic Guitar, Comb and Paper and Backing Vocal
Paul McCartney : Bass Guitar, Piano, Comb and Paper and Lead/Backing Vocal
George Harrison : Acoustic Guitar, Comb and Paper and Backing Vocal
Ringo Starr : Drums
George Martin : Piano

Lead vocal comes from Paul who also plays piano, although the honky-tonk piano in the middle is George Martin. John, Paul and George sing backing vocals and also use comb and paper to produce the 'sha, sha, sha' sound. The last 60 seconds include a fine blues/jazz piano from Paul and various grunting and groaning noises. The Beatles were to use a similar ending on the Magical Mystery Tour title track later in 1967.

Good Morning, Good Morning (Lennon–McCartney) 2:35

John Lennon : Lead/Backing Vocal
Paul McCartney : Bass Guitar, Lead Guitar and Backing Vocal
George Harrison : Lead Guitar
Ringo Starr : Drums
Sounds Incorporated : Three Saxophones, two Trombones and one French Horn

This lively track opens with the sound of a cock crowing and then some very solid brass (three saxophones, two trumpets and a French horn) played by Sounds Incorporated, a fellow Liverpool group who were great friends of the Beatles. The lead vocal is by John, joined by Paul for the chorus. The guitar solo is by Paul. The ending can only be described as recorded chaos. Amongst the sound effects used are : a fox-hunt (which gallops away across the stereo), bleating sheep, a mooing cow, and a clucking chicken which George Martin had noticed sounded like the opening guitar note of the next track. He carefully edited this so that the clucking sound blended into the guitar note, so we are transported from the farmyard back into the theatre.

Sgt. Pepper's Lonely Hearts Club Band (Reprise)
(Lennon–McCartney) 1:20

John Lennon : Maracas, Lead Guitar and Lead Vocal
Paul McCartney : Bass Guitar and Lead Vocal
George Harrison : Lead Guitar and Lead Vocal
Ringo Starr : Drums

Paul counts in 'one-two-three-four' to introduce the reprise of the opening track. (If you listen to the counting over headphones you will hear John say 'bye' between the 'two' and 'three' of the count-in.) There is no lead vocalist on this second version — everybody sings the amended lyrics. Unlike on the opening track, there are no horns here. The recording does not finish; as it fades out to the sound of an applauding audience, the acoustic guitar and piano of A Day In The Life fade in.

A Day In The Life (Lennon–McCartney) 5:03

John Lennon : Acoustic Guitar, Piano* and Lead Vocal
Paul McCartney : Bass Guitar, Piano, Piano* and Lead Vocal
George Harrison : Bongos and Piano*
Ringo Starr : Drums, Maracas and Piano*
George Martin : Harmonium*
Mal Evans : Voice Counting, Alarm Clock and Piano*
Session Musicians : 41 Piece Orchestra
*Finale Only

This must be one of the most controversial Beatle recordings. The song originally began by recounting the news from the daily papers, with a report of a car crash and subsequent death. The second news item was a report of 4,000 potholes in the roads of Blackburn that had been personally counted by a local councillor. John, having written the two segments, could not join them together, and asked Paul to fill in the middle section. Paul has been quoted as saying, 'The next bit was another song altogether but it just happened to fit. It was just me remembering what it was like to run up the road to catch a bus to school, having a smoke and going into class. We decided : "bugger this, we're going to write a turn-on song". It was a reflection of my school days — I would have a Woodbine then, and somebody would speak and I would go into a dream. This was the only one in the album written as a deliberate provocation. A stick-that-in-your-pipe . . . but what we want is to turn you on to the truth rather than pot.'

When the song begins it fades in from the applause of the previous track. John plays the guitar intro, with Paul joining in on piano. John's cold harsh vocal then begins. When he reaches 'I'd love to turn you on ' a 41 piece orchestra begins to play, climbing higher and higher up the musical scale, until suddenly, the noise stops and we hear the sound of an alarm clock. The lyrics continue, and for a second time repeat 'I'd love to turn you on'; the 41 piece orchestra repeats its cacophonous destruction of the musical scale, reaches a climax and suddenly stops. There is then the most unearthly crash on three pianos and a harmonium. The resultant chord is drawn out for a staggering 45 seconds. A few further details might be of interest. The voice that can be heard counting during the 24 bar cacophonous build-up of the orchestra belongs to Mal Evans. The alarm clock was not originally intended for inclusion in the track, but it couldn't be removed, so had to be left in. Paul made use of it to include the line 'woke up, fell out of bed'. The orchestra build-up was recorded four times and then dubbed one on top of the other, slightly out of synchronisation, to give a fuller sound. The three pianos and a harmonium at the end are played or struck by members of the Beatles plus George Martin. This was also recorded four times then synchronised to give an unearthly sound.

The 15,000 Hz Tone   0:08

This tone was added as a gesture from the Beatles to all the dogs in Britain so that there would be something on the L.P. for them too! This is included only on British copies of the album.

The Inner Groove   0:02

This two seconds of nonsense was a snippet of conversation which sounded good when edited from a recording of the party given by the Beatles after they had finished the piano parts at the end of A Day In The Life. They decided they would like to fill the inner groove with something and this is what they chose.

UK Release : 19 November 1976
Parlophone PCTC 255
US Release : 27 November 1967
Capitol MAL 2835 : SMAL 2835
Intl CD No : CDP 7 48062 2
Producer : George Martin
Running Time : 36:32

SIDE ONE : Magical Mystery Tour; The Fool On The Hill; Flying; Blue Jay Way; Your Mother Should Know; I Am The Walrus.

SIDE TWO : Hello Goodbye; Strawberry Fields Forever; Penny Lane; Baby You're A Rich Man; All You Need Is Love.

The idea for the film, of which the first side of this album is the sound track, was originally conceived by Paul McCartney as early as March 1967, although filming didn't begin until Monday 11 September 1967. The invitation to the Beatles to appear as the British contribution to the world-wide television broadcast *Our World* in which they performed All You Need Is Love (which is also included on this album) caused the delay between conception and realisation of the idea.

The Beatles invited various friends and fan club secretaries to be included in the film. Amongst these was their old mate, Victor Spinetti, who appears in the film as a recruiting sergeant. (He had also appeared in the Beatles' two previous films, *A Hard Day's Night* and *Help!*) The Beatles decided that the coach used in the film should have a special logo along the side. This logo can be found on the front cover of the album. The tour, on film, begins in a side street just off Baker Street by the London Planetarium and then continues through the West of England. In the main the film was ad-libbed; the result was interesting though somewhat crazy. Weird characters emerge from the imaginations of the Beatles to feature in the various songs in the film — characters such as 'The Fool On The Hill', 'The Walrus', 'The Man Of A Thousand Voices' and 'The Egg Men'.

The album, although not made available in Britain until 1976, was available in the USA from 1967. It consists of the contents of the two E.P. set issued in Britain on 8 December 1967 along with the A- and B-sides of the three singles the Beatles issued in 1967. When the album was issued in Britain, EMI did a straight pressing from the American album. This left much to be desired as three of the tracks, Penny Lane, Baby You're A Rich Man and All You Need Is Love, are in fake stereo.

In 1973, EMI decided to issue a cassette version of the Magical Mystery Tour album. This cassette contained stereo versions of all the tracks included on the album, including a stereo version of Baby You're A Rich Man, which had previously been unavailable in Britain, although it was included on European pressings of the album. The cassette also includes the re–recorded version of All You Need Is Love (see the Yellow Submarine album), although the album contains the original single version of the song. The album has the catalogue number PCTC 255, but the cassette, in addition to the usual cassette prefix of TC, has the confusing number PCS 3077, which places it in between the Rubber Soul (PCS 3075) and Revolver (PCS 7009) albums.

It is interesting that the Beatles' entire 1967 record releases are contained on the Sgt. Pepper's Lonely Hearts Club Band and Magical Mystery Tour albums.

SIDE ONE

Magical Mystery Tour (Lennon–McCartney)   2:48

John Lennon : Acoustic Guitar and Backing Vocal
Paul McCartney : Bass Guitar, Piano and Lead Vocal
George Harrison : Lead Guitar and Backing Vocal
Ringo Starr : Drums and Tambourine
Session Musicians : Three Trumpets

The strong opening track features Paul on lead vocal and he joins John and George to sing the answer-style backing.

The influences of Penny Lane and Lovely Rita show through on this track, with three trumpets and jazz/blues piano. The Beatles expanded their use of stereo on this track, placing sounds and voices to create the effect of the movement of the Magical Mystery Tour coach.

The Fool On The Hill (Lennon–McCartney)   3:00

John Lennon : Harmonica and Maracas
Paul McCartney : Piano, Recorder, Flute and Solo Vocal
George Harrison : Lead Guitar and Harmonica
Ringo Starr : Finger Cymbals

Paul is the solo vocalist accompanying himself on piano, double-tracked recorder and flute. John and George add harmonicas and Ringo joins in with finger cymbals. George can be heard on lead guitar in the backing. The song is in the classic McCartney ballad style and has become a standard, rating nearly as well as his classics Yesterday and Michelle.

Flying (Lennon–McCartney–Harrison–Starkey)   2:16

John Lennon : Mellotron and Chanting
Paul McCartney : Assorted Guitars and Chanting
George Harrison : Assorted Guitars and Chanting
Ringo Starr : Drums, Maracas and Chanting

The only track to have been issued and composed by all four Beatles, this is the second of only two instrumentals ever released by them. The other was the Lennon–Harrison 1961 composition Cry For A Shadow. John plays the main theme of this instrumental on a Mellotron. Paul and George add an assortment of guitars and all four Beatles produce the chanting heard later. The ending fades into an assortment of sound effects and backward-running tapes and tape loops put together by John and Ringo for this recording.

Blue Jay Way (Harrison)   3:50

John Lennon : Tambourine
Paul McCartney : Bass Guitar and Backing Vocal
George Harrison : Hammond Organ, Lead and Backing Vocal
Ringo Starr : Drums
Session Musician : Cello

George leaves Indian music for a while to record the story of Derek Taylor (the Beatles publicist) being lost in fog in Los Angeles whilst trying to find Blue Jay Way, where George was staying at the time. The recording fades in immediately after the previous track as if the two are joined together. This is the only track to feature phasing (an electronic effect produced by playing the recording on two tape machines, slightly out of synchronisation, to produce a swirling, swishing effect). George's double-tracked lead vocals, backed mainly by himself on Hammond organ and Ringo on drums, are all phased throughout — quite an achievement, as phasing tends to slip after a while. The backing also includes a cello, various electronic sounds and backing vocals played forwards and backwards.

Your Mother Should Know (Lennon–McCartney)   2:33

John Lennon : Organ and Backing Vocal
Paul McCartney : Bass Guitar, Piano and Lead/Backing Vocal
George Harrison : Tambourine, Tabla and Backing Vocal
Ringo Starr : Drums

Paul's fascination with the twenties and thirties began to show on When I'm Sixty-Four on Sgt. Pepper, when he did a very good Noel Coward impression. His fascination continues with this similar song. Paul sings lead vocal and joins John and George for the backing vocals, the backing also includes Paul on piano, John on organ and at the end, George on an Indian tabla. The vocals start off on the left-hand channel for the first verse and switch to the right-hand channel for the second verse, then back to the left-hand channel for the third and final verse.

I Am The Walrus (Lennon–McCartney)   4:35

John Lennon : Mellotron and Lead Vocal
Paul McCartney : Bass Guitar and Backing Vocal
George Harrison : Tambourine and Backing Vocal
Ringo Starr : Drums
Session Musicians : Eight Violins, four Cellos and three Horns
Choir : Six Boys and Six Girls (Children of Michael Sammes Singers)

Definitely the most intriguing track the Beatles recorded. There are seven separate edits of this recording; this one features the opening riff played by John on the Mellotron repeated four times (although the British E.P. has the opening riff repeated six times (see Chapter 50 *The Alternative Versions*). He is then joined by eight violins, four cellos and Ringo on drums. The nonsensical flow of John's lyrics brings to mind his two books, *In His Own Write* and *Spaniard In The Works*. Strange phrases like 'sitting on a cornflake', 'yellow matter custard', 'crabalocker fishwife', 'expert texpert choking smokers', 'semolina pilchard' and 'elementary penguin' seem to fit into the interwoven collage of sound that he wanted to create.

On the line 'yellow matter custard' John is joined by three horns, various voices, oscillations and discordant sounds from a radio plugged into the recording console. When the recording stops we hear a snatch of noise and oscillations from the radio, then the music starts again, this time in fake stereo. The sound is mixed into mono on the right-hand channel with the 'highs' from the mix on the left-hand channel.

The radio, as legend goes, was coming through live onto the tape and two lines spoken by two separate voices fit perfectly with the lyrics, for after John sings 'I am the egg man' the first voice says 'Are you sir?'. John then continues with 'They are the egg men' and the second voice says 'A man may take you for what you are'. It was apparently John's idea to plug the radio into the recording console, and it was him playing around with the dial, which caused the noises and voices to be added to the recording. In addition to the music and the radio in the backing are six boys and girls, the children of the Michael Sammes Singers. The boys can be heard singing 'Oompah, oompah, stick it up your jumpah', and the girls are singing 'Everybody's got one.' John then tunes the radio into a Shakespeare play and at the end of the recording we hear 'Sit ye down father, rest you.'

SIDE TWO

Hello Goodbye (Lennon–McCartney)   3:24

John Lennon : Lead Guitar, Organ and Backing Vocal
Paul McCartney : Bass Guitar, Piano, Bongos, Conga Drum and
　　Lead/Backing Vocal
George Harrison : Lead Guitar, Tambourine and Backing Vocal
Ringo Starr : Drums and Maracas
Session Musicians : Two Violas

This was released as a single three weeks prior to the Magical Mystery Tour double E.P. set, with I Am The Walrus, a 'taster' from the E.P. set, on the B-side. This is the only song, except for the six Magical Mystery Tour recordings, that features in the film. Paul sings lead and joins John and George for the backing vocals. The guitars are played by John and George, and Paul plays piano and the bongos and conga drum on the Maori finale. John also plays the organ that can be heard near the end of the song before the Maori finale begins; session men added the violas that crop up now and again throughout the recording.

Strawberry Fields Forever (Lennon–McCartney)   4:05

John Lennon : Lead Guitar, Harpsichord and Solo Vocal
Paul McCartney : Bass Guitar, Piano, Bongos and Flute
George Harrison : Lead Guitar and Timpani
Ringo Starr : Drums
Mal Evans : Tambourine
Philip Jones : Alto Trumpet
Session musicians : Two Cellos and two Horns

With this song John immortalised forever Strawberry Fields, a Salvation Army orphanage in Liverpool, not far from Penny Lane. He traces a slightly surrealistic trip to Strawberry Fields and reveals the confused state of an orphan's mind — 'nothing is real'. The Beatles made two recordings of Strawberry Fields Forever, and after listening to the playback John decided that he liked the first half of one recording and the second half of the other. There was one problem — they were in different keys. John entrusted the necessary editing to George Martin. To edit the two together, George Martin had to speed up the first section and slow down the second so that they were approximately in the same key.

There are two oddities on this recording of which only one has been publicised. The first is a Morse code message, tapped out just after John sings 'Let me take you down ...'. The Morse message consists of two letters, J and L.

It is surprising that this has not received more attention. The second oddity included on this recording sparked off rumours of Paul McCartney's death. At the end of the recording, John can be heard to say 'cranberry sauce'. Many people, however, decided that John was saying 'I buried Paul.'

Penny Lane (Lennon–McCartney)   3:00

John Lennon : Piano and Harmony Vocal
Paul McCartney : Bass Guitar, Arco String Bass, Flute and Lead Vocal
George Harrison : Conga Drum and Firebell
Ringo Starr : Drums
George Martin : Piano
David Mason : Piccolo Trumpet
Phillip Jones : Trumpet

Penny Lane has been known to Liverpool's residents for years as the name of a bus terminus. There is nothing particularly special about Penny Lane — it looks the same as any other road in the area — but like the Strawberry Fields Salvation Army Home, the Beatles have immortalised Penny Lane in the words of their song. Paul's reminiscence of Liverpool is finely displayed in his lyrics, although with a slight surrealism.

Paul's lead vocal is backed up by John, who with George Martin also adds piano. Paul besides singing lead also adds string bass and a flute. The piccolo trumpet which crops up here and there was added by David Mason of the London Symphony Orchestra. Phillip Jones, who was also with the LSO, plays the trumpet on this track and also on Strawberry Fields Forever.

When the record was circulated in late January 1967 to radio stations in the USA and Canada the ending had seven extra notes played by David Mason on piccolo trumpet over the final few seconds of the recording. When the record actually reached the shops those seven notes had been trimmed off, which, besides making the radio station copies different, also made them rather valuable.

Baby You're A Rich Man (Lennon–McCartney)   3:07

John Lennon : Clavioline, Piano and Lead Vocal
Paul McCartney : Bass Guitar, Piano and Harmony Vocal
George Harrison : Tambourine and Harmony Vocal
Ringo Starr : Drums and Maracas
Studio Engineer : Vibes

This started life as two different songs — One Of The Beautiful People (a song that John had written for a possible Sgt. Pepper Volume II album) and Baby, You're A Rich Man written by Paul. Although both songs were apparently recorded, neither has ever been issued in its original form. The two songs were joined together in a similar way to A Day In The Life with John singing the opening part of the song and then joining Paul and George for the Baby You're A Rich Man section.

The unusual 'pipes of Pan' sound is from a keyboard instrument called a clavioline. This is a rather strange device with a mind of its own and which will only play one note at a time.

John manages to play it and also piano. Paul plays his bass guitar and adds a second piano while an obliging engineer adds some vibes. The track in its present form was originally intended for the *Yellow Submarine* film, but was hurriedly included as the B-side of All You Need Is Love.

All You Need Is Love (Lennon–McCartney)   3:57

John Lennon : Harpsichord and Lead Vocal
Paul McCartney : Arco String Bass, Bass Guitar and Backing Vocal
George Harrison : Violin, Lead Guitar and Backing Vocal
Ringo Starr : Drums
George Martin : Piano
Chorus : Includes Mick Jagger, Marianne Faithfull, Keith Richard, Gary Brooker and Keith Moon.
Session Musicians : Four Violins, two Cellos, two Trumpets, two Trombones, two Saxophones and one Accordion

The BBC invited the Beatles to represent the UK in a world-wide television broadcast called *Our World*, which was part of the Canadian EXPO 67 festival. The Beatles were to be seen recording their new single All You Need Is Love. The recording was not all made live; the rhythm section was pre-recorded earlier in the day and simply played back at the time of the broadcast, although the Beatles were seen playing their guitars. All other parts of the song, the vocals, the backing vocals and the orchestra, were recorded at the time of broadcast, before an audience of approximately 200 million people. A second recording of the song, made during rehearsals for the broadcast, is included on the Yellow Submarine album. The day before the broadcast, the Beatles decided that they would release All You Need Is Love as soon as possible after the show. After listening to the playback, John's vocals were re-recorded and copies of the master tape were then flown all over the world and the record was on sale within weeks of being broadcast.

The Beatles asked the orchestra to dress in white dinner suits for the broadcast, and also invited a few of their friends along to join in on the backing vocals; these included Mick Jagger, Marianne Faithfull, Keith Richard, Gary Brooker from Procol Harum and Keith Moon. As it was to be a world-wide broadcast, the Beatles wanted to have an international flavour. George Martin suggested that they use the *Marseillaise* (the French national anthem) for the beginning, and for the ending he included Greensleeves and Glen Miller's In The Mood in the orchestral arrangement. Unfortunately, George had used Miller's own arrangement, not then out of copyright, and as soon as the record was released EMI was approached by the copyright holders. However, EMI agreed to pay and all was sorted out.

The initial rhythm track the Beatles recorded for All You Need Is Love ran for just over ten minutes and included John playing a harpsichord, Paul an Arco string bass with a bow, George a violin and Ringo on drums. For the actual broadcast the Beatles played their usual instruments, except John who just sang. The orchestra, conducted by Mike Vickers, consisted of 13 musicians playing four violins, two cellos, two saxophones, two trombones, two trumpets and an accordion; even George Martin joined in on piano. At the end, John comes in with an off-key rendition of She Loves You. The recording lasted for approximately six minutes, although it was later trimmed down to just under four. The broadcast took place on 25 June 1967 and the record, which was to become the international anthem for a generation, was on sale in Great Britain by 7 July 1967, and ten days later in the USA.

UK Release : 22 November 1968
Apple PMC 7067–8 : PCS 7067–8
US Release : 25 November 1968
Apple SWBO 101
Intl CD No : CDS 7 46443 8
Producer : George Martin
Running Time : 93:33

The BEATLES

SIDE ONE : Back In The U.S.S.R.; Dear Prudence; Glass Onion; Ob-La-Di, Ob-La-Da; Wild Honey Pie; The Continuing Story Of Bungalow Bill; While My Guitar Gently Weeps; Happiness Is A Warm Gun.
SIDE TWO : Martha My Dear; I'm So Tired; Blackbird; Piggies; Rocky Racoon; Don't Pass Me By; Why Don't We Do It In The Road?; I Will; Julia.

SIDE THREE : Birthday; Yer Blues; Mother Nature's Son; Everybody's Got Something To Hide Except Me And My Monkey; Sexy Sadie; Helter Skelter; Long, Long, Long.
SIDE FOUR : Revolution 1; Honey Pie; Savoy Truffle; Cry Baby Cry; Revolution 9; Good Night.

This album, more widely known as The White Album (although its working title was A Dolls House) was the Beatles' first album on their then newly formed Apple label which had made its first appearance three months earlier on 30 August 1968 with the single Hey Jude/Revolution (Apple R5722). Both tracks were recorded during the sessions for this album. With this album the Beatles appeared to return to the Revolver album of 1966, before their flight of fantasy into psychedelia during 1967.

Most of the 30 tracks on this double album were written during the Beatles' stay at the Maharishi Mahesh Yogi's Academy of Meditation just outside of the town of Rishikesh in northern India in early 1968. They show the Beatles' ever-increasing ability to write and perform all types of music from hard rock (Helter Skelter) to ballads (Blackbird and Mother Nature's Son) including a Hollywood-type number (Goodnight), send-ups of previously recorded songs (Glass Onion and Revolution 1) and the nightmarish Revolution 9.

The widening gap between John and Paul's writing styles begins to show on this album. John's lyrics are hard hitting and caustic, while Paul tends to write pleasant inoffensive ballads and love songs. Although these songs are jointly credited as being Lennon–McCartney compositions, the only track they did co-write on this album is Birthday. From this album on, all Lennon–McCartney credited songs can be more clearly defined as being written by the lead vocalist on the individual tracks. George Harrison, whose song-writing ability progresses with time, has four new songs on this album, While My Guitar Gently Weeps, Piggies, Long, Long, Long and Savoy Truffle, and Ringo has one, Don't Pass Me By.

At the time of recording this album, the Beatles were beginning to be disillusioned with the group; John wanted to leave, and Ringo did leave for a period of two weeks, but was eventually coaxed back. With the creation of APPLE the Beatles had gone from being just musicians to being businessmen. This, along with the death of Brian Epstein in 1967 and the arrival of Yoko Ono, all contributed to the beginning of the end of the Beatles. The tension of continual business meetings, musical differences and John's growing interest in working with Yoko, were all contributory factors to the break-up. When the sessions for this album were eventually finished the rift between the Beatles had grown so wide that none of them had much interest in what they had recorded. The Beatles had decided to issue two albums mainly to fulfil their contract with EMI as soon as possible, so they sifted through the tracks, of which there were 32, and rejected two of them. The tracks rejected were What's The New Mary Jane, which was continually reported as being their next single, which to date has not seen the light of day, and Not Guilty, which has yet to be released.

After the elaborate Sgt. Pepper sleeve the Beatles decided to have the simplest possible plain white sleeve, hence the unofficial title of The White Album. The outer part of the sleeve has only the title plus the catalogue number printed down the spine, with the words 'The Beatles' embossed into the cardboard on the front. The inner part of the sleeve gives the barest of information with song titles on one side and four black and white photographs of the Beatles on the other. The sleeve contains four separate colour photographs and a poster with a hodge podge of photographs — rather like a visual version of Revolution 9. On the back of the poster are the complete lyrics to all the songs.

SIDE ONE

Back In The U.S.S.R. (Lennon–McCartney) 2:45

John Lennon : Six-String Bass and Backing Vocal
Paul McCartney : Lead Guitar, Piano and Lead/Backing Vocal
George Harrison : Bass Guitar and Backing Vocal
Ringo Starr : Drums

The opening track, originally titled I'm Backing The U.S.S.R., fades in with the sound of a plane landing then goes straight into a great rock and roll song heavily influenced by Chuck Berry's Back In The U.S.A. Paul is on lead vocals with a Beach Boys style backing from both John and Paul. The lead guitar is played by Paul, as is the rocking piano. John can be heard playing a six-string bass and, for the first time on a Beatles' record, George plays a bass guitar. The Beatles also add handclapping to the backing for the first time since approximately 1964. The track ends in much the same way as it began, with the sound of an aircraft, which then fades into the following track.

Dear Prudence (Lennon–McCartney) 4:00

John Lennon : Lead Guitar, Tambourine and Lead/Backing Vocal
Paul McCartney : Bass Guitar, Piano, Flugelhorn and Backing Vocal
George Harrison : Acoustic Guitar and Backing Vocal
Ringo Starr : Drums
Mal Evans : Tambourine

As Back In The U.S.S.R. fades out to the sound of jet engines, Dear Prudence fades in with the sound of a rather persistent acoustic guitar which continues throughout the recording. The gentle beginning builds up into an extravagant and interesting climax that includes a complicated drumbeat from Ringo, with Paul on bass guitar, piano and flugelhorn. The lead vocal on this recording is a multi-tracked John Lennon with a three-part backing vocal from John, Paul and George. The song could almost be made up of two songs joined together, rock song and ballad, although there is no evidence to confirm this. John's lead vocal is double-tracked for the main lyrics with a further over-dubbing in places — an extremely interesting combination. The song was written by John for Prudence Farrow (sister of Mia Farrow) while the Beatles were in India. Prudence spent most of her day meditating in spite of John's attempts to persuade her to do otherwise.

Glass Onion (Lennon–McCartney) 2:10

John Lennon : Acoustic Guitar and Solo Vocal
Paul McCartney : Bass Guitar, Piano and Flute
George Harrison : Lead Guitar
Ringo Starr : Drums and Tambourine
Session Musicians : Orchestra

John's nonsensical lyrics are basically a series of unconnected comments, which include reference to Strawberry Fields Forever, Fixing A Hole, The

Fool On The Hill, Lady Madonna and I Am The Walrus. The track features an unusual combination of a Rain-style drumbeat, with an Eleanor Rigby-style orchestration and an All My Loving stop-start structure. The song sends up all those who tried to explain the Beatles' lyrics, and John includes a line especially for them : 'Well, here's a clue for you all.'

Ob-La-Di, Ob-La-Da (Lennon–McCartney)   3:10

John Lennon : Maracas and Backing Vocal
Paul McCartney : Piano, Bass Guitar and Lead Vocal
George Harrison : Acoustic Guitar and Backing Vocal
Ringo Starr : Drums
Session Musicians : Brass

On this lively track the Beatles, having attempted many forms of music, now try their hand at reggae. Paul is on piano and lead vocals, with John and George joining in for the chorus. The recording also features some Jamaican style brass. Paul took the expression 'ob-la-di, ob-la-da life goes on, bra' from a Jamaican friend, Jimmy Scott, who had been using the expression for years and had a band called Jimmy Scott and his Ob-La-Di, Ob-La-Da Band. At the time of release of this album Paul McCartney wanted to issue this track as a single but both John and George voted against.

Wild Honey Pie (Lennon–McCartney)   1:02

John Lennon : Not Present
Paul McCartney : Guitars, Drums and All Vocals
George Harrison : Not Present
Ringo Starr : Not Present

This bouncy semi-instrumental was written and performed solely by Paul. In addition to repeating the line 'honey pie' throughout the track he also plays drums, lead, bass and acoustic guitars. This was originally an experimental recording of a spontaneous sing-a-long, that Paul had thought up while the Beatles were staying in India, not intended for release, but Jane Asher, Paul's girlfriend, liked it so much that Paul edited it to its present length. The full track has yet to see the light of day.

The Continuing Story Of Bungalow Bill
(Lennon–McCartney)   3:05

John Lennon : Acoustic Guitar, Organ and Lead Vocal
Paul McCartney : Bass Guitar and Backing Vocal
George Harrison : Acoustic Guitar and Backing Vocal
Ringo Starr : Drums, Tambourine and Backing Vocal
Yoko Ono : Harmony Vocal
Chris Thomas : Mellotron
Chorus : Includes Yoko Ono and Maureen Starkey

The track opens with a Spanish/Mexican style acoustic guitar solo which leads straight into the sing-a-long chorus of 'Hey Bungalow Bill, what did you kill? Bungalow Bill'. The song, written by John who also sings lead, sounds rather like an updated version of Yellow Submarine. It's a pleasant track with, for the first and only time on a Beatles' record, harmony vocals from Yoko Ono on the third verse and also on chorus (where she is joined by Ringo's wife Maureen). The Beatles are also joined by assistant Chris Thomas, who adds the Mellotron near the end. The track doesn't fade out but is linked to the following track with an 'Ey up' introduction from John.

While My Guitar Gently Weeps (Harrison)   4:46

John Lennon : Acoustic Guitar, Organ and Harmony Vocal
Paul McCartney : Bass Guitar, Piano and Harmony Vocal
George Harrison : Acoustic Guitar, Lead Guitar and Lead Vocal
Ringo Starr : Drums, Castanets and Tambourine
Eric Clapton : Lead Guitar

The first of four tracks written by George, who seemed at this stage to have given up using Indian instruments on Beatles' recordings although he issued a solo album called Wonderwall consisting mainly of Indian instrumentals. Here he enlists the help of his long-time friend Eric Clapton to play the lead guitar. The lead vocal is by George, who double-tracks in part, and John and Paul join in on the chorus. The track has an extremely long fade-out which is really a showcase for Eric Clapton's lead guitar.

Happiness Is A Warm Gun (Lennon–McCartney)   2:47

John Lennon : Lead Guitar, Tambourine and Lead/Backing Vocal
Paul McCartney : Bass Guitar and Backing Vocal
George Harrison : Lead Guitar and Backing Vocal
Ringo Starr : Drums

This title is an interesting collage consisting of three separate songs which John had written but decided to join together into one song. The track begins as a gentle ballad with solo vocal from John who interweaves nonsensical one-line comments into the lyrics. The song slowly changes into a semi-rock song which builds up with the repetitive 'Mother Superior jumped the gun'. The third and final section has John shouting out the lyrics over a 'bang, bang — shoot, shoot' backing vocal which he recorded with Paul. John had the idea for the third section of the song after George Martin showed him an advertisement in a magazine proclaiming 'Happiness is a warm gun'.

Martha My Dear (Lennon–McCartney)   2:28

John Lennon : Bass Guitar
Paul McCartney : Piano and Solo Vocal
George Harrison : Lead Guitar
Ringo Starr : Drums
Session Musicians : Strings and Brass

This is a Paul McCartney thirties-influenced song written about his old English sheepdog. It features an orchestral/danceband backing and has a solo vocal from Paul who also plays piano.

I'm So Tired (Lennon–McCartney)   2:01

John Lennon : Acoustic Guitar, Lead Guitar, Organ and Lead Vocal
Paul McCartney : Bass Guitar and Harmony Vocal
George Harrison : Lead Guitar and Rhythm Guitar
Ringo Starr : Drums

Written by John about Yoko, this song features a lead vocal from John who also plays acoustic guitar and organ. Paul harmonises in places. The recording is structured in a similar way to Happiness Is A Warm Gun. It starts, builds up and then stops, only to start up again. The track finishes with a few seconds of nonsensical gibberish that has been interpreted as Ringo saying 'Paul is dead, man, miss him, miss him' backwards.

Blackbird (Lennon–McCartney)   2:20

John Lennon : Not Present
Paul McCartney : Acoustic Guitar, Bongos and Solo Vocal
George Harrison : Not Present
Ringo Starr : Not Present

This gentle song with inoffensive lyrics has a solo vocal from Paul who double tracks his lead vocal in part and backs it himself with an acoustic guitar. A metronomic beat is tapped out on what sounds like half of a set of bongos. Like several tracks on the album, this stops and starts up again, but here with the addition of a blackbird singing sweetly over the encore.

Piggies (Harrison)   2:04

John Lennon : Sound Effects
Paul McCartney : Bass Guitar
George Harrison : Acoustic Guitar and Solo Vocal
Ringo Starr : Tambourine
Chris Thomas : Harpsichord
Session Musicians : Strings

This song is a sarcastic swipe at the greedy, the 'piggies', always out to make money, and in particular out of the Beatles. Lead vocal is from George with double-tracking in parts. Chris Thomas plays harpsichord and the sound of grunting, snorting pigs is used to good effect.

Rocky Racoon (Lennon–McCartney)   3:33

John Lennon : Harmonium, Harmonica and Backing Vocal
Paul McCartney : Acoustic Guitar and Lead Vocal
George Harrison : Bass Guitar and Backing Vocal
Ringo Starr : Drums
George Martin : Piano

Written by Paul during one of his visits to India, this has a country-folk flavour, like his earlier I've Just Seen A Face, on Help! He sings lead vocal, and backing vocals are a three-part harmony from himself plus John and George. A harmonica is used, although sparingly, for the first time since the earlier recordings; a honky-tonk, bar-room style piano is added by George Martin and a harmonium by John.

Don't Pass Me By (Starkey)   3:52

John Lennon : Acoustic Guitar and Tambourine
Paul McCartney : Bass Guitar
George Harrison : Violin
Ringo Starr : Piano, Drums and Solo Vocal

After years of performing songs specially written for him by John and Paul, and co-writing only one song, What Goes On? on Rubber Soul, Ringo finally sings a solo on a self-penned song which he wrote in 1963, five years previously. The very bouncy backing includes a violin reputed to have been played by George Harrison, and the solid drum beat of course is provided by Ringo. This excellent first song from Ringo proved he too could write.

Why Don't We Do It In The Road? (Lennon–McCartney)   1:42

John Lennon : Not Present
Paul McCartney : Lead Guitar, Bass Guitar, Piano, Drums and Solo Vocal
George Harrison : Not Present
Ringo Starr : Not Present

Another multi-tracked solo vocal from Paul who sings and plays every instrument on this regrettably short track : piano, drums, lead and bass guitars.

I Will (Lennon–McCartney)   1:46

John Lennon : Not Present
Paul McCartney : Acoustic Guitar, Bass Guitar and Solo Vocal
George Harrison : Not Present
Ringo Starr : Drums, Bongos and Maracas.

This ballad is also a rather short track. Paul sings solo vocal and supplies a minimum backing with an acoustic guitar. Bongos are supplied by Ringo, together with drums and maracas.

Julia (Lennon–McCartney)   2:57

John Lennon : Acoustic Guitar and Solo Vocal
Paul McCartney : Not Present
George Harrison : Not Present
Ringo Starr : Not Present

This beautiful song, written by John, helped by Yoko, is mainly about his love for his dead mother. A reference to his love for Yoko is included with the words 'ocean child' (an English translation of Yoko is 'child of the ocean'). John sings solo vocal and backs himself with two acoustic guitars.

SIDE THREE

Birthday (Lennon–McCartney)   2:40

John Lennon : Lead Guitar and Lead Vocal
Paul McCartney : Piano and Lead Vocal
George Harrison : Bass Guitar and Tambourine
Ringo Starr : Drums
Chorus : Includes Yoko Ono and Patti Harrison

This is the only track on the two albums to have been co-written by John and Paul. It is basically an up-dated, noisier re-write of the traditional 'Happy Birthday' and was written in India for Patti Harrison, George's wife, who was celebrating her birthday. It races along with a heavy drumbeat from Ringo, a persistent lead guitar riff from George and a jangling piano (phased in places) from Paul. The lead vocal, also from Paul, is double-tracked onto each channel of the stereo (an effect not used since Revolver). John sings lead in places but is mainly confined to backing, with Yoko Ono and Patti Harrison.

Yer Blues (Lennon–McCartney)   4:01

John Lennon : Lead Guitar and Solo Vocal
Paul McCartney : Bass Guitar
George Harrison : Lead Guitar
Ringo Starr : Drums

This is John Lennon's send-up of the flourishing British electric blues scene of the late sixties. The music and lyrics are just as powerful as John's vocals and the stabbing, attacking lead guitar from George with Ringo's insistent drumbeat suit the track perfectly.

Mother Nature's Son (Lennon–McCartney)   2:46

John Lennon : Not Present
Paul McCartney : Acoustic Guitar, Bongos, Timpani and Solo Vocal
George Harrison : Not Present
Ringo Starr : Not Present
Session Musicians : Horns

Paul McCartney sets his vision of country life to pleasantly simple music. His solo vocal is backed by himself on acoustic guitar with a secondary acoustic guitar, bongos and a very distant timpani being over-dubbed also by himself. Some unobtrusive, pleasant horns are added by session musicians.

Everybody's Got Something To Hide Except Me And My Monkey (Lennon–McCartney)   2:25

John Lennon : Lead Guitar, Maracas and Lead Vocal
Paul McCartney : Bass Guitar and Backing Vocal
George Harrison : Rhythm Guitar and Firebell
Ringo Starr : Drums

This track was written by John in reply to a drawing depicting Yoko as a monkey sitting on his shoulders, digging long talons into his back, supposedly draining him of his talent. John dismissed it with this song, basically saying 'we've got nothing to hide, Yoko inspires me, she doesn't destroy my ability to write good songs'. This is a great piece of rock and roll with John on lead vocal, and backing vocals (in places) from John and Paul. It features a prominent lead guitar riff and extensive use of a firebell. The song began life with the reputed working title of Come On, Come On.

Sexy Sadie (Lennon–McCartney)   3:15

John Lennon : Acoustic Guitar, Rhythm Guitar, Organ and Lead/Backing Vocal
Paul McCartney : Piano, Bass Guitar and Backing Vocal
George Harrison : Lead Guitar and Backing Vocal
Ringo Starr : Drums and Tambourine

Written by John about the Maharishi, who, during the Beatles' stay at his academy of meditation in India, had made a very non-mystical approach to Mia Farrow, proving to John that he was not all he made out to be. John originally intended to write the song as 'Maharishi What Have You Done, You Made A Fool of Everyone' but in the end decided against it. The track features a lead vocal from John, who joins Paul and George for the partly phased backing vocals, which produce an unusual effect. John plays acoustic guitar, Paul piano and George a distorted lead guitar.

Helter Skelter (Lennon–McCartney)   4:30

John Lennon : Bass Guitar, Lead Guitar, Saxophone and Backing Vocal
Paul McCartney : Bass Guitar, Lead Guitar and Lead Vocal
George Harrison : Rhythm Guitar and Backing Vocal
Ringo Starr : Drums
Mal Evans : Trumpet

This is the heaviest sound that the Beatles ever produced, a sound first tried out in 1966 with tracks such as Rain and And Your Bird Can Sing.

Paul's lead vocals are screamed out of the speakers; the backing vocals from John and Paul add to the overall excited sound of the recording which includes various unexplainable bleeps and squeaks. At one point the guitars run down the musical scale and then dissolve into distorted feedback. Ringo starts the track up again with his drums but it fades out to a few seconds of silence and the recording seems to finish — but no, back it comes with all its heaviness then fades slightly only to reappear with Ringo Starr's famous statement 'I've got blisters on my fingers'. John plays saxophone and Mal Evans, one of the Beatles' roadies, plays trumpet. This recording was originally 25 minutes long but the Beatles realised that at that length it would take up an entire album side so it was edited to 4:30.

After the Charles Manson murders in 1969 — reportedly inspired, in part, by this song — John Lennon later appeared in court to defend this recording, saying that it was simply about a fairground slide and nothing else.

Long, Long, Long (Harrison)   3:08

John Lennon : Acoustic Guitar and Piano
Paul McCartney : Bass Guitar and Hammond Organ
George Harrison : Acoustic Guitar and Solo Vocal
Ringo Starr : Drums

George Harrison's third offering on the album is reminiscent of a funeral dirge. George's double-tracked lead vocal is mixed so far back that it's difficult to hear the lyrics above the acoustic guitar. The recording includes a very dramatic drumbeat from Ringo and features Paul playing both piano and Hammond organ. It ends with a rather unearthly screech which sounds as though it might have come from Yoko.

SIDE FOUR

Revolution 1 (Lennon–McCartney)   4:13

John Lennon : Lead Guitar, Acoustic Guitar and Lead/Backing Vocal
Paul McCartney : Bass Guitar, Acoustic Guitar, Piano and Backing Vocal
George Harrison : Rhythm Guitar and Backing Vocal
Ringo Starr : Drums
Session Musicians : Brass

This recording is a slower, almost acoustic version of the song issued as the B-side of the Hey Jude single, issued two or three months before the album. The double-tracked lead vocal is by John. The track has a false start and when it does begin the lead guitar, instead of being on the right-hand channel, as it is on the faster version, is on the left-hand channel. There is a do-wop backing which makes it sound rather like a send-up. Additional features are a brass section and Paul playing piano.

Honey Pie (Lennon–McCartney)   2:42

John Lennon : Lead Guitar
Paul McCartney : Piano and Solo Vocal
George Harrison : Bass Guitar
Ringo Starr : Drums
Session Musicians : 15-Piece Band

Like When I'm Sixty-Four and Your Mother Should Know this song is influenced by the music of the twenties. Paul wrote it, sings lead vocal and plays piano. John plays lead guitar and George (as on several tracks of this album) bass guitar. Ringo, of course, is on drums, and 15 session musicians add the danceband-type backing.

Savoy Truffle (Harrison)   2:55

John Lennon : Lead Guitar
Paul McCartney : Bass Guitar
George Harrison : Lead Guitar, Organ and Solo Vocal
Ringo Starr : Drums and Tambourine
Session Musicians : Brass

This song is dedicated to Eric Clapton's sweet tooth! George makes an uncomfortable reference to Ob-La-Di, Ob-La-Da which does not fit in with the other lyrics but rhymes with the following line. The recording has a solid brass backing, rather reminiscent of Got To Get You Into My Life.

Cry Baby Cry (Lennon–McCartney) 2:34

John Lennon : Acoustic Guitar, Piano, Organ and Solo Vocal
Paul McCartney : Bass Guitar
George Harrison : Lead Guitar
Ringo Starr : Drums and Tambourine
George Martin : Harmonium

John Lennon demonstrates his versatility on this track by playing almost every instrument. He plays guitar, piano and organ with help from George Martin on harmonium. The guitars at the beginning are phased and John experiments with the stereo, so that the verses appear in the centre while the chorus appears on the left-hand channel. John was inspired to write the song by a television commercial and his original verse was to have been 'make your mother buy' but he changed his mind and added more nonsensical lyrics.

Can You Take Me Back (Lennon–McCartney) 0:27

John Lennon : Not Present
Paul McCartney : Acoustic Guitar, Drums, Maracas, Bongos and Solo Vocal
George Harrison : Not Present
Ringo Starr : Not Present

This short track links Cry Baby Cry with Revolution 9, and possibly was originally intended to be part of one of these songs. The lyrics are not printed on the back of the poster with those of other songs on the album. The solo vocal is from Paul with backing provided by an acoustic guitar, drums and maracas (presumably all played by Paul). It does not seem to be an intro to Revolution 9 because it fades out completely before that track begins. It sounds rather like a first take which was initially dismissed, then included at the last moment.

Revolution 9 (Lennon–McCartney) 8:15

John Lennon : Voice, Mixing and Editing
Paul McCartney : Piano
George Harrison : Voice
Ringo Starr : Voice
Yoko Ono : Voice
George Martin : Mixing and Editing

What can be said about a Beatles recording that doesn't feature any music? The recording starts with a snatch of overheard conversation. A piano (played by Paul) begins, then an anonymous voice repeats 'Number 9, Number 9, Number 9'. From here the recording becomes a mixture of backward-running tapes, discordant sounds, laughter, snatches of conversation between John and George and crowd noises. It sounds rather like the memory of a nightmare portrayed in sound. This is one of John's experimental avant-garde recordings, many of which are featured on his Two Virgins album. It was created solely by John and Yoko, was rejected initially by the other three, but eventually included.

Good Night (Lennon–McCartney)   3:14

John Lennon : Not Present
Paul McCartney : Not Present
George Harrison : Not Present
Ringo Starr : Solo Vocal
Session Musicians : 30-Piece Orchestra, Harp and Choir

This was written by John specifically for Ringo and only him. The thirties, Hollywood-style backing is supplied by the George Martin orchestra, with a sweet-sounding female choir. One cannot resist the feeling that this track is a Lennon send-up.

UK Release : 17 January 1969
Apple PMC 7070 : PCS 7070
US Release : 13 January 1969
Apple SW 153
Intl CD No : CDP 7 46445 2
Producer : George Martin
Running Time : 40:15

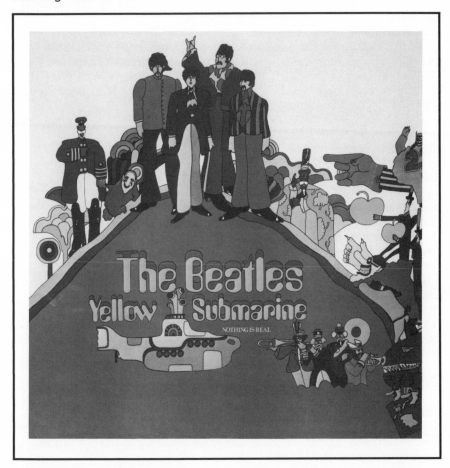

SIDE ONE : Yellow Submarine; Only A Northern Song; All Together Now; Hey Bulldog; It's All Too Much; All You Need Is Love.

SIDE TWO : Contains incidental music by George Martin and Orchestra as played in the film.

This is the soundtrack album for the feature-length cartoon film of the same name based loosely around the lyrics of Yellow Submarine.

The contract for the film and album, signed by Brian Epstein, stipulated that the Beatles were to supply at least three previously unreleased recordings for use in the soundtrack. The Beatles, who felt Brian Epstein had let them down, initially wanted nothing to do with the project, but eventually decided to supply songs that would not normally have been seriously considered for release. One song, however, Baby You're A Rich Man, originally recorded for inclusion on this album, was issued six months previously as the B-side to All You Need Is Love (see the Magical Mystery Tour album).

The four songs eventually given, albeit reluctantly, for use in the film (Only A Northern Song, All Together Now, Hey Bulldog and It's All Too Much) were considered by the Beatles to be 'throwaway' recordings. The original plan was to release the four new tracks as an E.P., but after consideration it seemed that an album would sell better. Unfortunately for Beatles' fans this turned out to be a one-sided Beatles' album with George Martin's orchestral score of the film's incidental music on the second side. The Beatles' previous soundtrack albums, when issued in Britain, had included on the second sides tracks not used in the respective films and it was a great pity that this album was not compiled in the same way.

The film soundtrack has these six album tracks plus parts or complete recordings of Sgt. Pepper's Lonely Hearts Club Band, With A Little Help From My Friends, Lucy In The Sky With Diamonds, Within You, Without You, When I'm Sixty-Four, A Day In The Life, Eleanor Rigby, Nowhere Man, Baby, You're A Rich Man, Think For Yourself and Love You To.

SIDE ONE

Yellow Submarine (Lennon–McCartney)   2:40

John Lennon : Acoustic Guitar and Backing Vocal
Paul McCartney : Acoustic Guitar and Backing Vocal
George Harrison : Tambourine and Backing Vocal
Ringo Starr : Drums and Lead Vocal
Chorus : Includes George Martin, Patti Harrison, Mal Evans, Neil Aspinall and Geoff Emerick
Session Musicians : Brass Band

Previously issued on Revolver, this is an eternally fresh song which does not seem to have dated at all.

Only A Northern Song (Harrison)   3:23

John Lennon : Piano and Various Discordant Instruments
Paul McCartney : Bass Guitar and Various Discordant Instruments
George Harrison : Organ, Various Discordant Instruments and Solo Vocal
Ringo Starr : Drums and Various Discordant Instruments

This track seems to reflect George Harrison's displeasure with the project. His one-line comments are thinly linked together into what can be loosely described as a song. The ironical title was also a sarcastic jibe at the publishing company, Northern Songs. The backing is a cacophonous 'tune-up' reminiscent of Tomorrow Never Knows and Revolution 9. Ringo's drums and Paul's bass guitar are the only musical parts of the backing. The organ intro is good, but gets lost amidst the continual burps and interruptions of off-key instruments. As this is a mono recording, it is difficult to tell if it continues throughout the recording. The track is not, at present, available anywhere in the world in stereo.

All Together Now (Lennon–McCartney)   2:08

John Lennon : Banjo and Backing Vocal
Paul McCartney : Acoustic Guitar, Bass Guitar and Lead Vocal
George Harrison : Harmonica and Backing Vocal
Ringo Starr : Drums and Finger Cymbals

Paul's contribution also sounds rather half-hearted. His lead vocal, with backing from John and George, seems to lack real enthusiasm, although it comes across reasonably well and is still enjoyable.

Hey Bulldog (Lennon–McCartney)   3:09

John Lennon : Piano, Lead Guitar and Lead Vocal
Paul McCartney : Bass Guitar and Harmony Vocal
George Harrison : Lead Guitar and Tambourine
Ringo Starr : Drums

John's sole contribution was, as he described it himself, 'a filler track for the album'. The recording was not intended for use in the film, as the contract demanded only three new songs, but it was finally included. John's lead vocal, without sounding over-enthusiastic, manages to give the recording power and excitement. He insisted on this title for the song, rather than the more obvious You Can Talk To Me, although nowhere in his original lyrics was there any reference to a bulldog. He then decided to include the words 'Hey Bulldog' right at the end of the song.

It's All Too Much (Harrison) 6:27

John Lennon : Lead Guitar and Harmony Vocal
Paul McCartney : Bass Guitar and Harmony Vocal
George Harrison : Lead Guitar, Organ and Lead Vocal
Ringo Starr : Drums and Tambourine
Session Musicians : Two Trumpets

George's lead vocals on this, his second contribution to Yellow Submarine, sound more enthusiastic than his first — probably because it was not recorded with the project in mind. This, and the recording used in the soundtrack (which has a verse not included here) are reputed to have been edited from a thirty-minute recording, although this has never been verified. George includes two rather odd lines. One is a line previously used in the Merseys' hit record Sorrow; the second is the mysterious line in which he sings 'we are dead'.

All You Need Is Love (Lennon–McCartney) 3:47

John Lennon : Harpsichord and Lead Vocal
Paul McCartney : Arco String Bass, Bass Guitar and Backing Vocal
George Harrison : Violin, Lead Guitar and Backing Vocal
Ringo Starr : Drums
George Martin : Piano
Chorus : Includes Mick Jagger, Marianne Faithfull, Keith Richard,
    Gary Brooker and Keith Moon
Session Musicians : Four Violins, two Cellos, two Trumpets, two Trombones,
    two Saxophones and one Accordion.

This is a completely different version of the track included on the Magical
Mystery Tour album. This recording, although using the same pre-recorded
rhythm track as the single, recorded during the *Our World* broadcast on 25
June 1967, has a different main track and lead vocal from John. This recording
is also ten seconds shorter than the single and is in stereo whereas the single
is in mono.

SIDE TWO

The George Martin Orchestra

Pepper Land (Martin) 2:18; **Sea Of Time** (Martin) 2:58; **Sea Of Holes**
(Martin) 2:14; **Sea Of Monsters** (Martin) 3:35; **March of the Meanies**
(Martin) 2:16; **Pepper Land Laid Waste** (Martin) 2:09; **Yellow Submarine
in Pepper Land** (Lennon–McCartney — arr. Martin) 2:10

UK Release : 26 September 1969
Apple PCS 7088
US Release : 26 September 1969
Apple SO 383
Intl CD No : CDP 7 46446 2
Producer : George Martin
Running Time : 46:54

SIDE ONE : Come Together; Something; Maxwell's Silver Hammer; Oh! Darling; Octopus's Garden; I Want You (She's So Heavy).

SIDE TWO : Here Comes The Sun; Because; You Never Give Me Your Money; Sun King; Mean Mr Mustard; Polythene Pam; She Came In Through The Bathroom Window; Golden Slumbers; Carry That Weight; The End; Her Majesty.

The Beatles, now on the verge of splitting up after the bad feeling created during the ill-fated Get Back sessions (see Chapter 19 *Let It Be*), briefly settled their personal and musical differences long enough to record Abbey Road, which was to be their last studio album. John suspended his Peace Campaign, Paul postponed a planned holiday, George broke off other recording sessions with Billy Preston and the Radha Krishna Temple and Ringo temporarily dropped his acting career.

The tension which had grown within the Beatles since the death of Brian Epstein had now reached the point where they could no longer agree on anything, particularly their music. John's concept of Abbey Road was for it to be a basic rock and roll album like Get Back. Paul, however, envisaged a 'pop opera' of different songs edited together into one long medley. In the end both got their way.

Side One of the album fulfils John's concept of individual tracks, which in the main are basically rock and roll. He contributes Come Together and I Want You (She's So Heavy), Paul his gutsy Oh! Darling and Maxwell's Silver Hammer, while George and Ringo contribute Something and Octopus's Garden, respectively.

Side Two has Paul's now famous 'Pop Opera' of ten different songs (of which only eight are listed) edited together along with George's Here Comes The Sun and John's Because, to form the sixteen-minute medley.

The album contains some of the Beatles' most technically perfect recordings and features some of the most intricate harmony singing the group has ever recorded. A number of tracks include the use of a synthesiser, an instrument suggested by George after he had recorded the album Electronic Sounds using only a synthesiser. That album and his other solo venture Wonderwall (a soundtrack album consisting almost entirely of Indian music) showed that George's musical interests were no longer fitting into the framework of the Beatles. John, too, now discontented with being a Beatle, had also begun to pursue a solo career. With the help of Yoko Ono he had recorded Two Virgins and Life With The Lions, two albums consisting entirely of avant-garde sound. He had also issued a solo single, Give Peace A Chance, under the name of The Plastic Ono Band. He was to continue his solo career by issuing The Wedding Album, a third album of avant-garde sound; Live Peace In Toronto, a live recording of The Plastic Ono Band; and Cold Turkey — all within weeks of the release of Abbey Road. In fact, John had apparently wanted the Beatles to record Cold Turkey as a new single, but neither Paul nor George were interested. John, along with Ringo, Eric Clapton and Klaus Voorman (the first real line-up of the Plastic Ono Band), recorded Cold Turkey and it was issued in direct competition with the Something/Come Together single (the first Beatles single issued in Britain from an album *after* the album had been issued).

Abbey Road, named after the location of the recording studios where the Beatles made most of their recordings, including this one, was the first Beatles' album to be issued solely in stereo. All previous Beatles' albums up to and including Yellow Submarine had been issued in both mono and stereo. This decision was made because the Beatles felt that their music should be heard in stereo and that the mono versus stereo argument of earlier years was now over, with most people accepting stereo.

The sleeve of the album, photographed by Iain Macmillan on 8 August 1969, shows the Beatles walking across a zebra crossing in Abbey Road, walking *away* from the recording studio. This, with the album's closing track The End, was regarded by many as being a cryptic message from the Beatles saying

'This is it, we've finished recording our final album, we're walking away and splitting up.' An announcement to that effect was to be made by Paul on 10 April 1970, almost six months after the release of this album.

SIDE ONE

Come Together (Lennon–McCartney)   4:16

Recorded : 21, 22, 23, 25, 29 and 30 July 1969, EMI Studios, Abbey Road, London

John Lennon : Rhythm Guitar, Lead Guitar, Tambourine and Lead Vocal
Paul McCartney : Bass Guitar, Electric Piano and Harmony Vocal
George Harrison : Lead Guitar and Maracas
Ringo Starr : Drums

Written by John, this was originally intended to be a campaign song for Timothy Leary , who was at one time proposing to run for the post of Governor of California. The idea was dropped after Leary decided not to run, and John changed the style of the song. It was eventually the subject of a law suit as Maurice Levy, owner of the American music publishers Big Seven Music, who hold the publishing rights to Chuck Berry's song You Can't Catch Me, claimed that John had used two of the song's lines in Come Together. To save months of legal arguments John apparently agreed to record, and include, You Can't Catch Me and Sweet Little Sixteen (also Berry's composition and published by Maurice Levy's company) on his 1975 solo album Rock And Roll.
   John also had another problem with the song; the BBC banned it, because of a reference to Coca-Cola which they deemed to be advertising. The recording, completed in nine takes plus overdubs, features a lead vocal from John with harmonies in places from Paul. It also features two lead guitars, one played by John, the other by George.

Something (Harrison)   2:59

Recorded : 2 and 5 May, 11 and 16 July and 15 August 1969, EMI Studios, Abbey Road, London and Olympic Studios, Church Road, Barnes, London

John Lennon : Lead Guitar
Paul McCartney : Bass Guitar and Backing Vocal
George Harrison : Lead Guitar and Lead Vocal
Ringo Starr : Drums
Billy Preston : Piano
Session Musicians : 21-piece Orchestra

Recorded in 36 takes, plus overdubs, this dramatic George Harrison rendition of his own song (which was inspired by his wife Patti) features a lead vocal from him with occasional backing vocals from Paul. Again, the recording makes use of the twin lead guitars of Messrs Lennon and Harrison and also features Billy Preston on piano. The song (which uses the title of James Taylor's Something In The Way She Moves as its opening line) must surely rank alongside some of the best Lennon–McCartney compositions as being one of the finest songs the Beatles ever recorded.

Maxwell's Silver Hammer (Lennon–McCartney)   3:24

Recorded : 9, 10 and 11 July and 6 August 1969, EMI Studios, Abbey Road, London

John Lennon : Acoustic Guitar and Lead Guitar
Paul McCartney : Bass Guitar, Piano, Synthesiser and Lead/Backing Vocal
George Harrison : Lead Guitar and Backing Vocal
Ringo Starr : Drums, Anvil and Backing Vocal
George Martin : Hammond Organ

Paul's first song on the album features himself on lead vocal with harmonies in places from George; they also get together for the backing vocals. The track, recorded in 21 takes plus overdubs, includes Paul on piano, Ringo banging a hammer on an anvil and for the first time on the album the use of a synthesiser, here played by Paul. The song's final line, 'silver hammer man', features a three-part harmony from Paul, George and Ringo. The Beatles can be seen, and heard, rehearsing this song in the film *Let It Be*.

Oh! Darling (Lennon–McCartney)   3:28

Recorded : 20 and 26 April, 18, 22 and 23 July and 8 and 11 August 1969, EMI Studios, Abbey Road, London

John Lennon : Piano and Backing Vocal
Paul McCartney : Bass Guitar, Lead Guitar, Piano, Tambourine and Lead/Backing Vocal
George Harrison : Lead Guitar and Backing Vocal
Ringo Starr : Drums

Before recording the vocals for this dramatic track, Paul spent a week going to the studios to practise and make his voice as harsh and gutsy as possible. Recorded in 26 takes with numerous overdubs, the track features John and Paul on two pianos and both Paul and George (via overdubs) on lead guitars. The recording also features a wordless backing vocal harmony from John, Paul and George.

Octopus's Garden (Starkey)   2:49

Recorded : 26 and 29 April and 17 and 18 July 1969, EMI Studios, Abbey Road, London

John Lennon : Lead Guitar
Paul McCartney : Bass Guitar, Piano, Sound Effects and Backing Vocal
George Harrison : Lead Guitar, Sound Effects and Backing Vocal
Ringo Starr : Drums, Percussion, Sound Effects and Lead Vocal

This is the second song written by Ringo to be included on a Beatles' album — the first, Don't Pass Me By, was included twelve months earlier on the double album The Beatles. Although he found it difficult to write songs, both are bouncy with infectious chorus lines. This song is reminiscent of Yellow

Submarine, particularly as it uses the same sound effects of water swirling around and bubbles being blown into water. Another interesting sound effect is the section of 'gargling' backing vocals from Paul and George. Ringo sings lead vocals with backing from Paul and George on this track which was recorded in 32 takes. As with other tracks on this album, two lead guitars are played by John and George, and Paul can be heard playing piano.

I Want You (She's So Heavy) (Lennon–McCartney) 7:49

Recorded : 22 February, 18 and 20 April and 8 and 11 August 1969, EMI Studios, Abbey Road, London and Trident Studios, Wardour Street, London

John Lennon : Multi-tracked Lead and Rhythm Guitars, Hammond Organ, Synthesiser, White Noise Generator and Lead/Harmony Vocal
Paul McCartney : Bass Guitar and Harmony Vocal
George Harrison : Multi-tracked Lead and Rhythm Guitars, Conga Drums and Harmony Vocal
Ringo Starr : Drums

With the exception of Revolution 9 this is the longest recording issued by the Beatles — even 38 seconds longer than Hey Jude, which clocks in at 7:11. The track is really two separate songs, I Want You and She's So Heavy, joined together, but without a link. Each is sung in segments throughout the recording with I Want You, sung repeatedly, predominating, and She's So Heavy inserted twice. Lead vocal and blues-style lead guitar are from John, with Paul and George harmonising here and there. The track, recorded in 35 takes with incalculable overdubs, features John and George both playing multi-tracked lead and rhythm guitars throughout. The ending features a persistent guitar riff being repeated maddeningly. Then John adds a synthesiser, building up the sound seemingly for ever until suddenly, it stops.

SIDE TWO

Here Comes The Sun (Harrison)   3:40

Recorded : 7, 8 and 16 July and 6, 11, 15 and 19 August 1969, EMI Studios, Abbey Road, London

John Lennon : Not Present
Paul McCartney : Bass Guitar, Handclapping and Backing Vocal
George Harrison : Acoustic Guitar, Lead Guitar, Harmonium, Synthesiser, Handclapping, Lead/Backing Vocal
Ringo Starr : Drums and Handclapping
Session Musicians : 17-Piece Orchestra

To escape the pressure of work, George took a day off from the recording session and sat in Eric Clapton's garden on one of the first days of spring and wrote this song. It's his second song on this album, on which he also sings lead vocal. Most of the instrumentation (with the obvious exception of the orchestral overdub) is also played by George, with only the bass guitar and drums being supplied by Paul and Ringo, respectively. The harmonies and backing vocals are also sung by George with help from Paul. The song, recorded in fifteen takes plus overdubs, starts on the left-hand channel with an acoustic guitar and synthesiser, then floats across the stereo to the right-hand channel as George begins to sing. This recording features the same instrumental break as Badge, a song co-written by George Harrison and Eric Clapton and recorded by Clapton's group Cream.

Because (Lennon–McCartney) 2:45

Recorded : 1, 4 and 5 August 1969, EMI Studios, Abbey Road, London

John Lennon : Lead Guitar and Lead/Harmony Vocal
Paul McCartney : Bass Guitar and Lead/Harmony Vocal
George Harrison : Synthesiser and Lead/Harmony Vocal
Ringo Starr : Not Present
George Martin : Harpsichord

John got the idea for this song when he heard Yoko play Beethoven's Moonlight Sonata. John suggested that she play the chord sequence backwards, which she did. He then slightly restructured it and added lyrics. It features a close-harmony vocal from John, Paul and George with George Martin supplying the harpsichord, and George adding a cleverly programmed synthesiser. Recorded in 23 takes, of which take 16 was selected as the master, the track also features John on lead guitar and Paul on bass.

You Never Give Me Your Money (Lennon–McCartney) 3:57

Recorded : 6 May and 1, 11, 15 and 31 July 1969, EMI Studios, Abbey Road, London and Olympic Studios, Church Road, Barnes, London

John Lennon : Distorted Lead Guitar and Backing Vocal
Paul McCartney : Bass Guitar, Piano, Tambourine, Chimes and Lead/Backing Vocal
George Harrison : Lead Guitar and Backing Vocal
Ringo Starr : Drums

This is a medley of four separate songs written by Paul. The first, You Never Give Me Your Money, features Paul singing solo and backing himself on piano. It was written about the boardroom squabbles at Apple and the arguments between the Beatles themselves. The second song, That Magic Feeling, features a honky-tonk style backing piano and Paul's vocals sound rougher — more like his Little Richard style. The third song, One Sweet Dream, is linked to That Magic Feeling by a wordless chorus from John, Paul and George. This is another up-beat rock and roll song featuring Paul in fine voice. The fourth song comes in only as the track fades, John, Paul and George repeat 'One-two-three-four-five-six-seven, all good children go to heaven.' These four songs have been successfully welded together to form one. The track, recorded in 36 takes, of which take 30 was selected for use for later overdubbing, has a long fade-out overlapping the intro of the following track.

Sun King (Lennon–McCartney)   2:31

Recorded : 24, 25 and 29 July 1969, EMI Studios, Abbey Road, London

John Lennon : Rhythm Guitar, Organ and Lead/Harmony Vocal
Paul McCartney : Bass Guitar, Piano and Harmony Vocal
George Harrison : Lead Guitar and Harmony Vocal
Ringo Starr : Drums and Percussion

John, who wrote this song, claimed that it came to him in a dream. This might explain the lyrics which are a mixture of Spanish, Italian, French and nonsense. The sound of crickets chirping opens the track with a bluesy lead guitar played by George. John's vocals are multi-tracked for the lead and also for the backing harmonies on which he is joined by Paul and George. Recorded in 35 takes, with later overdubs, this track features the same beautiful close-harmony vocals as used on Because earlier.

Mean Mr Mustard (Lennon–McCartney)   1:06

Recorded : 24, 25 and 29 July 1969, EMI Studios, Abbey Road, London

John Lennon : Rhythm Guitar, Organ and Lead/Harmony Vocal
Paul McCartney : Bass Guitar, Piano and Harmony Vocal
George Harrison : Electric Guitar and Harmony Vocal
Ringo Starr : Drums and Percussion

This really is the Beatles getting back to the three guitars and drums of earlier years; it's rather a pity the song didn't last a bit longer. Recorded in 35 takes together with the previous song Sun King, the track also includes an organ and piano played by John and Paul, respectively. Written by John whilst he was meditating in India, the song features a strong lead vocal from John in his best Liverpool accent with harmonies in places from Paul and George.

Polythene Pam (Lennon–McCartney)   1:13

Recorded : 25, 28 and 30 July 1969, EMI Studios, Abbey Road, London

John Lennon : Twelve-string Acoustic Guitar, Electric Piano, Lead Vocal
Paul McCartney : Bass Guitar, Piano and Backing Vocal
George Harrison : Lead Guitar, Acoustic Guitar and Backing Vocal
Ringo Starr : Drums and Percussion

Again written by John whilst in India and again sung with a strong Liverpool accent. The song, recorded in 40 takes, is about a mythical Liverpool prostitute. The backing is based around a persistent twelve-string guitar riff played by John and the wordless backing vocals are supplied by Paul and George.

She Came In Through The Bathroom Window
(Lennon–McCartney)   1:58

Recorded : 25, 28 and 30 July 1969, EMI Studios, Abbey Road, London

John Lennon : Twelve-string Acoustic Guitar, Electric Piano and
   Backing Vocal
Paul McCartney : Bass Guitar, Piano and Lead/Backing Vocal
George Harrison : Lead Guitar, Acoustic Guitar and Backing Vocal
Ringo Starr : Drums and Percussion

This song harks back to the days of the Beatles' early sixties American tours,
when fans would literally do anything to see their idols. One in particular,
undaunted by the fact that the Beatles were staying on the upper floors of a
hotel, scaled a drainpipe and broke into Paul's suite through the bathroom
window. Recorded, together with the previous song, in 40 takes, the track
features a lead vocal from Paul who joins John and George for the wordless
backing vocal.

Golden Slumbers (Lennon–McCartney)   1:31

Recorded : 2, 3, 4, 30 and 31 July and 15 August 1969, EMI Studios,
   Abbey Road, London

John Lennon : Not Present
Paul McCartney : Rhythm Guitar, Piano and Solo Vocal
George Harrison : Bass Guitar and Lead Guitar
Ringo Starr : Drums
Session Musicians : 30-piece Orchestra

During a stay at his father's home in Heswall, not far from Liverpool, Paul
wrote this lilting melody with dramatic overtones. He took the lyrics (originally
from a 400-year-old poem written by Thomas Dekker) from his step-sister's
music book. As he could not read the music to accompany himself on the
piano he improvised his own version. The track, recorded in seventeen takes
with various overdubs, features a solo vocal from Paul who accompanies
himself on piano, backed, not only by George and Ringo, but also a 30-piece
orchestra.

Carry That Weight (Lennon–McCartney)   1:37

Recorded : 2, 3, 4, 30 and 31 July and 15 August 1969, EMI Studios,
   Abbey Road, London

John Lennon : Not Present
Paul McCartney : Rhythm Guitar, Piano and Lead Vocal
George Harrison : Bass Guitar, Lead Guitar and Lead Vocal
Ringo Starr : Drums, Timpani and Lead Vocal
Session Musicians : 30-piece Orchestra

Paul McCartney reputedly wrote this song about the responsibility of keeping the Beatles together after Brian Epstein's death in 1967. The song, recorded together with Golden Slumbers in seventeen takes plus overdubs, is divided into three sections and features a reprise of the second verse of You Never Give Me Your Money, which appears earlier on the album. The first section has a three-part harmony from Paul, George and Ringo; the second section, as mentioned, is a reprise of You Never Give Me Your Money, and features a solo vocal from Paul. The track then returns to the original melody of Carry That Weight, with Paul, George and Ringo on vocals.

The End (Lennon–McCartney)   2:04

Recorded : 23 July and 5, 7, 8, 15 and 18 August 1969, EMI Studios, Abbey Road, London

John Lennon : Lead Guitar and Harmony Vocal
Paul McCartney : Bass Guitar, Lead Guitar, Piano and Lead Vocal
George Harrison : Lead Guitar and Harmony Vocal
Ringo Starr : Drums
Session Musicians : 30-piece Orchestra

Recorded in seven takes with numerous overdubs, this track, after starting with a one-verse solo vocal from Paul, then features the first, and only, drum solo by Ringo on a Beatles' record. The sixteen-second solo is followed by guitar solos from John, Paul and George (in that order), who also sing a monotonous 'love you' 24 times. As this section, which lasts for just under a minute, stops a piano begins and Paul, with harmonies in places from John, sings the final verse. There is a break of twenty seconds' silence before the last short track.

Her Majesty (Lennon–McCartney)   0:23

Recorded : 2 July 1969, EMI Studios, Abbey Road, London

John Lennon : Not Present
Paul McCartney : Acoustic Guitar and Solo Vocal
George Harrison : Not Present
Ringo Starr : Not Present

With a certain tongue-in-cheek irony, this three-take recording could be regarded as a rewritten version of the British National Anthem with Paul on solo vocal and acoustic guitar. It is the last track on the last Beatles' album.

UK Release : 21 May 1979
Parlophone PCS 7184
US Release : 26 February 1970
Apple SW 385
Intl CD No : None
Producer : George Martin
Running Time : 32:59

SIDE ONE : Can't Buy Me Love; I Should Have Known Better; Paperback Writer; Rain, Lady Madonna; Revolution.

SIDE TWO : Hey Jude; Old Brown Shoe; Don't Let Me Down; The Ballad Of John And Yoko.

Previously only available on import from the USA, this album was eventually released in Britain in May 1979 (nearly nine years after its first appearance in the US). The album includes most of the Beatles' later singles released in 1968 and 1969 together with both sides of the 1966 single Paperback Writer. Two rather odd (and out of sequence) inclusions are Can't Buy Me Love and I Should Have Known Better (both from the album A Hard Day's Night), which have been included in place of The Inner Light and Get Back even though their respective A- and B-sides, Lady Madonna and Don't Let Me Down, are included.

SIDE ONE

Can't Buy Me Love (Lennon–McCartney)   2:15

John Lennon : Rhythm Guitar
Paul McCartney : Bass Guitar and Solo Vocal
George Harrison : Lead Guitar
Ringo Starr : Drums

Previously included on the album A Hard Day's Night.

I Should Have Known Better (Lennon–McCartney)   2:42

John Lennon : Acoustic Guitar, Harmonica and Solo Vocal
Paul McCartney : Bass Guitar
George Harrison : Lead Guitar
Ringo Starr : Drums

Previously included on the album A Hard Day's Night.

Paperback Writer (Lennon–McCartney)   2:25

Recorded : 13 and 14 April 1966, EMI Studios, Abbey Road, London

John Lennon : Rhythm Guitar and Backing Vocal
Paul McCartney : Bass Guitar and Lead Vocal
George Harrison : Lead Guitar and Backing Vocal
Ringo Starr : Drums

This track was recorded in two takes (with one overdub) during the sessions for Revolver, and was issued as a single on 10 June 1966, some two months prior to that album. The song, written mainly by Paul, with John contributing some of the lyrics, was inspired by John Lennon's two books *In His Own Write* and *Spaniard In The Works*, and tells of Paul's wish to become a writer too. It begins with an a cappella introduction, followed by one of the best instrumental backings on any Beatles' records. The guitar sound on this record could be regarded as a foretaste of heavy metal. The lead vocal comes from Paul, who also joins John and George for the three-part harmony backing vocals, which are a combination of the title, together with a section of the French song *Frère Jacques*.

Rain (Lennon–McCartney)   2:59

Recorded : 14 and 16 April, 1966, EMI Studios, Abbey Road, London

John Lennon : Rhythm Guitar and Lead Vocal
Paul McCartney : Bass Guitar and Backing Vocal
George Harrison : Lead Guitar and Backing Vocal
Ringo Starr : Drums and Tambourine

Previously issued as the B-side to Paperback Writer, this track features a stronger heavy guitar sound than the A-side, making the latter sound (in comparison) rather tame. The sound was to influence artists such as The Who, Cream and Jimi Hendrix. The guitars attack from the beginning; Ringo's superb drumbeat accentuates the heaviness of the sound and John's laconic sententious lead vocal grinds out of the left-hand channel. At the end of this recording one line of John's vocal is played backwards : 'Rain, when the rain comes they run and hide their heads' (note the substitution of 'when' for 'if', which is used in the main recording). Apparently, John took a copy of the master tape home and accidentally played it backwards, liked it, and included it on the final record. After this experiment, backwards-playing tapes were also included on (amongst others) I'm Only Sleeping and Tomorrow Never Knows on the Revolver album. The instrumental track to this, which was played fast, was recorded on 14 April 1966 and then remixed with the tape running on slow/vari-speed. The vocal track was added two days later on 16 April 1966 and, after eight takes, the seventh was chosen for the released stereo version.

Lady Madonna (Lennon–McCartney)   2:17

Recorded : 3 and 6 February 1968, EMI Studios, Abbey Road, London

John Lennon : Rhythm Guitar and Backing Vocal
Paul McCartney : Bass Guitar, Piano and Lead Vocal
George Harrison : Lead Guitar and Backing Vocal
Ringo Starr : Drums and Backing Vocal
Ronnie Scott : Tenor Saxophone
Harry Klein : Baritone Saxophone
Bill Povey : Tenor Saxophone
Bill Jackman : Baritone Saxophone

This was the last single issued by the Beatles on the Parlophone label in 1968, before the dream of Apple became a reality later that year. It was written and sung by Paul, who also plays piano in true rock and roll style, showing the influence of (amongst others) Little Richard and Jerry Lee Lewis. The song is rather like a rock version of his earlier Eleanor Rigby with loneliness again as the main theme. It was recorded in five takes on 3 February 1968 and completed with the saxophone backing played by Ronnie Scot, Harry Klein, Bill Povey and Bill Jackman three days later. The saxophone segment in the middle (according to various reports) was apparently originally some fifteen to twenty seconds longer, but was then edited. The vocal backing, by all four Beatles, was reputed to have been achieved by them singing with their hands cupped around their mouths.

Revolution (Lennon–McCartney)   3:22

Recorded : 10–12 July 1968, EMI Studios, Abbey Road, London

John Lennon : Lead Guitar and Solo Vocal
Paul McCartney : Bass Guitar
George Harrison : Lead Guitar
Ringo Starr : Drums
Nicky Hopkins : Electric Piano

Previously issued as the B-side to the Beatles' first Apple single Hey Jude on 30 August 1968, this Lennon-written anti-war song (written by John in India) was recorded in sixteen takes between 10 and 12 July 1968 and features session man Nicky Hopkins on piano. The sound of a distorted guitar, played by John, is heard at the beginning of the record, to which Ringo then adds an electronically compressed drumbeat, giving the recording a solid 'heavy' sound. John's lead vocals (although recorded several times and rejected because he was dissatisfied with the result) were eventually completed after he had, as an experiment, lain on his back on the floor of the studio and sung them once more, finally achieving the sound he had originally wanted.

SIDE TWO

Hey Jude (Lennon–McCartney) 7:11

Recorded : 31 July and 1 August 1968, Trident Studios,
     Wardour Street, London

John Lennon : Acoustic Guitar and Backing Vocal
Paul McCartney : Piano and Lead Vocal
George Harrison : Lead Guitar and Backing Vocal
Ringo Starr : Drums
Session Musicians : 36-Piece Orchestra

This was the A-side of the first single issued by the Beatles on their own Apple label, on 30 August 1968. It was the longest single issued to that date, totalling with its B-side, Revolution, 10 minutes 33 seconds. Written by Paul, the song had started out as Hey Jules, about John's son Julian. The Beatles first attempted to record this at Abbey Road on 29 July 1968 but moved to Trident Studios in Soho where they recorded the song in four takes on 31 July (finally selecting take 1 for further overdubbing on 1 August). Paul sings lead vocal and accompanies himself on piano with backing vocals from John and George. The song starts simply, the main part lasting 3 minutes 11 seconds, but builds up until it finally explodes into a four-minute fade-out — the longest on a Beatles' record. The fade consists of all four Beatles plus a 36-piece orchestra (rather than the 100-piece which Paul had originally envisaged) playing and singing along to a one-line chorus of 'na, na-na-na-na-na, na'.

Old Brown Shoe (Harrison)   3:16

Recorded : 16 and 18 April 1969, EMI Studios, Abbey Road, London

John Lennon : Rhythm Guitar
Paul McCartney : Bass Guitar, Piano and Backing Vocal
George Harrison : Lead Guitar, Hammond Organ and Lead Vocal
Ringo Starr : Drums

Originally issued as the B-side to the 1969 single The Ballad Of John And Yoko, this was the second George Harrison song used as the B-side of a Beatles' single. (The first was The Inner Light on the B-side of Lady Madonna in 1968.) It was recorded in four takes on 16 and 18 April 1969, a few days after the completion of The Ballad Of John And Yoko. This, unlike the A-side, actually features all four Beatles and is quite an up-tempo song from George, who during the previous two years had been writing either Indian mantras or slower more doleful songs like While My Guitar Gently Weeps and Blue Jay Way.

Don't Let Me Down (Lennon–McCartney)   3:34

Recorded : 28 January 1969, Apple Studios, Savile Row, London

John Lennon : Lead Guitar and Lead Vocal
Paul McCartney : Bass Guitar and Harmony Vocal
George Harrison : Rhythm Guitar
Ringo Starr : Drums
Billy Preston : Organ

Previously issued as the B-side to the Get Back single on 11 April 1969, this recording, made within minutes of Get Back on 28 January 1969, features an extremely raw lead vocal from John, with harmony vocals from Paul. The Beatles are once again joined by Billy Preston who, whilst adding to the backing, also has a solo in the middle. The lyrics to this powerful blues-influenced song, written by John with Yoko in mind, are minimal with John simply repeating the title over and over.

The Ballad Of John And Yoko (Lennon–McCartney)   2:58

Recorded : 14 April 1969, EMI Studios, Abbey Road, London
John Lennon : Acoustic Guitar, Lead Guitar, Percussion and Lead Vocal
Paul McCartney : Bass Guitar, Drums, Piano, Maracas and Harmony Vocal
George Harrison : Not Present
Ringo Starr : Not Present

This was released as a single on 20 May 1969 while Get Back was still at No. 1. It was recorded in eleven takes (take ten being the released version) on 14 April 1969 (incidentally three days after the release of Get Back) at Abbey Road during an eight and a half hour session at which John and Paul played all the instruments heard. John is on lead vocal, acoustic and lead guitars and percussion, and Paul plays bass guitar, drums, piano and maracas together with supplying a harmony vocal in places. The song tells the story of John and Yoko's wedding in Gibraltar the previous month and their subsequent week-long bed-in for peace at the Amsterdam Hilton.

UK Release : 8 May 1970;
                   6 November 1970
Apple PXS 1 : PCS 7096
US Release : 18 May 1970
Apple AR 34001
Intl CD No : CDP 7 46447 2
Producers: George Martin and
                   Phil Spector
Running Time : 35:07

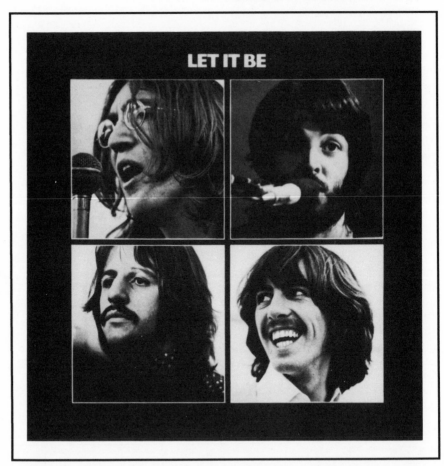

SIDE ONE : Two Of Us; Dig A Pony; Across The Universe; I Me Mine; Let It Be; Maggie Mae.

SIDE TWO : I've Got A Feeling; One After 909; The Long And Winding Road; For You Blue; Get Back.

It is interesting that Abbey Road was recorded *after* this album. Let It Be was originally called Get Back and intended as the soundtrack for a television film of the same name. It was to have been the official follow-up to the double album, The Beatles.

The idea originally came from John, who wanted to record an album that was not necessarily reliant upon technical tricks, overdubs or electronic wizardry. What he wanted was an album of up-to-date but basic Beatle music, without studio effects. Paul then suggested that they make a film showing the Beatles in the studio recording the album — and so recording and filming began on 2 January 1969 and finished on 30 January 1969 with the now famous concert on the roof of the Apple Office in London's Savile Row.

The album and film were not finally released until a year later, as they were delayed by Allen Klein, the Beatles' financial adviser. When released, the title was changed to Let It Be.

Klein had been called in originally by John against Paul's wishes to manage the Beatles' affairs, but initially proved valuable when he re-negotiated the contract with EMI to give the Beatles a higher royalty payment from their records. Now, with his eye on a better commercial proposition, he suggested that the proposed television film made originally in 16mm should be blown up to 35mm and marketed as a new Beatles' cinema film.

As this would take time, and as the Get Back single had been released already, in April 1969, Klein suggested that film and album be re-scheduled and retitled Let It Be and that a single of the same name be issued to promote both.

The Get Back album, which got as far as being pressed and sent to radio stations in both the USA and Canada, was never released to record stores because Klein felt that it could be improved. Originally it consisted of the following tracks : One After 909, Rocker, Save The Last Dance For Me, Don't Let Me Down, Dig A Pony, I've Got A Feeling, Get Back, For You Blue, Teddy Boy, Two Of Us, Maggie Mae, Dig It, Let It Be, The Long And Winding Road, and Get Back (reprise).

Klein also wanted the 'live' recordings of Get Back and Don't Let Me Down scrapped and replaced with studio recordings although the first made it through to the Let It Be album.

Because of the delay between recording and release of the final album, the Beatles lost interest in the possibility of themselves improving the original album, so John invited Phil Spector (who had worked with him on Instant Karma, and who was to work with both John and George later) to produce the album as Let It Be. Spector sifted through 24 hours of recorded material in which there were many different versions of each song. He eventually salvaged the album, which he remixed, and overdubbed strings on Let It Be, Across The Universe and I Me Mine, and strings *and* a heavenly choir on The Long And Winding Road to the apparent dissatisfaction of Paul McCartney who had envisioned the recording with only himself on vocals and piano, and John on bass guitar.

This was the first album since the Beatles signed with EMI for which George Martin did not have complete responsibility. Although he had produced the original recordings, the final production was left to Spector whose syrupy technique did little to hide the Beatles' sloppy playing. One wonders if he really did choose the best possible versions of each track as the inevitable bootlegs, such as Sweet Apple Tracks, include far better alternatives.

The album was packaged as a boxed set complete with book (exactly as had been planned for Get Back). It was also given the catalogue number held for the original Get Back album package (PXS 1). It went on sale in Britain on 8 May 1970 at £1 more than other albums, and sold poorly. After six months the album was re-issued on 6 November 1970, separately, without the book (as PCS 7096), but because of the time lag it did not sell well although it picked up sales at Christmas.

From 96 hours of recorded film, *Let It Be* finally emerged as a 90-minute semi-documentary, about the recording of the Get Back album. The film is as embarrassing to watch as the album is to listen to. It shows four rather unhappy-looking individuals involved in petty squabbles. After one scene, where Paul and George are seen arguing over a guitar riff, George left for three days and filming had to be halted until he returned. It is a sad spectacle, showing the public break-up of one of the world's greatest pop groups. One can only hope that one day enough will be salvaged from the remaining 94½ hours of footage to make a second movie. Certainly the Beatles were captured on film performing many rock and roll standards and reworkings of a number of their old songs. The most exciting surviving part of the film, shown at the end of the movie, is the impromptu concert on the roof of the Apple office in London's Savile Row. This shows the stunned and excited reaction of lunchtime shoppers and office workers in the area to the unbelievable noise of a Beatles' concert drifting down from the roof to the streets below. The Beatles manage to perform five songs (I Dig A Pony, I've Got A Feeling, One After 909, Don't Let Me Down and Get Back) before the arrival of the police to stop the concert.

An interesting postscript is that Get Back was not the only album to be planned from the material which never reached the shops. There were two more, which, although taken to the final stages, were never given working titles. The second was to have been re-recordings of old Beatles' tracks. Love Me Do, Norwegian Wood and She Said, She Said were announced as prospective tracks. The third album was to have consisted of fourteen old rock and roll standards without any Beatle-written songs. Tracks recorded for this included Shake Rattle and Roll, Lawdy Miss Clawdy, Blue Suede Shoes and Tracks Of My Tears.

It is also interesting to document the events which followed Let It Be. After the recording sessions for Abbey Road (after this album) finished in August 1969 both Paul and Ringo began work on their first solo albums (John and George had already done so). Ringo's first solo album, Sentimental Journey, a run-through of twelve standards, was issued on 27 March 1970 and Paul McCartney's album, McCartney, a selection of left-over Beatles' songs and instrumentals, was issued on 17 April 1970, a few weeks prior to the release of the Let It Be album. John, George and Ringo were not pleased that Paul was about to issue a solo album in competition with a Beatles' album. As he could not be persuaded otherwise, Ringo was sent by John to try and change his mind. On 10 April 1970, exactly one week prior to the release of the McCartney album, Paul announced that he was leaving the Beatles, a statement that shook and saddened all Beatles' fans. Many also thought that Paul's statement was a little too well timed to tie in with the release of his first solo album.

After Paul left the group John, George and Ringo considered recruiting Klaus Voormann (on bass) and forming The Ladders. This line-up did get together once in 1973 with Billy Preston when they recorded the track I'm The Greatest for Ringo's solo album Ringo (Apple PCTC 252).

Two Of Us (Lennon–McCartney)   3:33

John Lennon : Acoustic Guitar and Lead Vocal
Paul McCartney : Acoustic Guitar and Lead Vocal
George Harrison : Lead Guitar
Ringo Starr : Drums

Just before this track begins a snatch of studio conversation is included and John proclaims 'I dig a pygmy by Charles Hawtrey and the Deaf Aids — Phase one, in which Doris gets her oats.' Two Of Us was written by Paul as a duet for himself and John, possibly as a reaction to the arrival of Yoko Ono who was claiming all of John's attention. When the song was originally recorded it was called On Our Way Home. After the Get Back album was scrapped Paul gave the song to one of Apple's latest signings, a New York trio called Mortimer, who recorded the song under its original title in May 1969. The recording, produced by Paul, never appeared and nothing has been heard of Mortimer since.

The track is a close harmony duet between John and Paul (who also play acoustic guitars) with Paul soloing in places. George adds lead guitar with Ringo on drums (memories of the 'three guitars and drums' sound of the early sixties). The song is featured twice in the film Let It Be; first, in rehearsal, slightly up-tempo when John and Paul ad-lib the lyrics, and secondly, when they play the complete song which is the version issued on this album.

Dig A Pony (Lennon–McCartney)   3:55

John Lennon : Lead Guitar and Lead Vocal
Paul McCartney : Bass Guitar and Harmony Vocal
George Harrison : Rhythm Guitar
Ringo Starr : Drums
Billy Preston : Organ

The first of the four 'live' recordings (taken from the 30 January 1969 rooftop concert) included on the album, this was written by John as two separate songs, All I Want Is You and Dig A Pony. When the track listing for the Get Back album was announced, this track was called All I Want Is You, but when the album was compiled the title was changed to Dig A Pony. It has a false start then a lead vocal from John with harmonies from Paul. The lyrics sound as if they could have been made up on the spot. John makes references to the Rolling Stones and Johnny and The Moondogs (one of the Beatles' earlier names). At the end of the recording John can be heard complaining that his hands are cold. The recording sounds rough both in instrumentation and in the falsetto harmonies from John and Paul.

It should be noted that the album's American sleeve lists this track as I Dig A Pony.

Across The Universe (Lennon–McCartney)   3:51

John Lennon : Acoustic Guitar, Lead Guitar and Lead Vocal
Paul McCartney : Piano
George Harrison : Tamboura and Maracas
Ringo Starr : Drums and Tomtoms
Session Musicians : (Overdubbed) 35-Piece Orchestra and 14-Piece Choir

The original recording of this song, which appeared on the charity album No One's Gonna Change Our World (Regal Starline SRS 5018) and which now appears on Past Masters — Volume Two (Parlophone BPM 2), is a far superior version. Unfortunately Phil Spector's heavenly choir and slushy orchestra, overdubbed on to this version in April 1970, have destroyed the original simplicity of the song. This recording is slightly slower than the original, as if it has been deliberately slowed down from its original recorded speed, which unfortunately gives John's voice a whining quality. The original recording featured backing vocals from Paul and George and two female singers (see Past Masters — Volume Two); these are not included on this version.

I Me Mine (Harrison)   2:25

John Lennon : Not Present
Paul McCartney : Bass Guitar, Electric Piano and Backing Vocal
George Harrison : Acoustic Guitar, Lead Guitar, Organ and
    Lead/Backing Vocal
Ringo Starr : Drums
Session Musicians : (Overdubbed) 35-Piece Orchestra

Recorded on 3 January 1970 at the first of two final recording sessions by the Beatles (although John Lennon was absent) and the last song ever recorded by them. Bearing a distinct resemblance to Harrison's earlier Savoy Truffle on The White Album, it opens with a dramatic organ from George (who also plays acoustic guitar), Paul on electric piano and Ringo on drums. The vocals are mainly a solo from George but are supplemented by backing from Paul on the chorus. This track, like the preceding Across The Universe, also has an overdubbed 35-piece orchestra, but thankfully Phil Spector has not mixed them too far forward.

Dig It (Lennon–McCartney–Starkey–Harrison)   0:51

John Lennon : Bass Guitar and Solo Vocal
Paul McCartney : Piano
George Harrison : Lead Guitar
Ringo Starr : Drums
Billy Preston : Organ

The original recording of this track lasts for nearly twelve and a half minutes, of which only a mere 51 seconds is included here (an extract lasting nearly four minutes was included on the Get Back album). This short extract fades in with John singing odd, unconnected lines held together with the insistent chorus of 'dig it'. As the track fades John announces 'That was "Can you dig it"

Georgie Wood, now we'd like to do "Ark The Angels Come"'; Let It Be then begins.

Let It Be (Lennon–McCartney)   4:01

John Lennon : Bass Guitar
Paul McCartney : Piano, Maracas and Lead/Harmony Vocal
George Harrison : Lead Guitar and Harmony Vocal
Ringo Starr : Drums
Billy Preston : Organ
Session Musicians : Brass and Cellos

Paul (sounding rather like a choirboy singing a hymn at a requiem mass) leads the Beatles through this song, which was originally recorded on 31 January 1969, during the ill-fated Get Back sessions.

This and the version released as a single on 6 March 1970 (Apple R5833) are, in effect, the same basic recording. They both originate from the same eight-track master tape which contains two lead guitar tracks (one of which was an overdub). When Phil Spector was asked to produce an album from the Get Back tapes he used the original recording of this (together with the sloppy lead guitar) and remixed the track entirely. In doing so he ruined the original arrangement and his mixing is disastrous; near the end Paul's vocal battles with George's lead guitar which has been mixed too far forward.

Maggie Mae (Trad. Arr.–Lennon–McCartney–Harrison–Starkey)   0:39

John Lennon : Acoustic Guitar and Lead Vocal
Paul McCartney : Acoustic Guitar and Harmony Vocal
George Harrison : Bass Guitar and Harmony Vocal
Ringo Starr : Drums

Here, the Beatles interpret a traditional old Liverpool song. John is on lead vocal with Paul and George harmonising. John and Paul play acoustic guitars and Ringo, drums. The Beatles quite often did short renditions of songs like this to 'warm up' their recordings sessions. This is one of only a few such tracks to be released (see Chapter 51 *The Unreleased Tracks*).

SIDE TWO

I've Got A Feeling (Lennon–McCartney)   3:38

John Lennon : Lead Guitar and Lead Vocal
Paul McCartney : Bass Guitar and Lead Vocal
George Harrison : Rhythm Guitar
Ringo Starr : Drums
Billy Preston : Organ

The second 'live' recording on the album taken from the rooftop concert on 30 January 1969 sounds as rough as the previous live track, Dig A Pony, on side one. George's heavily distorted rhythm guitar provides the intro. The verses are split between John and Paul with Paul on lead vocal for the first two. John leads on the second two and finally there is an interesting interchange between stereo channels, with Paul on the left, repeating the first two verses, and John on the right-hand channel, repeating the third and fourth verses. The line-up is John on lead guitar, Paul on bass guitar, George on rhythm guitar, Ringo on drums and Billy Preston on organ.

One After 909 (Lennon–McCartney)   2:52

John Lennon : Lead Guitar and Lead Vocal
Paul McCartney : Bass Guitar and Lead Vocal
George Harrison : Rhythm Guitar
Ringo Starr : Drums
Billy Preston : Organ

This is one of John's earliest songs, which he revived especially for the Get Back project. Again this is a rough-sounding recording, also taken from the rooftop concert. The vocals are a duet between John and Paul with John singing solo for one verse.

At the end of the track John goes into an off-the-cuff rendition of Danny Boy, not credited on either record label or sleeve.

The Long And Winding Road (Lennon–McCartney)   3:40

John Lennon : Bass Guitar
Paul McCartney : Piano and Solo Vocal
George Harrison : Lead Guitar
Ringo Starr : Drums
Session Musicians : (Overdubbed) 35-Piece Orchestra and
   14-Piece Choir

Paul McCartney's ballad is overlaid with Spector's choirs and orchestras. Originally, Paul backed himself on piano while John, George and Ringo supplied a gentle accompaniment.

For You Blue (Harrison)   2:33

John Lennon : Steel Guitar
Paul McCartney : Bass Guitar and Piano
George Harrison : Acoustic Guitar and Solo Vocal
Ringo Starr : Drums

Prior to this track another snatch of studio chat can be heard from John : 'The Queen says no to pot-smoking FBI members.' Musically this is quite good, but at the same time it still seems like a rehearsal recording. It features a lead vocal from George, who also plays acoustic guitar, with John on a steel guitar, Paul on bass and Ringo on drums. Although the Beatles' music changed between 1962 and 1970 the return to a basic four-instrument sound is quite evident on this recording. Curiously, although this track is called For You Blue, the title is not mentioned anywhere in the lyrics.

Get Back (Lennon–McCartney)   3:09

John Lennon : Lead Guitar and Harmony Vocal
Paul McCartney : Bass Guitar and Lead Vocal
George Harrison : Rhythm Guitar
Ringo Starr : Drums
Billy Preston : Organ

The recording starts with Paul saying 'Rosetta, Oh Rosetta' which prompts John to launch into 'Sweet Rosetta Fart, she thought she was a cleaner, but she was a frying pan'. Although a live recording, the quality is comparable with the studio version issued as a single instead of this one as planned. The track features a lead vocal from Paul, who wrote the song, with harmonies in places from John. This recording omits the final verse of the song which is included on the studio version. The track ends with John saying poignantly 'I'd like to say "thank you" on behalf of the group and ourselves. I hope we've passed the audition.'

UK Release : 20 April 1973
Apple PCSP 717
US Release : 2 April 1973
Apple SKBO 3403
Intl CD No: To be released
Producer : George Martin
Running Time : 61:26

SIDE ONE : Love Me Do; Please Please Me; From Me To You; She Loves You; I Want To Hold Your Hand; All My Loving; Can't Buy Me Love
SIDE TWO : A Hard Day's Night; And I Love Her; Eight Days A Week; I Feel Fine; Ticket To Ride; Yesterday.

SIDE THREE : Help!; You've Got To Hide Your Love Away; We Can Work It Out; Day Tripper; Drive My Car; Norwegian Wood (This Bird Has Flown).
SIDE FOUR : Nowhere Man; Michelle; In My Life; Girl; Paperback Writer : Eleanor Rigby; Yellow Submarine.

UK Release : 20 April 1973
Apple PCSP 718
US Release : 2 April 1973
Apple SKBO 3404
Intl CD No : To be released
Producers : George Martin and
            Phil Spector
Running Time : 98:51

The Beatles / 1967-1970

SIDE ONE : Strawberry Fields Forever; Penny Lane; Sgt. Pepper's Lonely Hearts Club Band; With A Little Help From My Friends; Lucy In The Sky With Diamonds; A Day In The Life; All You Need Is Love.
SIDE TWO : I Am The Walrus; Hello Goodbye; The Fool On The Hill; Magical Mystery Tour; Lady Madonna; Hey Jude; Revolution.

SIDE THREE : Back In The U.S.S.R.; While My Guitar Gently Weeps; Ob-La-Di, Ob-La-Da; Get Back; Don't Let Me Down; The Ballad Of John And Yoko; Old Brown Shoe.
SIDE FOUR : Here Comes The Sun; Come Together; Something; Octopus's Garden; Let It Be; Across The Universe; The Long And Winding Road.

Although it was three years after the Let It Be album of May 1970 before the next Beatles' album was released, it was worth waiting for. It was not one album but four, compiling the Beatles' greatest hits, selected by themselves. Although its release was planned to combat the ever-growing numbers of bootleg compilations it is excellent, nonetheless. The four albums, as the titles suggest, trace the Beatles' recording history from the first single Love Me Do in 1962 to 1970 and Let It Be. All the Beatles' number one hit songs are included, plus all the A-sides of the singles and a fair selection of tracks from almost every L.P. released. Every one of the 54 tracks is Beatle-written, either by Lennon and McCartney, George Harrison or Ringo Starr. In a way, it is sad that one or two of the 24 non-Beatle written tracks were not included, but as they wrote so many highly commercial songs, there just wasn't room for any songs they didn't write. Similarly, although the Beatles' solo material was also considered, there was not sufficient space.

The first double album, The Beatles 1962–1966, contains all the A-sides of the Beatles' singles issued on Parlophone up to the end of 1966, plus a selection of album tracks from the same period, namely, All My Loving from With The Beatles, Eight Days A Week from Beatles For Sale, Yesterday from Help! and Norwegian Wood and Michelle from Rubber Soul. These two albums consist solely of Lennon–McCartney songs.

The second double album, The Beatles 1967–1970, compiles the remaining A-sides of singles, plus a further selection of album tracks issued during that period. Of the 28 tracks, three (While My Guitar Gently Weeps, Old Brown Shoe and Something) are written by George Harrison. Octopus's Garden is written by Ringo and the remaining 24 tracks are written by Lennon and McCartney.

The sleeves of these two double albums show two photographs, taken eight years apart, of the Beatles in the same pose. The first is that used in 1963 for the Please Please Me album; the second taken in 1969 had been planned for the unreleased Get Back album. It was good that this was not scrapped as the two make an effective pair. They differ in their coloured borders — the first is red, the second blue, reputedly picked by the Beatles themselves for their Liverpool fans to show the colours of Liverpool's two football clubs, Liverpool and Everton. In the late 1970s when coloured vinyl records became popular, these two double albums were re-issued on coloured vinyl, the first on red, the second on blue. To date, these are the only Beatles' albums available in Britain on coloured vinyl, although other albums are available elsewhere in the world in varying colours. Because of this they have the additional letters R and B (for Red and Blue) in their catalogue number prefixes. They make interesting (although expensive if you already own the black vinyl copies) additions to a Beatles collection.

THE BEATLES 1962–1966

Side One
Love Me Do   2:1
Please Please Me   2:00
From Me To You   1:55
She Loves You   2:18
I Want To Hold Your Hand   2:24
All My Loving   2:04
Can't Buy Me Love   2:15

Side Two
A Hard Day's Night   2:32
And I Love Her   2:27
Eight Days A Week   2:43
I Feel Fine   2:19
Ticket To Ride   3:03
Yesterday   2:04

Side Three
James Bond Theme (Norman) 0:16*
Help!   2:16
You've Got To Hide Your Love
   Away   2:08
We Can Work It Out   2:10
Day Tripper   2:37
Drive My Car   2:25
Norwegian Wood (This Bird Has
   Flown)   2:00

The George Martin Orchestra (U.S. copies only)

Side Four
Nowhere Man   2:40
Michelle   2:42
In My Life   2:23
Girl   2:26
Paperback Writer   2:25
Eleanor Rigby   2:11
Yellow Submarine   2:40

THE BEATLES 1967–1970

Side One
Strawberry Fields Forever   4:05
Penny Lane   3:00
Sgt. Pepper's Lonely Hearts Club
   Band   1:59
With A Little Help From My Friends
   2:46
Lucy In The Sky With
   Diamonds   3:25
A Day In The Life   5:03
All You Need Is Love   3:57

Side Two
I Am The Walrus   4:35
Hello Goodbye   3:24
The Fool On The Hill   3:00
Magical Mystery Tour   2:48
Lady Madonna   2:17
Hey Jude   7:11
Revolution   3:22

Side Three
Back In The U.S.S.R.   2:45
While My Guitar Gently Weeps
   (Harrison)   4:46
Ob-La-Di, Ob-La-Da   3:10
Get Back   3:11
Don't Let Me Down   3:34
The Ballad of John And Yoko   2:58
Old Brown Shoe (Harrison)   3:16

Side Four
Here Comes The Sun
   (Harrison)   3:04
Come Together   4:16
Something (Harrison)   2:59
Octopus's Garden (Starkey)   2:49
Let It Be   3:50
Across The Universe   3:51**
The Long And Winding
   Road   3:40**

**Produced by George Martin/Phil Spector; all others produced by George Martin.*

All Lennon–McCartney songs except where stated.

UK Release : 11 June 1976
Parlophone PCSP 719
US Release : 7 June 1976
Capitol SKBO 11537
Intl CD No : None
Producers: George Martin and
Phil Spector
Running Time : 72:44

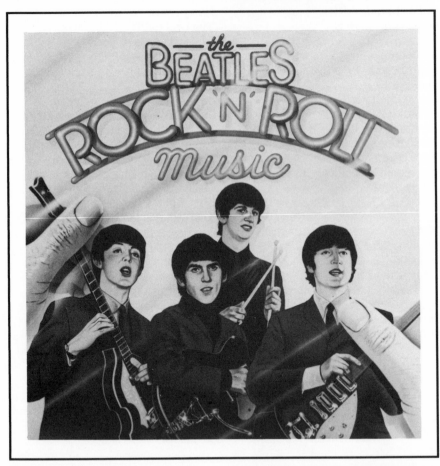

SIDE ONE : Twist And Shout; I Saw Her Standing There; You Can't Do That; I Wanna Be Your Man; I Call Your Name; Boys; Long Tall Sally.
SIDE TWO : Rock And Roll Music; Slow Down; Kansas City/Hey Hey Hey Hey; Money; Bad Boy; Matchbox; Roll Over Beethoven.

SIDE THREE : Dizzy Miss Lizzy; Any Time At All; Drive My Car; Everybody's Trying To Be My Baby; The Night Before; I'm Down; Revolution.
SIDE FOUR : Back In The U.S.S.R.; Helter Skelter; Taxman; Got To Get You Into My Life; Hey Bulldog; Birthday; Get Back.

After the release of the four-album set, but prior to the release of this album, the Beatles' contract expired and EMI decided in 1976 to re-issue every Beatles' single — at the same time! This obviously caused chaos in the British record charts. No less than six reached the top 40 : Help (37), Strawberry Fields Forever (32), Paperback Writer (23), Hey Jude (12), Get Back (28) and a specially issued single of Yesterday (8). As could be expected, other record companies were irate as this was spoiling the chances of newer artists.

Decca Records, the Rolling Stones record company throughout the sixties, replied by re-promoting the Rolling Stones' singles with advertisements stating 'The Rolling Stones singles are, and always have been available : none have ever been deleted'. Although this seemed like a 'Battle of the Giants' created by the two record companies of the sixties, none of the Rolling Stones' singles were placed a second time in the top forty in 1976 (although their new single Fool To Cry : RS19131, issued on their own label, reached number 6 on 1 May 1976).

It seemed hopeful that after the re-release of the old Beatles' singles some of the unreleased tracks would then be issued. Instead, the idea for this album, Rock and Roll Music, came from Bhaskar Menon, the head of Capitol Records in the U.S.A. Menon, after trying unsuccessfully to contact one or all of the Beatles for approval of the track listing for this new double album, eventually gave up and contacted George Martin, their producer. When Martin was told of the plan to release this compilation of old Beatles' tracks as a new album he flew to the Hollywood offices of Capitol.

After hearing some of the older tracks with bad background noise and poor stereo Martin was appalled at the prospect of their reissue and set about filtering and remixing every track included on this album. On some of the older tracks, such as Twist and Shout and I Saw Her Standing There, he reversed the stereo and brought the vocal track away from the edge into the centre, adding a slight echo for a more modern sound. He also filtered out the bass from the rhythm track and placed that also in the centre of the stereo, and with the aid of filters and equalisers gave the recordings a crisper sound.

When he had finished his work, Martin took a copy of these tapes back to EMI Records in Britain, but the Company was horrified as the Beatles had issued official instructions that the tapes must not be 'touched, added to, edited or mutilated in any way'. EMI Records took this edict rather too literally, i.e. that if they were to be re-issued, the tapes should be exactly as originally recorded. Thus George Martin's remixed and filtered versions of the original tracks were not included on the Rock and Roll Music album when released in Britain.

In 1980, however, EMI Records relented and decided to issue the remixed recordings. They split the two albums, put them into new sleeves (after receiving numerous complaints about the original sleeve) and issued them on the Music For Pleasure label as Rock and Roll Music, Volumes 1 and 2: MFP 50506 and 50507. These two albums are worth buying if only to compare the original recordings with the re-mixes.

The following track listing, complete with timings, applies to both the original double album and the two remixed Music For Pleasure albums Rock and Roll Music Volumes 1 and 2 (MFP50506 and 50507) issued in 1980.

Side One
Twist And Shout
  (Medley–Russell)   2:32
I Saw Her Standing There   2:50
You Can't Do That   2:33
I Wanna Be Your Man   1:59
I Call Your Name   2:02
Boys (Goffin–King)   2:24
Long Tall Sally
  (Johnson–Penniman–
  Blackwell)   1:58

Side Two
Rock and Roll Music (Berry)   2:02
Slow Down (Williams)   2:54
Kansas City (Leiber/Stoller)/Hey
  Hey Hey Hey (Penniman)   2:30
Money (Bradford–Gordy)   2:47
Bad Boy (Williams)   2:17
Matchbox (Perkins)   1:37
Roll Over Beethoven (Berry)   2:44

Side Three
Dizzy Miss Lizzy (Williams)   2:51
Any Time At All   2:10
Drive My Car   2:25
Everybody's Trying To Be My Baby
  (Perkins)   2:24
The Night Before   2:33
I'm Down   2:30
Revolution   3:22

Side Four
Back In the U.S.S.R.   2:45
 Helter Skelter   4:30
Taxman (Harrison)   2:36
Got To Get You Into My Life   2:31
Hey Bulldog   3:09
Birthday   2:40
Get Back   3:09*

*Produced by George Martin and Phil Spector; all
others produced by George Martin.*

All Lennon–McCartney songs except where stated.

UK Release : 6 May 1977
Parlophone EMTV 4
US Release : 2 May 1977
Capitol SMAS 11638
Intl CD No : To be released
Producers : Voyle Gilmore and
George Martin
Running Time : 33:50

SIDE ONE : Twist And Shout; She's A Woman; Dizzy Miss Lizzy; Ticket To Ride; Can't Buy Me Love; Things We Said Today; Roll Over Beethoven.

SIDE TWO : Boys; A Hard Day's Night; Help!; All My Loving; She Loves You; Long Tall Sally.

The release of a 'live' album by the Beatles recorded at the Hollywood Bowl had been announced in the music press at various intervals during the 1970s. In 1972 it was announced to combat the increasing number of bootleg albums appearing on the market. Eighteen months later the album was announced again. Details were given that the album would be a live recording of the Hollywood Bowl concert on 23 August 1964, with the following tracks:

Side One : Twist And Shout, You Can't Do That, All My Loving, She Loves You, Things We Said Today, Roll Over Beethoven.

Side Two : Can't Buy Me Love, If I Fell, I Want To Hold Your Hand, Boys, A Hard Day's Night, Long Tall Sally.

However, once again the album did not appear.

In 1977 the release of a live album by the Beatles was announced yet again. This time it was to include some of the recordings from the 1964 concert with some from a second concert held on 29 August 1965. The album did appear this time and was worth waiting for. The excitement of a Beatles' concert is captured perfectly, complete with the sound of 17,000 screaming Beatles' fans, the only disadvantage being that because of the noise, the album is neither technically nor musically perfect. Of the thirteen tracks, six (All My Loving, She Loves You, Things We Said Today, Roll Over Beethoven, Boys and Long Tall Sally) are from the 1964 concert. The remaining seven ('Twist and Shout, She's A Woman, Dizzy Miss Lizzy, Ticket To Ride, Can't Buy Me Love, A Hard Day's Night, and Help!) are from the 1965 concert. They have been edited together successfully by George Martin to make a highly enjoyable live album.

Because the original recordings were made on old-fashioned three-track machines, it was necessary to first transfer them on to sixteen-track tape before George Martin and his studio engineer, Geoff Emerick, could filter, equalise and edit them. The major problem was that with continual use the tape heads of these old machines overheated and melted the magnetic tape. The resourceful Martin hit on the idea of using hair dryers, blowing cold air, to cool down the tape heads.

As a postscript, it is interesting to note that the biggest concert ever given by the Beatles was neither of these Hollywood Bowl concerts but was one given two weeks previously at New York's Shea Stadium on 15 August 1965, before 65,000 fans. It was recorded and also filmed. Nine months after the concert, on 1 May 1966, the BBC premièred the film on British television. Unlike the recording of the Hollywood Bowl Concert, the Shea Stadium Concert has never been officially released, although it is available on bootleg albums.

Side One   17:57

Twist And Shout
  (Medley–Russell)   1:20
She's A Woman   2:45
Dizzy Miss Lizzy (Williams)   3:00
Ticket To Ride   2:18
Can't Buy Me Love   2:08
Things We Said Today   2:07
Roll Over Beethoven (Berry)   2:10

Side Two   15:53

Boys (Dixon–Farrell)   1:57
A Hard Day's Night   2:30
Help!   2:16
All My Loving   1:55
She Loves You   2:10
Long Tall Sally
  (Johnson–Penniman–
  Blackwell)   1:54

All Lennon–McCartney songs except where stated.

UK Release : 28 November 1977
Parlophone PCSP 721
US Release : 24 November 1977
Capitol SKBL 11711
Intl CD No : None
Producers : George Martin and
          Phil Spector
Running Time : 59:25

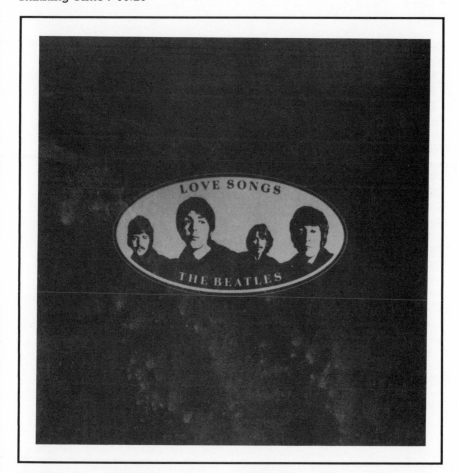

SIDE ONE : Yesterday; I'll Follow The Sun; I Need You; Girl; In My Life; Words Of Love; Here, There And Everywhere.
SIDE TWO : Something; And I Love Her; If I Fell; I'll Be Back; Tell Me What You See; Yes It Is.

SIDE THREE : Michelle; It's Only Love; You're Going To Lose That Girl; Every Little Thing; For No One; She's Leaving Home.
SIDE FOUR : The Long And Winding Road; This Boy; Norwegian Wood (This Bird Has Flown); You've Got To Hide Your Love Away; I Will; P.S. I Love You.

This album is mainly a compilation of tracks previously available on other Beatles' albums. The only two not previously issued on British albums are This Boy and Yes It Is and these are simply mono recordings re-channelled into fake stereo, even though This Boy is available in stereo on a Canadian single.

The album was issued just in time for Christmas 1977, so sales were guaranteed to a certain extent. In addition to taking these buyers for a ride, the record of course exploited dedicated fans and collectors who always bought Beatles' albums. To add insult to injury there were many other tracks available, which would have made a far better compilation album. One good feature of the album package is the inclusion of the 1967 Richard Avedon poster.

Side One
Yesterday   2:04
I'll Follow The Sun   1:46
I Need You (Harrison)   2:28
Girl   2:26
In My Life   2:23
Words Of Love (Holly)   2:10
Here, There And
    Everywhere   2:29

Side Two
Something (Harrison)   2:59
And I Love Her   2:27
If I Fell   2:16
I'll Be Back   2:22
Tell Me What You See   2:35
Yes It Is   2:40

Side Three
Michelle   2:42
It's Only Love   1:53
You're Going To Lose That
    Girl   2:18
Every Little Thing   2:01
For No One   2:03
She's Leaving Home   3:24

Side Four
The Long And Winding
    Road   3:40*
This Boy   2:11
Norwegian Wood (This Bird Has
    Flown)   2:00
You've Got To Hide Your Love
    Away   2:08
I Will   1:46
P.S. I Love You   2:02

*Produced by George Martin/Phil Spector. All others produced by George Martin.

All Lennon–McCartney songs except where stated.

UK Release : 15 December 1978
Parlophone/Apple BC 13
US Release : None
Intl CD No : See Individual Albums
Producers: George Martin and
                Phil Spector
Running Time : See Individual Albums

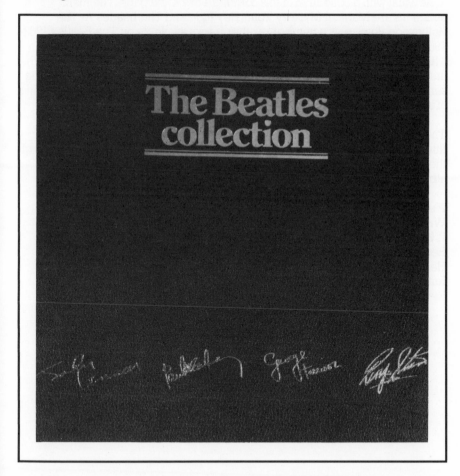

A boxed set containing the following albums; Please Please Me; With The Beatles; A Hard Day's Night; Beatles For Sale; Help!; Rubber Soul; Revolver; Sgt. Pepper's Lonely Hearts Club Band; The Beatles; Yellow Submarine; Abbey Road; Let It Be; The Beatles Rarities.

This collection of the main Beatles' albums as a boxed set was inevitable. Unfortunately, it is by no means a complete collection of the Beatles' recordings issued by EMI/Parlophone between 1962 and 1970. Rather it is a collection of the Beatles' studio albums, issued by EMI in Britain during that period. Curiously, A Collection of Beatles Oldies is excluded, although included is a brand new album The Beatles' Rarities, (a collection of B-sides from singles, plus a few tracks not previously available on British Beatles' albums).

As usual with a collection of this sort there are a few gaps. The main omissions are Magical Mystery Tour, Hey Jude and The Beatles At The Hollywood Bowl, plus a number of other tracks available on The Beatles 1962–1966 and The Beatles 1967–1970.

Overall it is a good collection for either younger Beatles' fans buying for the first time or older fans who would like to renew their Beatles' albums. For the serious collector, who has bought everything issued since 1962, the only thing of interest is the box.

The Beatles Collection comes neatly packaged in a dark blue box, with the title and the four Beatles' autographs printed in gold on the front. It consists of the stereo versions of the twelve studio albums, plus The Beatles Rarities album.

Please Please Me (PCS 3042)
With The Beatles (PCS 3045)
A Hard Day's Night (PCS 3058)
Beatles For Sale (PCS 3062)
Help! (PCS 3071)
Rubber Soul (PCS 3075)
Revolver (PCS 7009)

Sgt. Pepper's Lonely Hearts Club Band (PCS 7027)
The Beatles (PCS 7067/8)
Yellow Submarine (PCS 7070)
Abbey Road (PCS 7088)
Let It Be (PCS 7096)
The Beatles Rarities (PSLP 261)

UK Release : October 1979
Parlophone PSLP 261 : PCM 1001
US Release : None
Intl CD No : None
Producer : George Martin
Running Time : 43:29

SIDE ONE : Across The Universe; Yes It Is; This Boy; The Inner Light; I'll Get You; Thank You Girl; Komm, Gib Mir Deine Hand; You Know My Name (Look Up The Number); Sie Liebt Dich.

SIDE TWO : Rain; She's A Woman; Matchbox; I Call Your Name; Bad Boy; Slow Down; I'm Down; Long Tall Sally.

Originally included as a free addition to the 1978 boxed set, The Beatles Collection, this album was issued separately in 1979 after EMI had received complaints that the only way of obtaining this 'free' album was to pay for the box and its duplicate copies of Beatles' albums. For most British fans the only rare tracks are Across The Universe, previously available only on the now deleted charity album No One's Gonna Change Our World, and the German-language versions of She Loves You and I Want To Hold Your Hand, previously unavailable in Britain. The sleeve notes proclaim the remaining fourteen tracks, which are a collection of B-sides and E.P. tracks, were not available on earlier British Beatles' albums. In fact eight of the seventeen tracks were previously available (Long Tall Sally, I Call Your Name, Slow Down, Matchbox and I'm Down are on the Rock and Roll Music album; Yes It Is and This Boy on Love Songs; and Rain on the Hey Jude album).

Although the album contains very little in the way of rare tracks, it is an intelligent compilation of some of the material previously only available on B-sides, E.P.s and foreign releases.

Beatles fans who play this album expecting to find the long-awaited stereo versions of tracks will be disappointed. Only four of the seventeen tracks (Across The Universe; Komm, Gib Mir Deine Hand; Sie Leibt Dich and Bad Boy) are actually in stereo. The remaining thirteen (of which four — Long Tall Sally, I Call Your Name, Slow Down and Matchbox — were issued as the Long Tall Sally E.P.) are the original mono mixes issued as the B-sides to various singles.

As a collection of B-sides and E.P. tracks (together with three actual rarities), this album is a good start towards making some rare and semi-rare tracks available and is certainly cheaper than buying all of the singles and trying to track down copies of long-deleted records. But an album of real rarities would be a much more exciting prospect.

SIDE ONE

Across The Universe (Lennon–McCartney) 3:41

Recorded : 4 and 8 February 1968, EMI Studios, Abbey Road, London

John Lennon : Acoustic Guitar, Lead Guitar and Lead/Backing Vocal
Paul McCartney : Piano and Harmony/Backing Vocal
George Harrison : Tamboura, Maracas and Backing Vocal
Ringo Starr : Tomtoms
Lizzie Bravo : Backing Vocal
Gayleen Pease : Backing Vocal

Recorded in eight takes on 4 and 8 February 1968 during the same period as Lady Madonna, this was considered as a possible rival for the March 1968 single, but Lady Madonna was chosen instead.

Shortly after being rejected in favour of Lady Madonna, this was given to the World Wildlife Fund who included it on the charity album No One's Gonna Change Our World which was released on 12 December 1969 (Regal Starline SRS 5013). A different mix of the recording (minus the sound effects and a considerable amount of the original backing) then appeared with an orchestral and choral backing some four months later on the Let It Be album.

The track begins with the sound of birds (added for the purposes of the charity album) which then 'flies' across the stereo. When it fades the track proper begins, featuring John singing lead vocal on his own song, with Paul harmonising in places. The backing vocals were added by two young women, Lizzie Bravo and Gayleen Pease, who (whilst waiting outside to see the Beatles) were invited into the studio by Paul to add the falsetto harmony to John's lead vocal.

The lyrics to this song are some of John's most imaginative, with his incessant chorus line 'Nothing's gonna change my world' accentuating their dreamy effect.

Yes It Is (Lennon–McCartney)   2:40

Recorded : 16 February 1965, EMI Studios, Abbey Road, London

John Lennon : Acoustic Guitar and Lead Vocal
Paul McCartney : Bass Guitar and Backing Vocal
George Harrison : Lead Guitar and Backing Vocal
Ringo Starr : Drums

The B-side to Ticket To Ride (included on the Help! album) released on 9 April 1965 was this beautiful ballad, which was recorded in fourteen takes on 16 February 1965 and written by John. The song is very reminiscent of his earlier This Boy and features a similar three-part harmony from John, Paul and George, with John singing solo in parts. The whining guitar in the backing is played by George, who achieved the effect with a volume/tone control pedal with which he had been experimenting at the time.

This Boy (Lennon–McCartney)   2:11

Recorded : 17 October 1963, EMI Studios, Abbey Road, London

John Lennon : Acoustic Guitar and Lead Vocal
Paul McCartney : Bass Guitar and Harmony Vocal
George Harrison : Lead Guitar and Harmony Vocal
Ringo Starr : Drums

This track was originally released in 1963 as the B-side to the Beatles' multi-million seller I Want To Hold Your Hand. This Boy was recorded at the same 17 October 1963 session as I Want To Hold Your Hand, and also went to seventeen takes before the fifteenth was finally chosen for release.

The song is dominated by a close three-part harmony from John, Paul and George, with an extremely powerful solo vocal from John. For the film *A Hard Day's Night*, George Martin produced an orchestral version of this which was retitled Ringo's Theme and used in the film as the soundtrack to a section featuring Ringo, who, amongst other things, is seen walking along the banks of the River Thames.

The Inner Light (Harrison)   2:36

Recorded : (Instrumental Track) 12 January 1968, EMI Studios, Bombay, India
   (Vocal Track) 6 and 8 February 1968, EMI Studios, Abbey Road, London

John Lennon : Backing Vocal
Paul McCartney : Backing Vocal
George Harrison : Lead Vocal
Ringo Starr : Not Present
Session Musicians : All Instruments

Issued originally in 1968 as the B-side of Lady Madonna, this was George's first song to be released on a Beatles' single. It is the last of three Beatles' tracks by George Harrison featuring almost entirely Indian instrumentation. The previous two were Love You To, included on Revolver, and Within You, Without You, featured on Sgt. Pepper's Lonely Hearts Club Band. The instrumental track was recorded in five takes on 12 January 1968 at EMI studios in Bombay, India, with some of India's virtuoso musicians, during the recording of George's Wonderwall album. The vocal track (including a brief backing from John and Paul) was overdubbed nearly a month later on 6 and 8 February 1968 at Abbey Road. Extracts from a Japanese poem by Roshi, translated into English by R. H. Bluth, formed the basis of George's lyrics for this interesting, and introspective, song.

I'll Get You (Lennon–McCartney)   2:04

Recorded : 1 July 1963, EMI Studios, Abbey Road, London

John Lennon : Rhythm Guitar, Harmonica and Lead Vocal
Paul McCartney : Bass Guitar and Harmony Vocal
George Harrison : Lead Guitar and Harmony Vocal
Ringo Starr : Drums

Originally considered as an A-side for the follow-up to From Me To You, this was released in 1963 as the B-side to She Loves You. The song is reminiscent of She Loves You with the opening 'Oh yeah' and the duet by John and Paul on lead vocals. John's overdubbed harmonica is prominent at the beginning and ending but is mixed back during the rest of the track. The take details of this, and She Loves You, are unknown. This is due to the studio master having been erased shortly after the session, which also accounts for the lack of stereo versions of both these tracks.

Thank You Girl (Lennon–McCartney)   2:01

Recorded : 5 and 13 March 1963, EMI Studios, Abbey Road, London

John Lennon : Acoustic Guitar, Harmonica and Lead Vocal
Paul McCartney : Bass Guitar and Lead Vocal
George Harrison : Lead Guitar
Ringo Starr : Drums

This exciting track dates back to April 1963 when it was originally released as the B-side of the Beatles' third Parlophone single From Me To You. It has a predominant harmonica from John and the usual John and Paul lead vocal duet featured on most of their 1963 singles. The recording was completed in thirteen takes on 5 March 1963 and some additional edit sections were recorded on 13 March 1963.

Komm, Gib Mir Deine Hand (Lennon–McCartney–Nicolas–Hellmer)   2:24

Recorded : (Instrumental Track) 17 October 1963, EMI Studios, Abbey Road, London
(Vocal Track) 29 January 1964, Pathé Marconi Studios, Paris, France

John Lennon : Rhythm Guitar and Lead Vocal
Paul McCartney : Bass Guitar and Lead Vocal
George Harrison : Lead Guitar
Ringo Starr : Drums

The German-language versions of I Want To Hold Your Hand and She Loves You were not recorded, as many thought, as a tribute to the Beatles' early days in Hamburg, but in answer to a request from EMI in Germany, who wanted authentic versions for the German market. The Beatles were far from enthusiastic about the idea but George Martin eventually persuaded them to record the tracks in the EMI studios in Paris, where they were at the time. The two recordings were subsequently released in Germany as a double A-sided single on 5 March 1964 (Odeon 22671). The German lyrics of both songs were written by two German songwriters, one of whom was present at the recording session to ensure that the songs were sung with the correct accent.
    For this version of the song the Beatles used the original backing track as used for the English version and, in eleven takes, added the new German vocals plus hand-claps.

You Know My Name (Look Up The Number)
(Lennon–McCartney)   4:20

Recorded : 17 May, 7 and 8 June 1967 and 30 April 1969, EMI Studios, Abbey Road, London

John Lennon : Maracas and Lead Vocal
Paul McCartney : Piano, Bass Guitar and Lead Vocal
George Harrison : Vibraphone and Backing Vocal
Ringo Starr : Drums, Bongos and Lead Vocal
Mal Evans : Backing Vocal
Brian Jones : Alto Saxophone

This intriguing off-beat track began life on 17 May 1967 shortly after the Sgt. Pepper's album had been completed, when a section of the backing track was recorded. On 7 and 8 June 1967 further sections were recorded and these were then edited together on 9 June the same year to form a final master track. Following that, it was abandoned. On 30 April 1969, John and Paul resurrected it and added the vocals and the sound effects, together with Mal Evans, but again it was shelved. On 26 November 1969 John edited the track down from its original six minutes to its current length of just under four and a half minutes and planned to issue it, together with another unreleased Beatles track, What's The New Mary Jane, as a single under the banner of The Plastic Ono Band. At the last minute, despite being given the catalogue number Apples 1002 and a release date of 5 December 1969, it was withdrawn without explanation.

The track then finally emerged on 6 March 1970 when it was issued as the B-side of the Let It Be single. One of the interesting points concerning that release is that the catalogue number of Apples 1002 is stamped in the run-off groove.

The lyrics to this Lennon-conceived track are basically a repetition of the title, with various additional comments and sound effects thrown in for good measure. The jazz piano is supplied by Paul McCartney and the saxophone solo by Brian Jones of the Rolling Stones.

As this track (despite being originally planned as a Plastic Ono Band release) is the B-side to the Beatles' final single it is interesting to note that, right at the end of the track, the final comment is 'Goodbye'.

Sie Liebt Dich (Lennon–McCartney–Nicolas–Montague) 2:18

Recorded : 29 January 1964, Pathé Marconi Studios, Paris, France

John Lennon : Rhythm Guitar and Lead Vocal
Paul McCartney : Bass Guitar and Lead Vocal
George Harrison : Lead Guitar and Harmony Vocal
Ringo Starr : Drums

This German-language version of She Loves You shares the same basic history as Komm, Gib Mir Deine Hand. But unlike Komm, Gib Mir Deine Hand, which used the backing track from I Want To Hold Your Hand, Sie Liebt Dich is a brand-new recording. The Beatles, unable to use the backing track to She Loves You for Sie Leibt Dich, due to the original studio master having been erased, had to make a completely new recording.

SIDE TWO

Rain (Lennon–McCartney) 2:59

Recorded : 14 and 16 April 1966, EMI Studios, Abbey Road, London

John Lennon : Rhythm Guitar and Lead Vocal
Paul McCartney : Bass Guitar and Backing Vocal
George Harrison : Lead Guitar and Backing Vocal
Ringo Starr : Drums and Tambourine

Originally released as the B-side to Paperback Writer on 10 June 1966, this track was then included, together with Paperback Writer, on the Hey Jude album in 1970 (see discussion of that album for review).

She's A Woman (Lennon–McCartney) 2:57

Recorded : 8 October 1964, EMI Studios, Abbey Road, London

John Lennon : Rhythm Guitar
Paul McCartney : Bass Guitar, Piano and Solo Vocal
George Harrison : Lead Guitar
Ringo Starr : Drums and Percussion

This great chunk of syncopated rock and roll, written and sung by Paul in his best rock and roll style, was recorded in seven takes and originally issued as the B-side of I Feel Fine on 27 November 1964.

Matchbox (Perkins) 1:37

Recorded : 1 June 1964, EMI Studios, Abbey Road, London

John Lennon : Rhythm Guitar
Paul McCartney : Bass Guitar
George Harrison : Lead Guitar
Ringo Starr : Drums and Solo Vocal
George Martin : Piano

This was recorded in five takes during the same session as Slow Down and released as part of the Long Tall Sally E.P. Ringo gives a rousing rendition of this 1957 Carl Perkins song which was recorded with Perkins present (although not participating) during the session.

I Call Your Name (Lennon–McCartney) 2:02

Recorded : 1 March 1964, EMI Studios, Abbey Road, London

John Lennon : Rhythm Guitar and Solo Vocal
Paul McCartney : Bass Guitar
George Harrison : Lead Guitar
Ringo Starr : Drums

This was originally written for Billy J. Kramer and The Dakotas, who recorded and issued it as the B-side to another Lennon–McCartney composition, Bad To Me. When John (who wrote it) discovered it had been buried on a B-side he decided that the Beatles should also record and issue it. So with John on lead vocals the Beatles recorded the song (which has a similar feel, both musically and vocally, to John's later You Can't Do That) in seven takes (the released version being an edit of takes five and seven) during the same session that produced Long Tall Sally. Like Long Tall Sally, this was issued as part of the American album The Beatles Second on 10 April 1964, and then in Britain on 19 June 1964 as part of the Long Tall Sally E.P.

Bad Boy (Williams) 2:17

Recorded : 10–11 May 1965, EMI Studios, Abbey Road, London

John Lennon : Rhythm Guitar, Hammond Organ and Solo Vocal
Paul McCartney : Bass Guitar and Electric Piano
George Harrison : Lead Guitar
Ringo Starr : Drums and Tambourine

This was originally issued as part of the American album Beatles VI on 14 June 1965 and later included on the British album A Collection Of Beatles Oldies released on 9 December 1966. The recording, which was completed in four takes, features a solo vocal from John and a very enthusiastic backing from the rest of the Beatles. This and another Larry Williams song, Dizzy Miss Lizzy (recorded during the same session), were the last two songs (leaving aside the rather short rendition of Maggie Mae on Let It Be) issued by the Beatles during their collective career that they did not write themselves.

Slow Down (Williams) 2:54

Recorded : 1 and 4 June 1964, EMI Studios, Abbey Road, London

John Lennon : Rhythm Guitar and Solo Vocal
Paul McCartney : Bass Guitar
George Harrison : Lead Guitar
Ringo Starr : Drums
George Martin : Piano

Released as part of the Long Tall Sally E.P. on 19 June 1964, this track, partially recorded during six takes on 1 June and completed on 4 June, which features John on lead vocal, is an extremely enthusiastic rendition of this little-known Larry Williams song. It is the first of three Williams songs which the Beatles recorded and released.

I'm Down (Lennon–McCartney) 2:30

Recorded : 14 June 1965, EMI Studios, Abbey Road, London

John Lennon : Hammond Organ and Backing Vocal
Paul McCartney : Bass Guitar and Lead Vocal
George Harrison : Lead Guitar and Backing Vocal
Ringo Starr : Drums and Bongos

This is the Beatles at their rock and roll best! This superb McCartney-written track, similar in style to Little Richard's Long Tall Sally, was originally issued on 23 July 1965 as the B-side of Help! (included on the album of the same name). The recording, completed in seven takes, rattles along at an incredible pace with Paul shouting out the lyrics in true Little Richard style while John hammers away at the Hammond organ. Unbelievably, this recording was made during the same session that produced Yesterday.

Long Tall Sally (Johnson–Penniman–Blackwell)   1:58

Recorded : 1 March 1964, EMI Studios, Abbey Road, London

John Lennon : Rhythm Guitar
Paul McCartney : Bass Guitar and Solo Vocal
George Harrison : Lead Guitar
Ringo Starr : Drums
George Martin : Piano

This Little Richard song, originally released as part of the American album
The Beatles Second on 10 April 1964 and then in Britain on 19 June 1964 as the
title track of an E.P., provides Paul with a perfect vehicle for his voice. Here,
his solo vocal sounds just as enthusiastic and spontaneous as John's does on
the classic Twist And Shout. In fact, like Twist And Shout, this was recorded in
one take. The Beatles had used both songs for years during their live
performances, which invariably opened with Twist And Shout and closed with
Long Tall Sally — a format they were to continue with for their later, larger-
scale concert performances.

UK Release : 20 October 1980
Parlophone PCS 7214
US Release : None
Intl CD No : None
Producers : George Martin and
Phil Spector
Running Time : 58:29

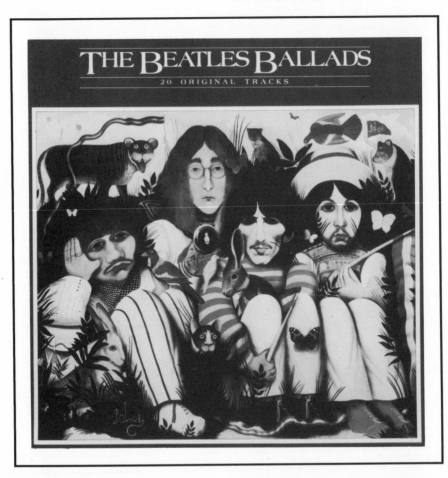

SIDE ONE : Yesterday; Norwegian Wood (This Bird Has Flown); Do You Want To Know A Secret; For No One; Michelle; Nowhere Man; You've Got To Hide Your Love Away; Across The Universe; All My Loving; Hey Jude.

SIDE TWO : Something; The Fool On The Hill; Till There Was You; The Long And Winding Road; Here Comes The Sun; Blackbird; And I Love Her; She's Leaving Home; Here, There And Everywhere; Let It Be.

Most of these tracks appear on Love Songs. Although a better compilation
album than Love Songs, it contains nothing new — no previously unreleased
tracks or even stereo versions of former mono recordings. A remixed version
of Norwegian Wood is included with the backing track now on the right-hand
channel instead of the left and the vocals mixed into the centre. Also, someone
in the depths of EMI seems to have confused and reversed the stereo on
Yesterday, You've Got To Hide Your Love Away, She's Leaving Home and
Here, There and Everywhere.

The possible permutations of material for compilation albums boggle the
mind. We have had the rock and roll music, the love songs, and on this album
the ballads. Presumably one album still to be compiled is The Songs The
Beatles Didn't Write. After all, there are 24 of them. There could even be four
separate albums — John Lennon and the Beatles, Paul McCartney and the
Beatles, George Harrison and the Beatles, and Ringo Starr and the Beatles.
This is not such a ridiculous idea when you consider that the album The Best of
George Harrison (Parlophone PAS 10011) has on side one Something, If I
Needed Someone, Here Comes The Sun, Taxman, Think For Yourself, For
You Blue and While My Guitar Gently Weeps.

Side One
Yesterday 2:04
Norwegian Wood (This Bird Has
  Flown) 2:00
Do You Want To Know A
  Secret 1:55
For No One 2:03
Michelle 2:42
Nowhere Man 2:40
You've Got To Hide Your Love
  Away 2:08
Across The Universe 3:41
All My Loving 2:04
Hey Jude 7:11

Side Two
Something (Harrison) 2:59
The Fool On The Hill 3:00
Till There Was You (Willson) 2:12
The Long And Winding
  Road* 3:40
Here Comes The Sun
  (Harrison) 3:40
Blackbird 2:20
And I Love Her 2:27
She's Leaving Home 3:24
Here, There And
  Everywhere 2:29
Let It Be 3:50

** Produced by George Martin/Phil Spector. All others
produced by George Martin.*

All Lennon–McCartney songs except where stated.

UK Release : 12 March 1982
Parlophone PCS 7218
US Release : 12 March 1982
Capitol SV 12199
Producers : George Martin and
Phil Spector
Running Time : 42:03

SIDE ONE : A Hard Day's Night; I Should Have Known Better; Can't Buy Me Love; And I Love Her; Help!; You've Got To Hide Your Love Away; Ticket To Ride; Magical Mystery Tour.

SIDE TWO : I Am The Walrus; Yellow Submarine; All You Need Is Love; Let It Be; Get Back; The Long And Winding Road.

Rock and Roll Music, Love Songs, The Beatles Ballads. . . . Now we have a further compilation, Reel Music, a selection of songs from the Beatles' films.

The album features four songs from A Hard Day's Night, three from Help!, two from Magical Mystery Tour, two from Yellow Submarine and three from Let It Be. Unfortunately, from the way the album is arranged, there is no real sense of 'flow' to the Reel Music. For a Beatles' album to have Ticket To Ride followed by Magical Mystery Tour, and I Am The Walrus followed by Yellow Submarine suggests some peculiar criteria for selection of tracks.

The album cover, which depicts the Beatles — in their five different roles as film stars, arriving at a film theatre — reflects the album's contents, indicating a rapidly produced piece of merchandise.

The sleeve notes consist of a six-paragraph potted history of the Beatles and their film career. These words are aimed mainly at the newer, younger Beatles fans, many of whom were not even born when the 'fab four' broke up. For the fans' benefit, the sleeve also credits the individual Beatles as composers, the first album to do so since With The Beatles in 1963.

The album is complete with a twelve-page 'Souvenir Program' which contains a brief resumé of each of the five Beatles movies along with selected stills. The inner sleeve has a further selection of stills and other photographs.

Following the 1981–2 worldwide success of the Stars on 45 medley by the Dutch 'Beatles soundalike' group Starsound (a medley which contained some very believable John Lennon-sounding vocals), Capitol Records decided to put together their own Beatle medley using the original Beatles' master tapes. The record, entitled The Beatles Movie Medley, contains excerpts from Magical Mystery Tour, All You Need Is Love, You've Got To Hide Your Love Away, I Should Have Known Better, A Hard Day's Night, Ticket To Ride and Get Back. The recording was issued as a single (Capitol B-5107) on 30 March 1982.

The editing, which is questionable, was carried out by John Palladino of Capitol Records. Unfortunately, the inclusion of You've Got To Hide Your Love Away within the medley seems to spoil the rhythm of the medley as a whole, which has a running time of 3 minutes 56 seconds.

When the first promotional copies of this record were pressed the B-side contained an edited press conference interview from 1964. When the record reached the stores, the B-side had been changed to I'm Happy Just To Dance With You.

In Britain, EMI Records decided that the editing of Beatles' recordings was unacceptable and withheld release of the record (but still allocated it a catalogue number, just in case). Demand for imported copies of the U.S. record was so high that EMI conceded and eventually issued it on 25 May 1982 (Parlophone R6055).

Side One

A Hard Day's Night   2:32
I Should Have Known Better   2:42
Can't Buy Me Love   2:15
And I Love Her   2:27
Help!   2:16
You've Got To Hide Your Love
    Away   2:08
Ticket To Ride   3:03
Magical Mystery Tour   2:48

Side Two

I Am The Walrus   4:35
Yellow Submarine   2:40
All You Need Is Love   3:47
Let It Be   4:01*
Get Back   3:09*
The Long And Winding
    Road   3:40*

Produced by George Martin and Phil Spector. All others produced by George Martin.

UK Release : 27 October 1980
Parlophone/World Records
SM 701–8
US Release : None
Intl CD No : None
Producers : George Martin and
Phil Spector
Running Time : See Individual
Albums

Track listings for the eight albums in the box are given on the following pages.

This collection is a must for any Beatles' fan or collector. A masterpiece, it spans the entire recording career of the Beatles from Love Me Do to Let It Be and is even better than The Beatles 1962–66 and 1967–70 albums.

The eight albums that make up The Beatles Box contain 124 tracks of what can definitively be classed as the Beatles' greatest hits — a tribute to the group's achievement, as there cannot be many artists whose 'greatest hits' would fill eight albums. Another good point is that The Beatles Box consists of eight *new* albums, not re-packages like The Beatles Collection issued in 1978. Amongst the 124 tracks are ten of particular interest.

The first is the original single version of Love Me Do with Ringo on drums (this is *not* the version included on the Please Please Me album). All My Loving in this version was previously only available on the German album Beatles Greatest (Odeon SMO 83991) and features a five-tap hi-hat intro. It makes its first appearance on a British Beatles' album here. And I Love Her, as heard here, was previously unavailable in Britain but was on the German album Something New (Odeon 1C 072–04 600). The final riff is repeated here six times whereas on the album A Hard Day's Night it is repeated only four times. She's A Woman was previously only available in Britain in mono. This is the stereo version which had been available only on the East Asian/Australian album The Beatles Greatest Hits Vol. 2 (Parlophone LPEA 1002). I Feel Fine is the much talked about 'whispering version' previously included on the album The Beatles 1962–66. It is the same stereo recording as on the album A Collection Of Beatles Oldies but includes two seconds of mysterious whisperings at the beginning. Day Tripper is a different stereo mix from that available on the album A Collection Of Beatles Oldies. Previously available only on the American album Yesterday . . . And Today (Capitol ST 2553) it has the guitar intro mixed into the left-hand channel instead of across the stereo. Paperback Writer is the re-mixed version from Hey Jude with the stereo reversed and the backing vocals mixed further forward than on A Collection Of Beatles Oldies. Penny Lane in this version was previously unavailable anywhere in the world. It was distributed to radio stations in America and Canada prior to the release of the single. It features seven extra piccolo trumpet notes played over the ending of the recording which had been edited out by the time the record reached the stores. Baby, You're A Rich Man is in stereo for the first time in Britain. I Am The Walrus, previously unavailable anywhere in the world in this format, is included in full, combining the oddities of three previous versions. The British single features the organ intro repeated four times, the stereo version on the Magical Mystery Tour two E.P. set, six times, and the American single with the organ intro repeated four times also has a few extra beats in the middle between the lines 'I'm crying' and 'Yellow matter custard'. These are missing from both British versions but are combined here.

Other tracks of interest are the stereo version of Long Tall Sally, I Call Your Name, Matchbox, Slow Down and I'm Down. Previously included on the rather messy compilation album Rock and Roll Music, these five tracks are presented here in a far superior way. On record six, All You Need Is Love is the original mono single not the re-recorded version from Yellow Submarine. Get Back, Let It Be and Across The Universe are the recordings from the album Let It Be, and not, in the case of the first two, the versions released as singles.

The eight albums, complete with individual sleeve notes, come packaged in a cardboard box looking rather like a wooden crate. This album set is only available through EMI's mail order division, World Records.

THE BEATLES BOX — RECORD 1
Parlophone/World Records SM701
Producer : George Martin
Running Time : 31:57

THE BEATLES BOX — RECORD 2
Parlophone/World Records SM702
Producer : George Martin
Running Time : 38:13

Side One
Love Me Do   2:22
P.S. I Love You   2:02
I Saw Her Standing There   2:50
Please Please Me   2:00
Misery   1:43
Do You Want To Know A
   Secret   1:55
A Taste Of Honey (Marlow–
   Scott)   2:02
Twist And Shout
   (Medley–Russell)   2:32

Side Two
From Me To You   1:55
Thank You Girl   2:01
She Loves You   2:18
It Won't Be Long   2:11
Please Mister Postman
   (Holland)   2:34
All My Loving   2:07
Roll Over Beethoven (Berry)   2:44
Money (Bradford–Gordy)   2:47

All Lennon–McCartney songs
   except where stated.

Side One
I Want To Hold Your Hand   2:24
This Boy   2:11
Can't Buy Me Love   2:15
You Can't Do That   2:33
A Hard Day's Night   2:32
I Should Have Known Better   2:42
If I Fell   2:16
And I Love Her   2:36

Side Two
Things We Said Today   2:35
I'll Be Back   2:22
Long Tall Sally (Johnson–
   Penniman–Blackwell)   1:58
I Call Your Name   2:02
Matchbox (Perkins)   1:37
Slow Down (Williams)   2:54
She's A Woman   2:57
I Feel Fine   2:19

All Lennon–McCartney songs
   except where stated.

THE BEATLES BOX — RECORD 3
Parlophone/World Records SM703
Producer : George Martin
Running Time : 38:12

Side One
Eight Days A Week   2:43
No Reply   2:15
I'm A Loser   2:31
I'll Follow The Sun   1:46
Mr Moonlight (Johnson)   2:35
Every Little Thing   2:01
I Don't Want To Spoil The
    Party   2:33
Kansas City (Lieber–Stoller)/Hey
    Hey Hey Hey (Penniman)   2:30

Side Two
Ticket To Ride   3:03
I'm Down   2:30
Help!   2:16
The Night Before   2:33
You've Got To Hide Your Love
    Away   2:08
I Need You (Harrison)   2:28
Another Girl   2:02
You're Going To Lose That
    Girl   2:18

All Lennon–McCartney songs
    except where stated.

THE BEATLES BOX — RECORD 4
Parlophone/World Records SM704
Producer : George Martin
Running Time : 38:49

Side One
Yesterday   2:04
Act Naturally (Morrison–
    Russell)   2:27
Tell Me What You See   2:35
It's Only Love   1:53
You Like Me Too Much
    (Harrison)   2:34
I've Just Seen A Face   2:04
Day Tripper   2:37
We Can Work It Out   2:10

Side Two
Michelle   2:42
Drive My Car   2:25
Norwegian Wood (This Bird Has
    Flown)   2:00
You Won't See Me   3:19
Nowhere Man   2:40
Girl   2:26
I'm Looking Through You   2:20
In My Life   2:23

All Lennon–McCartney songs
    except where stated.

THE BEATLES BOX — RECORD 5
Parlophone/World Records SM705
Producer : George Martin
Running Time : 34:13

THE BEATLES BOX — RECORD 6
Parlophone/World Records SM706
Producer : George Martin
Running Time : 47:07

Side One
Paperback Writer   2:25
Rain   2:59
Here, There And
   Everywhere   2:29
Taxman (Harrison)   2:36
I'm Only Sleeping   2:58
Good Day Sunshine   2:08
Yellow Submarine   2:40

Side Two
Eleanor Rigby   2:11
And Your Bird Can Sing   2:02
For No One   2:03
Dr. Robert   2:14
Got To Get You Into My Life   2:31
Penny Lane   3:00
Strawberry Fields Forever   4:05

All Lennon–McCartney songs
   except where stated.

Side One
Sgt. Pepper's Lonely Hearts Club
   Band   1:59
With A Little Help From My
   Friends   2:46
Lucy In The Sky With
   Diamonds   3:25
Fixing A Hole   2:33
She's Leaving Home   3:24
Being For The Benefit Of Mr.
   Kite   2:36
A Day In The Life   5:03

Side Two
When I'm Sixty-Four   2:38
Lovely Rita   2:43
All You Need Is Love   3:57
Baby, You're A Rich Man   3:07
Magical Mystery Tour   2:48
Your Mother Should Know   2:33
The Fool On The Hill   3:00
I Am The Walrus   4:35

All Lennon–McCartney songs.

THE BEATLES BOX — RECORD 7
Parlophone/World Records SM707
Producer : George Martin
Running Time : 48:17

THE BEATLES BOX — RECORD 8
Parlophone/World Records SM708
Producers : George Martin and
　　　　　　　　Phil Spector
Running Time : 52:11

Side One
Hello Goodbye　3:24
Lady Madonna　2:17
Hey Jude　7:11
Revolution　3:22
Back In The U.S.S.R.　2:45
Ob-La-Di, Ob-La-Da　3:10
While My Guitar Gently Weeps
　(Harrison)　4:46

Side Two
The Continuing Story Of Bungalow
　Bill　3:05
Happiness Is A Warm Gun　2:47
Martha My Dear　2:28
I'm So Tired　2:01
Piggies (Harrison)　2:04
Don't Pass Me By (Starkey)　3:52
Julia　2:57
All Together Now　2:08

All Lennon–McCartney songs
　except where stated.

Side One
Get Back　3:09
Don't Let Me Down　3:34
The Ballad Of John And Yoko　2:58
Across The Universe　3:51
For You Blue (Harrison)　2:33
Two Of Us　3:33
The Long And Winding Road　3:40
Let It Be　4:01

Side Two
Come Together　4:16
Something (Harrison)　2:59
Maxwell's Silver Hammer　3:24
Octopus's Garden (Starkey)　2:49
Here Comes The Sun
　(Harrison)　3:04
Because　2:45
Golden Slumbers　1:31
Carry That Weight　1:37
The End　2:04
Her Majesty　0:23

All Lennon–McCartney songs
　except where stated.

UK Release : 9 April 1979
EMI Nut 18
US Release : None
Intl CD No : None
Producer : Various (See individual tracks)
Running Time : 46:14

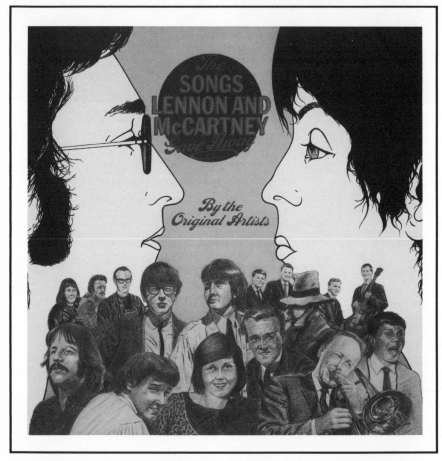

SIDE ONE : I'm The Greatest (Ringo Starr); One And One Is Two (The Strangers with Mike Shannon); From A Window (Billy J. Kramer and The Dakotas); Nobody I Know (Peter and Gordon); Like Dreamers Do (The Applejacks); I'll Keep You Satisfied (Billy J. Kramer and The Dakotas); Love Of The Loved (Cilla Black); Woman (Peter and Gordon); Tip Of My Tongue (Tommy Quickly); I'm In Love (The Fourmost).

SIDE TWO : Hello Little Girl (The Fourmost); That Means A Lot (P.J. Proby); It's For You (Cilla Black); Penina (Carlos Mendes); Step Inside Love (Cilla Black); World Without Love (Peter and Gordon); Bad To Me (Billy J. Kramer and The Dakotas); I Don't Want To See You Again (Peter and Gordon); I'll Be On My Way (Billy J. Kramer and The Dakotas); Catcall (The Chris Barber Band).

During their career as the main song writers for the Beatles, John Lennon and Paul McCartney wrote a number of songs which they gave away to other artists, many of whom were old friends from Liverpool. Amongst those friends were Billy J. Kramer and The Dakotas who are featured on four songs : From A Window, I'll Keep You Satisfied, Bad To Me and I'll Be On My Way; Cilla Black with Love Of The Loved, It's For You and Step Inside Love; and The Fourmost with Hello Little Girl and I'm In Love.

Curiously, the first song which Lennon and McCartney gave away — I'll Be On My Way, which was recorded by Billy J. Kramer in 1963 — is also the only song of which the Beatles made an 'official' recording when they recorded a version for the BBC on 4 April 1963.

Although recordings by John Lennon, Paul McCartney or the Beatles exist of the other songs which are featured on this album, most, if not all, were recorded as demonstration recordings for the artists who were to eventually record the song.

Only one song on this album does not come from the Beatles' collective recording career : I'm The Greatest, a song written by John Lennon which he gave to Ringo for his 1973 album, Ringo. The nineteen remaining tracks performed by ten other artists were given away during the Beatles' career from 1962 to 1969. Most were not written specifically for the artists who recorded them, with the exceptions of Step Inside Love, written for Cilla Black by Paul McCartney in 1968, and the Peter and Gordon recordings on the album, also written for them by McCartney.

Seven other John Lennon and/or Paul McCartney songs which were given away between 1963 and 1969 and recorded by other artists are mentioned at the end of the album listing here. These are relevant although they do not appear on the album.

SIDE ONE

I'm The Greatest (John Lennon) 3:23

Ringo Starr
UK Release : 9 November 1973
Apple PCTC 252 (L.P. Ringo)
US Release : 2 November 1973
Apple SWAL 3413 (L.P. Ringo)
Producer : Richard Perry

John Lennon : Piano and Harmony Vocal
Paul McCartney : Not Present
George Harrison : Lead Guitar
Ringo Starr : Drums and Lead Vocal
Klaus Voormann : Bass Guitar
Billy Preston : Organ

This is the only song on the album that does not come from the Beatles' collective recording career, but it is also the only recording on this album that could almost be termed 'a Beatles recording'. As can be seen from the line-up (which, incidentally, John Lennon thought about putting together in 1970) the only Beatle missing here is Paul McCartney.

Written by John Lennon for Ringo's 1973 album, Ringo, the lyrics refer to, amongst other things, the Beatles, Sgt. Pepper's and Yoko Ono. The music has snatches reminiscent of I Want You (She's So Heavy), Golden Slumbers, Being For The Benefit of Mr. Kite, Revolution and Cry Baby Cry.

One And One Is Two (Lennon–McCartney)   2:10

The Strangers with Mike Shannon
UK Release : 8 May 1964
Phillips BF 1335
US Release : None
Producer : Unknown

From A Window (Lennon–McCartney)   1:55

Billy J. Kramer and The Dakotas
UK Release : 17 July 1964
Parlophone R5156
US Release : 12 August 1964
Imperial 66051
Producer : George Martin

Nobody I Know (Lennon–McCartney)   2:27

Peter and Gordon
UK Release : 27 May 1964
Columbia DB 7292
US Release : 15 June 1964
Capitol 5211
Producer : John Burgess

Like Dreamers Do (Lennon–McCartney)   2:30

The Applejacks
UK Release : 5 May 1964
Decca F11916
US Release : 6 July 1964
London 9681
Producer : Mike Smith

I'll Keep You Satisfied (Lennon–McCartney)   2:04

Billy J. Kramer and The Dakotas
UK Release : 1 November 1963
Parlophone R5073
US Release : 11 November 1963
Liberty 55643
Producer : George Martin

Love Of The Loved (Lennon–McCartney)   2:00

Cilla Black
UK Release : 27 September 1963
Parlophone R5065
US Release : None
Producer : George Martin

Woman (Paul McCartney as B. Webb)   2:21

Peter and Gordon
UK Release : 11 February 1966
Columbia DB 7834
US Release : 10 January 1966
Capitol 5579
Producer : John Burgess

Tip Of My Tongue (Lennon–McCartney)   2:02

Tommy Quickly
UK Release : 30 July 1963
Piccadilly 7N 35137
US Release : None
Producer : Les Reed

I'm In Love (Lennon–McCartney)   2:07

The Fourmost
UK Release : 15 November 1963
Parlophone R5078
US Release : 10 February 1964
Atco 6285
Producer : George Martin

SIDE TWO

Hello Little Girl (Lennon–McCartney)   1:50

The Fourmost
UK Release : 30 August 1963
Parlophone R5056
US Release : 15 November 1963
Atco 6280
Producer : George Martin

That Means A Lot (Lennon–McCartney) 2:31

P. J. Proby
UK Release : 17 September 1965
Liberty LBF 10215
US Release : 23 August 1965
Liberty LST 7421 (L.P. P. J. Proby)
Producer : Ron Richards

It's For You (Lennon–McCartney) 2:20

Cilla Black
UK Release : 31 July 1964
Parlophone R5162
US Release : 17 August 1964
Capitol 5258
Producer : George Martin

Penina (Paul McCartney) 2:36

Carlos Mendes
UK Release : None : Portugal only, July 1969
Parlophone QMSP 16459
US Release : None
Producer : Unknown

Step Inside Love (Lennon–McCartney) 2:20

Cilla Black
UK Release : 8 March 1968
Parlophone R5674
US Release : 6 May 1968
Bell 726
Producer : George Martin

World Without Love (Lennon–McCartney) 2:38

Peter and Gordon
UK Release : 28 February 1964
Columbia DB 7225
US Release : 27 April 1964
Capitol 5175
Producer : Norman Newell

Bad To Me (Lennon–McCartney) 2:18

Billy J. Kramer and The Dakotas
UK Release : 26 July 1963
Parlophone R5049
US Release : 23 September 1963
Liberty 55626
Producer : George Martin

I Don't Want To See You Again (Lennon–McCartney)   1:59

Peter and Gordon
UK Release : 11 September 1964
Columbia DB 7356
US Release : 21 September 1964
Capitol 5272
Producer : Norman Newell

I'll Be On My Way (Lennon–McCartney)   1:38

Billy J. Kramer and The Dakotas
UK Release : 26 April 1963
Parlophone R5023
US Release : 10 June 1963
Liberty 55586
Producer : George Martin

Catcall (Paul McCartney)   3:05

The Chris Barber Band
UK Release : 20 October 1967
Marmalade 598–005
US Release : None
Producers : Chris Barber, Giorgio Gomelsky, Reggie King

The following seven songs, written by John Lennon and/or Paul McCartney, and recorded by other artists up to the end of 1969, but not included on this album, are:

Theme From The Family Way (Paul McCartney)   2:05

The George Martin Orchestra
UK Release : 23 December 1966
United Artists UP 1165
US Release: None
Producer : George Martin

Love In The Open Air (Paul McCartney)   2:18

The George Martin Orchestra
UK Release : 23 December 1966
United Artists UP 1165
US Release : 24 April 1967
United Artists UA 50148
Producer : George Martin

Thingumybob (Paul McCartney) 1:51

John Fosters and Sons Ltd. Black Dyke Mills Band
UK Release : 6 September 1968
Apple 4
US Release : 28 August 1968
Apple 1800
Producer : Paul McCartney

Goodbye (Lennon–McCartney) 2:23

Mary Hopkin
UK Release : 28 March 1969
Apple 10
US Release : 7 April 1969
Apple 1806
Producer : Paul McCartney

Give Peace A Chance (Lennon–McCartney) 4:49

The Plastic Ono Band
UK Release : 4 July 1969
Apple 13
US Release : 7 July 1969
Apple 1809
Producers : John Lennon and Yoko Ono

Cold Turkey (John Lennon) 4:59

The Plastic Ono Band
UK Release : 24 October 1969
Apple 1001
US Release : 20 October 1969
Apple 1813
Producers : John Lennon and Yoko Ono

Come And Get It (Paul McCartney) 2:21

Badfinger
UK Release : 5 December 1969
Apple 20
US Release : 12 January 1970
Apple 1815
Producer : Paul McCartney

THE AMERICAN ALBUMS

Capitol ST 2047
Producer : George Martin
Release Date : 20 January 1964
Running Time : 26:43

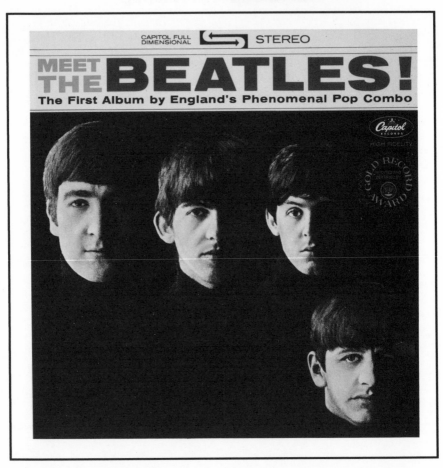

SIDE ONE : I Want To Hold Your Hand; I Saw Her Standing There; This Boy; It Won't Be Long; All I've Got To Do; All My Loving.

SIDE TWO : Don't Bother Me; Little Child; Till There Was You; Hold Me Tight; I Wanna Be Your Man; Not A Second Time.

After almost twelve months of rejecting the Beatles, Capitol Records put together this first 'official' American Beatles' album. Previously, Beatles' records (as issued on Parlophone in the UK) had been issued on a variety of record labels in the USA such as Vee Jay, Tollie and Swan. When Beatlemania swept America, Capitol, fully aware that they had originally rejected the Beatles, were desperate to take up the option of issuing their records.

Meet the Beatles, which has a similar jacket to the British album With The Beatles, also contains nine of the 14 tracks from that album, plus I Saw Her Standing There from Please Please Me and the Beatles' latest British single at the time, I Want To Hold Your Hand/This Boy.

Capitol also issued I Want To Hold Your Hand with the B-side I Saw Her Standing There as a single from this album.

Side One

I Want To Hold Your Hand   2:24
(See A Collection Of Beatles Oldies
   Album PCS 7016)
I Saw Her Standing There   2:50
(See Please Please Me Album PCS
   3042)
This Boy   2:11
(See British Rarities Album PCM
   1001)
It Won't Be Long   2:11
(See With The Beatles Album PCS
   3045)
All I've Got To Do   2:05
(See With The Beatles Album PCS
   3045)
All My Loving   2:04
(See With The Beatles Album PCS
   3045)

Side Two

Don't Bother Me (Harrison)   2:28
(See With The Beatles Album PCS
   3045)
Little Child   1:46
(See With The Beatles Album PCS
   3045)
Till There Was You (Willson)   2:12
(See With The Beatles Album PCS
   3045)
Hold Me Tight   2:30
(See With The Beatles Album PCS
   3045)
I Wanna Be Your Man   1:59
(See With The Beatles Album PCS
   3045)
Not A Second Time   2:30
(See With The Beatles Album PCS
   3045)

All Lennon–McCartney songs except where stated.

Capitol ST 2020
Producer : George Martin
Release Date : 10 April 1964
Running Time : 26:12

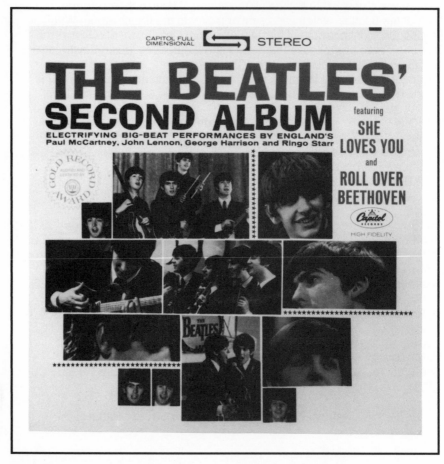

SIDE ONE : Roll Over Beethoven; Thank You Girl; You Really Got A Hold On Me; Devil In Her Heart; Money; You Can't Do That.

SIDE TWO : Long Tall Sally; I Call Your Name; Please Mr. Postman; I'll Get You; She Loves You.

Within four months of issuing Meet The Beatles, Capitol Records, now fully aware of the surge of Beatlemania in America, issued this album which includes the remaining five tracks from With The Beatles, Along with You Can't Do That (the B-side of Can't Buy Me Love which, at the time, was Capitol Records' latest Beatles' single which was also to be included on the soundtrack and album of A Hard Day's Night), She Loves You and I'll Get You (both previously issued as a single by Swan Records for which Capitol had now acquired the rights), Long Tall Sally and I Call Your Name (issued on the E.P. Long Tall Sally in Britain) and the stereo recording of Thank You Girl (yet to be issued in Britain).

Side One

Roll Over Beethoven (Berry)   2:44
(See With The Beatles Album PCS
   3045)
Thank You Girl   2:01
(See British Rarities Album PCM
   1001)
You Really Got A Hold On Me
   (Robinson)   2:58
(See With The Beatles Album PCS
   3045)
Devil In Her Heart (Drapkin)   2:23
(See With The Beatles Album PCS
   3045)
Money (Bradford–Gordy)   2:47
(See With The Beatles Album PCS
   3045)
You Can't Do That   2:33
(See British A Hard Day's Night
   Album PCS 3058)

Side Two

Long Tall Sally (Johnson–
   Penniman–Blackwell)   1:58
(See British Rarities Album PCM
   1001)
I Call Your Name   2:02
(See British Rarities Album PCM
   1001)
Please Mr. Postman (Holland)   2:34
(See With The Beatles Album PCS
   3045)
I'll Get You   2:04
(See British Rarities Album PCM
   1001)
She Loves You   2:18
(See A Collection Of Beatles Oldies
   Album PCS 7016)

All Lennon–McCartney songs except where stated.

United Artists UAS 6366
Producer : George Martin
Release Date : 26 June 1964
Running Time : 29:21

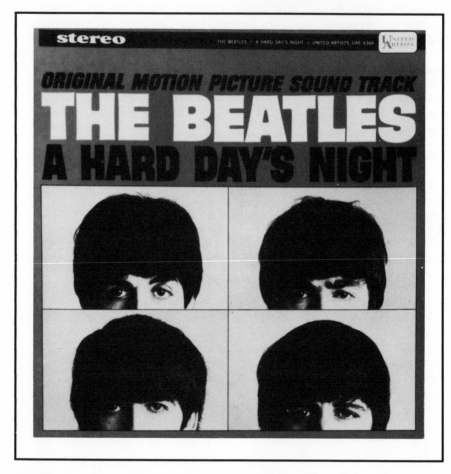

SIDE ONE : A Hard Day's Night; Tell Me Why; I'll Cry Instead; (I Should Have Known Better); I'm Happy Just To Dance With You; (And I Love Her).

SIDE TWO : I Should Have Known Better; If I Fell; And I Love Her; (Ringo's Theme — This Boy); Can't Buy Me Love; (A Hard Day's Night).

The Beatles' first movie soundtrack album bears little resemblance to the British album of the same name, although it does include all the new material used in the film plus George Martin's orchestral contributions. The seven new songs heard in the film are spread between the two album sides (whereas they are all on side one of the British album) with I'll Cry Instead, which was dropped from the film at the last minute.

Side One

A Hard Day's Night   2:28
(See British A Hard Day's Night
   Album PCS 3058)
Tell Me Why   2:04
(See British A Hard Day's Night
   Album PCS 3058)
I'll Cry Instead   2:06
(See British A Hard Day's Night
   Album PCS 3058)
I Should Have Known Better*   2:16
I'm Happy Just To Dance With
   You   1:59
(See British A Hard Day's Night
   Album PCS 30358)
And I Love Her*   3:42

Side Two

I Should Have Known Better   2:42
(See British A Hard Day's Night
   Album PCS 3058)
If I Fell   2:16
(See British A Hard Day's Night
   Album PCS 3058)
And I Love Her   2:27
(See British A Hard Day's Night
   Album PCS 3058)
Ringo's Theme (This Boy)*   3:06
Can't Buy Me Love   2:15
(See British A Hard Day's Night
   Album PCS 3058)
A Hard Day's Night*   2:00

*The George Martin Orchestra

Capitol ST 2108
Producer : George Martin
Release Date : 20 July 1964
Running Time : 24:23

SIDE ONE : I'll Cry Instead; Things We Said Today; Any Time At All; When I Get Home; Slow Down; Matchbox.

SIDE TWO : Tell Me Why; And I Love Her; I'm Happy Just To Dance With You; If I Fell; Komm, Gib Mir Deine Hand.

Although this album claims to be 'something new', five of the eleven tracks were previously issued on the American album A Hard Day's Night. Of the remaining six tracks, three have been extracted from the British album A Hard Day's Night, whilst Slow Down and Matchbox come from the British E.P. Long Tall Sally. The final track, Komm, Gib Mir Deine Hand, is the German language version of I Want To Hold Your Hand, which although issued in both Germany and America was not issued in Britain until 1978 on the Rarities album.

Side One
I'll Cry Instead   1:44
(See British A Hard Day's Night
   Album PCS 3058)
Things We Said Today   2:35
(See British A Hard Day's Night
   Album PCS 3058)
Any Time At All   2:10
(See British A Hard Day's Night
   Album PCS 3058)
When I Get Home   2:14
(See British A Hard Day's Night
   Album PCS 3058)
Slow Down (Williams)   2:54
(See British Rarities Album PCM
   1001)
Matchbox (Perkins)   1:37
(See British Rarities Album PCM
   1001)

Side Two
Tell Me Why   2:04
(See British A Hard Day's Night
   Album PCS 3058)
And I Love Her   2:27
(See British A Hard Day's Night
   Album PCS 3058)
I'm Happy Just To Dance With
   You   1:59
(See British A Hard Day's Night
   Album PCS 3058)
If I Fell   2:16
(See British A Hard Day's Night
   Album PCS 3058)
Komm, Gib Mir Deine Hand
   (Lennon–McCartney–Nicolas–
   Hellmer)   2:24
(See British Rarities Album PCM
   1001)

All Lennon–McCartney songs except where stated.

Capitol STBO 2222
Producers : Gary Usher and
Roger Christian
Release Date : 23 November 1964
Running Time : 49:54

SIDE ONE : On Stage With The Beatles; How Beatlemania Began; Beatlemania In Action; Man Behind The Beatles — Brian Epstein; John Lennon; Who's A Millionaire?
SIDE TWO : Beatles Will Be Beatles; Man Behind The Music — George Martin; George Harrison.

SIDE THREE : A Hard Day's Night — Their First Film; Paul McCartney; Sneaky Haircuts And More About Paul.
SIDE FOUR : The Beatles Look At Life; 'Victims' Of Beatlemania, Beatle Medley; Ringo Starr; Liverpool And All The World!

Many Beatles' interview albums appeared in the USA during 1964, and Capitol Records put together this 'biography in sound' of the Beatles. It gives an approximate 50-minute history of the Beatles, from their beginnings in Liverpool as The Quarrymen and their days in Hamburg, to their eventual world-wide success. It is compiled and narrated by John Babcock in association with Al Wiman and Roger Christian of radio station KFWB, Hollywood, California, and (with the exception of the brief snatches of Beatles' records produced by George Martin) is produced by Gary Usher and Roger Christian.

Overall, the album is a rather glossy biography of the Beatles and includes interviews with them and some of their hysterical fans after the 1964 Hollywood Bowl concert (which incidentally is where the 'live' recording of Twist And Shout on side four comes from). Interspersed with the interviews and narration are fourteen Beatles' recordings, which are not credited on the album's jacket or record label. In addition to Twist and Shout the remaining thirteen tracks are : I Want To Hold Your Hand; Slow Down; This Boy; You Can't Do That; If I Fell; A Hard Day's Night; And I Love Her; Things We Said Today; I'm Happy Just To Dance With You; Little Child; Long Tall Sally; She Loves You; Boys.

Throughout the album the narrators give brief biographies of each of the Beatles, also of Brian Epstein (their manager) and George Martin (their record producer). They try to explain Beatlemania but somehow don't succeed. Even so the album does manage to capture the spirit and excitement of Beatlemania in America at the height of the Beatles' success.

Side One
On Stage With The Beatles   1:03
How Beatlemania Began   1:18
Beatlemania in Action   2:24
Man Behind the Beatles — Brian
    Epstein   3:01
John Lennon   4:24
Who's A Millionaire?   0:43

Side Two
Beatles Will Be Beatles   7:37
Man Behind The Music — George
    Martin   0:47
George Harrison   4:43

Side Three
A Hard Day's Night — Their First
    Movie   3:45
Paul McCartney   1:55
Sneaky Haircuts and More About
    Paul   3:38

Side Four
The Beatles Look At Life   1:51
'Victims' Of Beatlemania   1:21
Beatle Medley   3:36
Ringo Starr   6:19
Liverpool And All The World!   1:09

Capitol ST 2228
Producer : George Martin
Release Date : 15 December 1964
Running Time : 25:10

SIDE ONE : No Reply; I'm A Loser; Baby's In Black; Rock And Roll Music; I'll Follow The Sun; Mr. Moonlight; Honey Don't.

SIDE TWO : I'll Be Back; She's A Woman; I Feel Fine; Everybody's Trying To Be My Baby.

The first side of this album is in essence side one of the British album Beatles For Sale without the last track, Kansas City. The second side contains two further tracks from Beatles For Sale — Honey Don't and Everybody's Trying To Be My Baby, along with the thirteenth and remaining track from the British album A Hard Day's Night, I'll Be Back, plus I Feel Fine and She's A Woman, issued as a single a week after the release of this album.

Side One

No Reply   2:15
(See Beatles For Sale Album PCS 3062)
I'm A Loser   2:31
(See Beatles For Sale Album PCS 3062)
Baby's In Black   2:02
(See Beatles For Sale Album PCS 3062)
Rock and Roll Music (Berry)   2:02
(See Beatles For Sale Album PCS 3062)
I'll Follow The Sun   1:46
(See Beatles For Sale Album PCS 3062)
Mr. Moonlight (Johnson)   2:35
(See Beatles For Sale Album PCS 3062)

Side Two

Honey Don't (Perkins)   2:56
(See Beatles For Sale Album PCS 3062)
I'll Be Back   2:22
(See British A Hard Day's Night Album PCS 3058)
She's A Woman   2:57
(See British Rarities Album PCM 1001)
I Feel Fine   2:20
(See A Collection of Beatles Oldies Album PCS 7016)
Everybody's Trying To Be My Baby (Perkins)   2:24
(See Beatles For Sale Album PCS 3062)

All Lennon–McCartney songs except where stated.

Capitol ST 2309
Producer : George Martin
Release Date : 22 March 1965
Running Time : 25:31

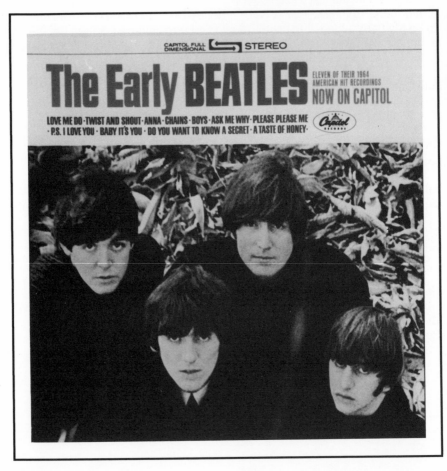

SIDE ONE : Love Me Do; Twist And Shout; Anna (Go To Him); Chains; Boys; Ask Me Why.

SIDE TWO : Please Please Me; P.S. I Love You; Baby It's You; A Taste Of Honey; Do You Want To Know A Secret.

Because Capitol Records rejected the Beatles in 1963, Veejay Records issued an album called Introducing The Beatles. When Beatlemania reached its peak at the end of 1964, Capitol acquired the rights of the Veejay recordings and issued this album which is a rather truncated version of the British album Please Please Me, without I Saw Her Standing There (already on Capitol's Meet The Beatles album) and without Misery and There's A Place (not to be issued on a Capitol album until 1980).

Side One
Love Me Do   2:19
(See Please Please Me Album PCS 3042)
Twist And Shout (Medley–
  Russell)   2:32
(See Please Please Me Album PCS 3042)
Anna (Go To Him)
  (Alexander)   2:56
(See Please Please Me Album PCS 3042)
Chains (Goffin–King)   2:21
(See Please Please Me Album PCS 3042)
Boys (Dixon–Farrell)   2:24
(See Please Please Me Album PCS 3042)
Ask Me Why   2:24
(See Please Please Me Album PCS 3042)

Side Two
Please Please Me   2:00
(See Please Please Me Album PCS 3042)
P.S. I Love You   2:02
(See Please Please Me Album PCS 3042)
Baby It's You (David–Bacharach–
  Williams)   2:36
(See Please Please Me Album PCS 3042)
A Taste Of Honey (Marlow–
  Scott)   2:02
(See Please Please Me Album PCS 3042)
Do You Want To Know A
  Secret   1:55
(See Please Please Me Album PCS 3042)

All Lennon–McCartney songs except where stated.

Capitol ST 2358
Producer : George Martin
Release Date : 14 June 1965
Running Time : 27:24

SIDE ONE : Kansas City/Hey Hey Hey Hey; Eight Days A Week; You Like Me Too Much; Bad Boy; I Don't Want To Spoil The Party; Words Of Love.

SIDE TWO : What You're Doing; Yes It Is; Dizzy Miss Lizzie; Tell Me What You See; Every Little Thing.

With Beatlemania still at its height in America, Capitol Records came up with Beatles VI, a compilation of the remaining six tracks left over from the British album Beatles For Sale, plus three tracks pulled from the British Help! album. They also put the B-side (Yes It Is) of the current single (Ticket To Ride) on this album, leaving the A-side which is featured in the film *HELP!* for that album. The only curio on this album is Bad Boy, which although obviously recorded in 1965 was not released in Britain until some eighteen months later when it was included on the album A Collection Of Beatles Oldies.

Side One

Kansas City (Leiber–Stoller)/Hey Hey Hey Hey (Penniman)   2:30
(See Beatles For Sale Album PCS 3062)
Eight Days A Week   2:43
(See Beatles For Sale Album PCS 3062)
You Like Me Too Much (Harrison)   2:34
(See British Help! Album PCS 3071)
Bad Boy (Williams)   2:17
(See A Collection of Beatles Oldies Album PCS 7016)
I Don't Want To Spoil The Party   2:23
(See Beatles For Sale Album PCS 3062)
Words Of Love (Holly)   2:10
(See Beatles For Sale Album PCS 3062)

Side Two

What You're Doing   2:30
(See Beatles For Sale Album PCS 3062)
Yes It Is   2:40
(See British Rarities Album PCM 1001)
Dizzy Miss Lizzy (Williams)   2:51
(See British Help! Album PCS 3071)
Tell Me What You See   2:35
(See British Help! Album PCS 3071)
Every Little Thing   2:01
(See Beatles For Sale Album PCS 3062)

All Lennon–McCartney songs except where stated.

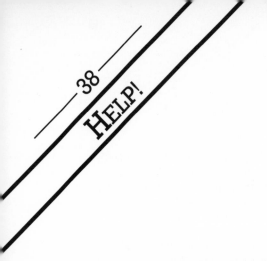

Capitol **SMAS 2386**
Producer : George Martin
Release Date : 13 August 1965
Running Time : 28:40

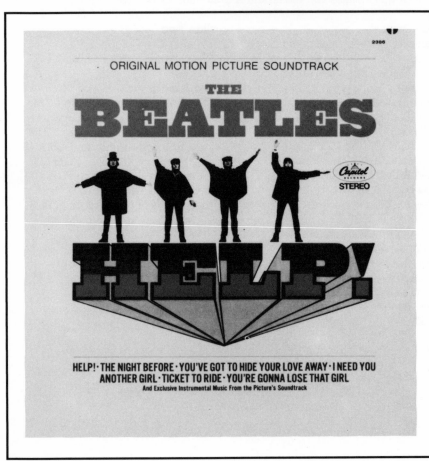

SIDE ONE : (The James Bond Theme); Help!;
The Night Before; (From Me To You Fantasy);
You've Got To Hide Your Love Away; I Need
You; (In The Tyrol).

SIDE TWO : Another Girl; (Another Hard Day's
Night); Ticket To Ride; (The Bitter End/You
Can't Do That; You're Going To Lose That Girl;
(The Chase).

The soundtrack of the Beatles' second movie includes not only the new songs specially written for the film, but also the incidental music played by the George Martin Orchestra. When this album was released in the USA many fans were annoyed to find that it had been issued as a de-luxe package (thereby increasing the price) but included only seven Beatles' tracks. On the sleeve, the four photographs of the Beatles have been inadvertently rearranged so that the semaphore message spells out a nonsensical H-P-E-L!. Also, unlike the British track listing, this album cover offers the version You're Gonna Lose That Girl; this spelling only occurs elsewhere on Record 3 of the Beatles Box.

Side One
The James Bond Theme (Norman)*
  0:16
Help! 2:16
(See British Help! Album PCS 3071)
The Night Before 2:33
(See British Help! Album PCS 3071)
From Me To You Fantasy* 2:03
You've Got To Hide Your Love
  Away 2:08
(See British Help! Album PCS 3071)
I Need You (Harrison) 2:28
(See British Help! Album PCS 3071)
In The Tyrol (Wagner–Arr.
  Thorne)* 2:21

Side Two
Another Girl 2:02
(See British Help! Album PCS 3071)
Another Hard Day's Night* 2:28
Ticket To Ride 3:03
(See British Help! Album PCS 3071)
The Bitter End (Thorne)/You Can't
  Do That 2:20
You're Going to Lose That
  Girl 2:18
(See British Help! Album PCS 3071)
The Chase (Thorne)* 2:24

The George Martin Orchestra

All Lennon–McCartney songs except where stated.

Capitol ST 2442
Producer : George Martin
Release Date : 6 December 1965
Running Time : 28:46

SIDE ONE : I've Just Seen A Face; Norwegian Wood (This Bird Has Flown); You Won't See Me; Think For Yourself; The Word; Michelle.

SIDE TWO : It's Only Love; Girl; I'm Looking Through You; In My Life; Wait; Run For Your Life.

Although the title and sleeve of the American Rubber Soul album are the same as the British, the contents are different. As the American Help! album had used only seven tracks from the British album, leaving four over, two of these (I've Just Seen A Face and It's Only Love) were included on the American Rubber Soul plus ten tracks from the British Rubber Soul. (The remaining tracks from the British albums — two from Help! and four from Rubber Soul — were issued on yet another album by Capitol, Yesterday ... and Today.)

Side One
I've Just Seen A Face   2:04
(See British Help! Album PCS 3071)
Norwegian Wood (This Bird Has
   Flown)   2:00
(See British Rubber Soul Album
   PCS 3075)
You Won't See Me   3:19
(See British Rubber Soul Album
   PCS 3075)
Think For Yourself (Harrison)   2:16
(See British Rubber Soul Album
   PCS 3075)
The Word   2:42
(See British Rubber Soul Album
   PCS 3075)
Michelle   2:42
(See British Rubber Soul Album
   PCS 3075)

Side Two
It's Only Love   1:53
(See British Help! Album PCS 3071)
Girl   2:26
(See British Rubber Soul Album
   PCS 3075)
I'm Looking Through You   2:27
(See British Rubber Soul Album
   PCS 3075)
In My Life   2:23
(See British Rubber Soul Album
   PCS 3075)
Wait   2:13
(See British Rubber Soul Album
   PCS 3075)
Run For Your Life   2:21
(See British Rubber Soul Album
   PCS 3075)

All Lennon–McCartney songs except where stated.

Capitol ST 2553
Producer : George Martin
Release Date : 20 June 1966
Running Time : 26:40

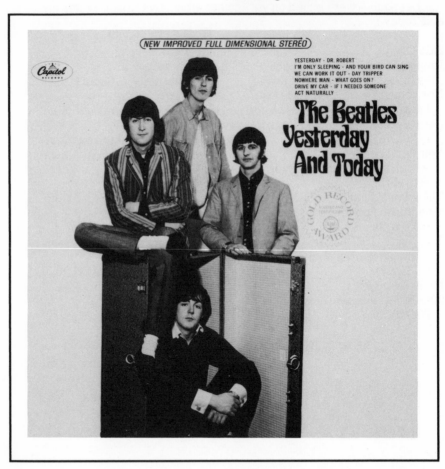

SIDE ONE : Drive My Car; I'm Only Sleeping; Nowhere Man; Dr. Robert; Yesterday; Act Naturally.

SIDE TWO : And Your Bird Can Sing; If I Need Someone; We Can Work It Out; What Goes On?; Day Tripper.

When Capitol Records revealed their intention to release this album, the Beatles decided to register a protest against the way their albums had been butchered, and were photographed for the sleeve dressed in butchers' aprons, holding pieces of meat and decapitated baby dolls. (See inner photograph on US Rarities sleeve.)

The public outcry was so great that this sleeve was withdrawn, the present sleeve quickly printed and substituted, and the album reissued. Because so many of the original sleeves had been printed, many simply had the new photograph pasted over the offending one. These examples are now quite valuable.

Tracks include Yesterday and Act Naturally from Help!, Drive My Car, Nowhere Man, If I Needed Someone and What Goes On? from Rubber Soul, plus three tracks originally planned for Revolver (and included on the British Revolver album) : I'm Only Sleeping, Dr. Robert, and And Your Bird Can Sing. To complete the album Capitol included We Can Work It Out and Day Tripper, issued as a double A-sided single, six months previously.

Side One

Drive My Car   2:24
(See British Rubber Soul Album
   PCS 3075)
I'm Only Sleeping   2:58
(See British Revolver Album PCS
   7009)
Nowhere Man   2:40
(See British Rubber Soul Album
   PCS 3075)
Dr. Robert   2:14
(See British Revolver Album PCS
   7009)
Yesterday   2:04
(See British Help! Album PCS 3071)
Act Naturally (Morrison–
   Russell)   2:27
(See British Help! Album PCS 3071)

Side Two

And Your Bird Can Sing   2:02
(See British Revolver Album PCS
   7009)
If I Needed Someone
   (Harrison)   2:19
(See British Rubber Soul Album
   PCS 3075)
We Can Work It Out   2:10
(See A Collection Of Beatles Oldies
   Album PCS 7016)
What Goes On? (Lennon–
   McCartney–Starkey)   2:44
(See British Rubber Soul Album
   PCS 3075)
Day Tripper   2:37
(See A Collection Of Beatles Oldies
   Album PCS 7016)

All Lennon–McCartney songs except where stated.

Capitol ST 2576
Producers : George Martin
Release Date : 8 August 1966
Running Time : 27:47

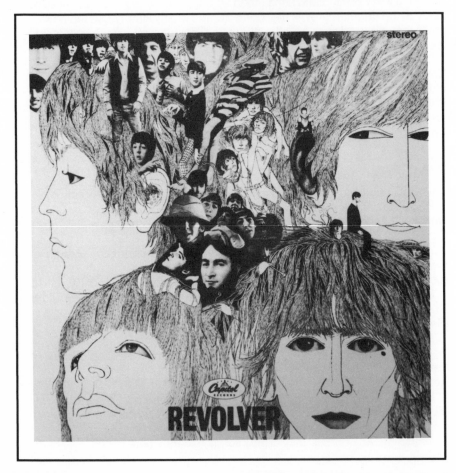

SIDE ONE : Taxman; Eleanor Rigby; Love You To; Here, There And Everywhere; Yellow Submarine; She Said, She Said.

SIDE TWO : Good Day Sunshine; For No One; I Want To Tell You; Got To Get You Into My Life; Tomorrow Never Knows.

This is the first Beatles album to be issued in the USA bearing any resemblance to its UK equivalent. With the exception of three tracks included on Yesterday ... And Today, the tracks on this album are the same as on the British album. All subsequent albums except Rarities had identical American and British editions.

Side One

Taxman (Harrison)   2:36
(See British Revolver Album PCS 7009)
Eleanor Rigby   2:11
(See British Revolver Album PCS 7009)
Love You To (Harrison)   3:00
(See British Revolver Album PCS 7009)
Here, There And Everywhere   2:29
(See British Revolver Album PCS 7009)
Yellow Submarine   2:40
(See British Revolver Album PCS 7009)
She Said, She Said   2:39
(See British Revolver Album PCS 7009)

Side Two

Good Day Sunshine   2:08
(See British Revolver Album PCS 7009)
For No One   2:03
(See British Revolver Album PCS 7009)
I Want To Tell You (Harrison)   2:30
(See British Revolver Album PCS 7009)
Got To Get You Into My Life   2:31
(See British Revolver Album PCS 7009)
Tomorrow Never Knows   3:00
(See British Revolver Album PCS 7009)

All Lennon–McCartney songs except where stated.

Capitol SHAL 12060
Producer : George Martin
Release Date : 24 March 1980
Running Time : 41:04

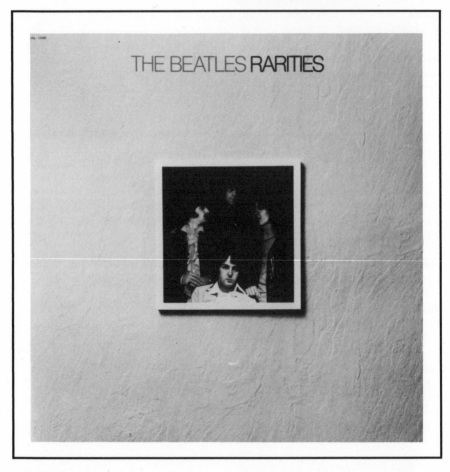

SIDE ONE : Love Me Do; Misery; There's A Place; Sie Liebt Dich; And I Love Her; Help!; I'm Only Sleeping; I Am The Walrus.

SIDE TWO : Penny Lane; Helter Skelter; Don't Pass Me By; The Inner Light; Across The Universe; You Know My Name (Look Up The Number); Sgt. Pepper Inner Groove.

When Capitol Records in America informed EMI of their intention to release a Rarities album; EMI assumed they meant the album as included in the box-set The Beatles Collection; so EMI also decided to release it as a separate album (changing the catalogue number from PSLP 261 to PCM 1001) on 29 October 1979. However Capitol's plans differed somewhat from the album that EMI had compiled. What Capitol had planned (which was also what they released) was an album of tracks which were rare in America. Virtually the entire contents of the British album were already included on American albums, so Capitol saw very little point in releasing that album in America. What they did was to collect together those tracks not previously included on albums along with various rarities from around the world.

The tracks included here which, although previously released in America, make their first appearance on a US album are : Misery, There's A Place, Sie Liebt Dich, The Inner Light and You Know My Name (Look Up The Number).

Of the remaining ten tracks, seven : Love Me Do, Help!, I'm Only Sleeping, Helter Skelter, Don't Pass Me By, Across The Universe and Sgt. Pepper Inner Groove, originate from British releases; whilst the version of And I Love Her included here was originally included on the German version of the album Something New (Odeon IC 072–04 600). The remaining two tracks, I Am The Walrus and Penny Lane, are newly created versions edited together from other versions. In the case of I Am The Walrus, this was edited together using the British stereo version and editing in a few extra beats which originally only appeared on the US single. The version of Penny Lane included here was also edited together using the British stereo version plus a few extra notes of a piccolo trumpet which had originally been included on a mono version of promotional copies distributed to radio stations in America and Canada.

What Capitol released was an album rather more worthy of the title Rarities than the album released in Britain by EMI which was basically a compilation of Beatle B-sides.

Side One

Love Me Do   2:22
(See Please Please Me Album PCS 3042)
Misery · 1:43
(See Please Please Me Album PCS 3042)
There's A Place   1:44
(See Please Please Me Album PCS 3042)
Sie Liebt Dich (Lennon–McCartney–Nicolas–Montague)   2:18
(See Past Masters — Vol 1 Album BPM 1)
And I Love Her   2:36
(See British A Hard Day's Night Album PCS 3058)
Help!   2:16
(See British Help! Album PCS 3071)
I'm Only Sleeping   2:58
(See British Revolver Album PCS 7009)
I Am The Walrus   4:35
(See Magical Mystery Tour Album PCTC 255)

Side Two

Penny Lane   3:00
(See Magical Mystery Tour Album PCTC 255)
Helter Skelter   3:38
(See The Beatles Album PCS 7067–8)
Don't Pass Me By   3:45
(See The Beatles Album PCS 7067–8)
The Inner Light (Harrison)   2:36
(See Past Masters — Vol 2 Album BPM 2)
Across The Universe   3:41
(See Past Masters — Vol 2 Album BPM 2)
You Know My Name (Look Up The Number)   4:20
(See Past Masters — Vol 2 Album BPM 2)
Sgt. Pepper Inner Groove   0:02
(See Sgt. Pepper's . . . Album PCS 7027)

All Lennon–McCartney songs except where stated.

20 GREATEST HITS

Capitol SV 12245
Producers : George Martin and
Phil Spector
Release Date : 18 October 1982
Running Time : 58:59

SIDE ONE : She Loves You; Love Me Do; I Want To Hold Your Hand; Can't Buy Me Love; A Hard Day's Night; I Feel Fine; Eight Days A Week; Ticket To Ride; Help!; Yesterday; We Can Work It Out; Paperback Writer.

SIDE TWO : Penny Lane; All You Need Is Love; Hello Goodbye; Hey Jude; Get Back; Come Together; Let It Be; The Long And Winding Road.

The release of a Beatles' greatest hits album in both the UK and USA must obviously pose a minor problem for the compilers. Do they compile an international greatest hits album or compile albums tailor-made for the individual market concerned? For this album Capitol in America (and Parlophone in Britain) decided on the latter and, using the Billboard charts, compiled an album of the Beatles' American greatest hits. Some of the recordings included on this American album are not on the British version and vice versa. Included here are Eight Days A Week, Yesterday, Penny Lane, Come Together, Let It Be and The Long And Winding Road, in place of From Me To You, Day Tripper, Yellow Submarine, Eleanor Rigby, Lady Madonna and The Ballad of John And Yoko (which are included on the British version). Eight Days A Week, Yesterday and The Long And Winding Road were (unlike in Britain) issued as singles and, together with the rest of the tracks on this version of the album (which, unlike the British version, covers the whole of the Beatles' Parlophone recording career from 1962 to 1970) they all reached No. 1 in the Billboard singles chart.

One interesting inclusion on the American album is a shorter version of Hey Jude which fades out just over 2 minutes earlier than the full version and clocks in at 5 minutes 5 seconds.

The sleeves of both the British and American albums are very similar except that the British sleeve, unlike the American one, has the album contents printed across the top.

Following the release of this album Capitol also reissued Love Me Do (which had originally been issued by Tollie Records (Tollie 9008) on 27 April 1964) on 12 November 1982 and not 10 October, as was expected, to tie in with its British re-release.

Side One
She Loves You   2:18
(See Past Masters — Vol 1 Album BPM 1)
Love Me Do   2:19
(See Please Please Me Album PCS 3042)
I Want To Hold Your Hand   2:24
(See Past Masters — Vol 1 Album BPM 1)
Can't Buy Me Love   2:15
(See British A Hard Day's Night Album PCS 3058)
A Hard Day's Night   2:32
(See British A Hard Day's Night Album PCS 3058)

I Feel Fine   2:19
(See Past Masters — Vol 1 Album BPM 1)
Eight Days A Week   2:43
(See Beatles For Sale Album PCS 3062)
Ticket To Ride   3:03
(See British Help! Album PCS 3071)
Help!   2:16
(See British Help! Album PCS 3071)
Yesterday   2:04
(See British Help! Album PCS 3071)
We Can Work It Out   2:10
(See Past Masters — Vol 2 BPM 2)
Paperback Writer   2:25
(See Past Masters — Vol 2 BPM 2)

Side Two

Penny Lane   3:00
(See Magical Mystery Tour Album
   PCTC 255)
All You Need Is Love   3:47
(See Magical Mystery Tour Album
   PCTC 255)
Hello Goodbye   3:42
(See Magical Mystery Tour Album
   PCTC 255)
Hey Jude   5:05
(See Past Masters — Vol 2 Album
   BPM 2)

Get Back   3:11
(See Past Masters — Vol 2 Album
   BPM 2)
Come Together   4:16
(See Abbey Road Album PCS 7088)
Let It Be   3:50
(See Let It Be Album PCS 7096)
*The Long And Winding
   Road   3:40
(See Let It Be Album PCS 7096)

*Produced by George Martin/Phil Spector. All others
produced by George Martin.

FURTHER BRITISH ALBUMS

UK Release : 18 October 1982
Parlophone PCTC 260
US Release : None
Intl CD No : None
Producer : George Martin
Running Time : 56:12

SIDE ONE : Love Me Do; From Me To You; She Loves You; I Want To Hold Your Hand; Can't Buy Me Love; A Hard Day's Night; I Feel Fine; Ticket To Ride; Help!; Day Tripper; We Can Work It Out.

SIDE TWO : Paperback Writer; Yellow Submarine; Eleanor Rigby; All You Need Is Love; Hello Goodbye; Lady Madonna; Hey Jude; Get Back; The Ballad Of John And Yoko.

Issued on 18 October 1982, two weeks after the re-release of Love Me Do, this album contains the A-sides of the Beatles' 17 British No. 1 singles starting with From Me To You released in 1963 and going through to 1969 and The Ballad Of John And Yoko. The three remaining tracks included are Day Tripper and Eleanor Rigby (two B-sides) together with Love Me Do.

Originally, this was planned as a double album entitled The Beatles Greatest Hits and was to have contained the A-sides of every one of the twenty-six Beatles' singles issued on Parlophone in Britain. The album got as far as the test pressing stage and was even given a catalogue number (EMTVS 34), but at the last moment was scrapped in favour of a single album to tie in with the American release. Although both albums use the same title, they have somewhat differing contents; the American album also includes a shorter version of Hey Jude not featured on the British album (see page 202).

The sleeve, which is not as cheap looking as some previous ones, is basically the same for both albums and is the first Beatles' album sleeve to ever feature recording information i.e. recording date, release date and chart position achieved.

For the twentieth anniversary re-release of Love Me Do on 4 October 1982, almost exactly twenty years to the day of its first release, EMI Records pressed the record with a red Parlophone label similar to the one used on the original release, and issued it in a special picture sleeve — they even used the original catalogue number (R4949). Unfortunately, the only thing not original about the record is the recording. As is widely known, there are two versions of Love Me Do, the original single version (which features Ringo Starr on drums) and the album version (which features session drummer Andy White). It is the latter of these that was used on the reissued single.

The record was also issued as a limited edition picture disc (RP4949) and, following the release of this album, was also issued as a twelve-inch single (12R4949) on 1 November 1982. This, unlike the ordinary single, does actually contain the original version of Love Me Do together with the album version and the single's original B-side, P.S. I Love You.

Love Me Do was to become the Beatles' second top ten hit of 1982 when it reached No. 4 in the British charts (its highest previous position had been No. 17). The Beatles' Movie Medley, issued earlier in the year, had reached No. 10 — not bad for a group that had split up some twelve years previously.

Side One

Love Me Do   2:19
From Me To You   1:55
She Loves You   2:18
I Want To Hold Your Hand   2:24
Can't Buy Me Love   2:15
A Hard Day's Night   2:32
I Feel Fine   2:19
Ticket To Ride   3:03
Help!   2:16
Day Tripper   2:37
We Can Work It Out   2:10

Side Two

Paperback Writer   2:25
Yellow Submarine   2:40
Eleanor Rigby   2:11
All You Need Is Love   3:47
Hello Goodbye   3:24
Lady Madonna   2:17
Hey Jude   7:11
Get Back   3:11
The Ballad Of John And Yoko   2:58

UK Release : 26 April 1984
Parlophone **CAV 1**
US Release : None
Intl CD No : None
Producers : George Martin and
Walter J. Ridley
Running Time : 38:30

SIDE ONE : Bad To Me (Billy J. Kramer and The Dakotas); Hello Little Girl (The Fourmost); You'll Never Walk Alone (Gerry and The Pacemakers); Hippy Hippy Shake (The Swinging Blue Jeans); Little Children (Billy J. Kramer and The Dakotas); You're No Good (The Swinging Blue Jeans); It's For You (Cilla Black); Ferry 'Cross The Mersey (Gerry and The Pacemakers).

SIDE TWO : Love Me Do; I Saw Her Standing There; Twist And Shout; She Loves You; Money; I Want To Hold Your Hand; Can't Buy Me Love; A Hard Day's Night.

This custom-pressed album is available exclusively at the Cavern Club in Mathew Street, Liverpool and was produced for it by EMI to celebrate its rebuilding and reopening on 26 April 1984.

After many years of virtually no interest on the part of Liverpool City Council in recognising the city's most famous sons the local commercial radio station, Radio City, decided to lead the way by buying up an enormous amount of Beatles memorabilia and opening Beatle City in Seel Street, where in the early sixties, Allan Williams, the Beatles' first manager, had The Blue Angel Club.

Prior to the opening of Beatle City, The Liverpool Beatles Appreciation Society, a group of fans including many original Cavern Club members, had been campaigning to have a statue or some other form of permanent tribute erected in the city. Impressed by their enthusiasm, the Liverpool-based Royal Insurance Company decided to build 'Cavern Walks' on the original site of the Cavern Club.

Opened in 1984, Cavern Walks contains a rebuilt Cavern Club (located slightly further up Mathew Street than the original) plus a shopping arcade (complete with a bronze statue of the Beatles). Following that, in early 1985, the British-born entertainer Tommy Steele presented the people of Liverpool with a bronze statue of Eleanor Rigby, for which he charged the City of Liverpool half a sixpence. This statue is sited in Stanley Street just around the corner from the Cavern Club. Since then, The Beatles Shop in Mathew Street, has also opened, selling mainly Beatles records and memorabilia, plus records by other Merseyside artists.

This album could almost be called The Greatest Hits of Merseybeat, as it contains some of the most famous recordings to emerge from that era. Besides the Beatles tracks which are featured on side two, it also includes other Merseybeat artists such as Gerry and The Pacemakers and Cilla Black.

One of the other interesting aspects of this album is the inclusion of sleeve notes written by Tony Barrow who wrote the sleeve notes for a number of the Beatles' early albums and E.P.s.

Side One
Bad To Me   2:18
Billy J. Kramer and The Dakotas
Hello Little Girl   1:50
The Fourmost
You'll Never Walk Alone   2:40
(Rodgers–Hammerstein II)
Gerry and The Pacemakers
Hippy Hippy Shake   1:44*
(Romero)
The Swinging Blue Jeans
Little Children   2:47
(Shuman–McFarland)
Billy J. Kramer and The Dakotas
You're No Good   2:16*
(C. Ballard Jnr)
The Swinging Blue Jeans
It's For You   2:20
Cilla Black

Ferry 'Cross The Mersey   2:38
(Marsden)
Gerry and The Pacemakers

Side Two
Love Me Do   2:19
I Saw Her Standing There   2:50
Twist And Shout (Medley–Russell)   2:32
She Loves You   2:18
Money (Bradford–Gordy)   2:47
I Want To Hold Your Hand   2:24
Can't Buy Me Love   2:15
A Hard Day's Night   2:32

Produced by Walter J. Ridley. All others produced by George Martin.

All Lennon–McCartney songs except where stated.

UK Release : 30 June 1986
Parlophone SMMC 151
(Cassette only)
US Release : None
Intl CD No : None
Producer : George Martin
Running Time : 33:10

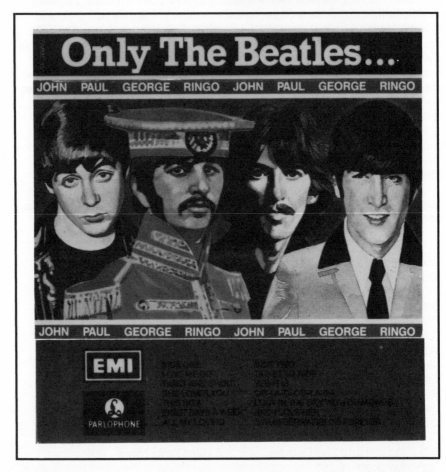

SIDE ONE : Love Me Do; Twist And Shout; She Loves You; This Boy; Eight Days A Week; All My Loving.

SIDE TWO : Ticket To Ride; Yes It Is; Ob-La-Di, Ob-La-Da; Lucy In The Sky With Diamonds; And I Love Her; Strawberry Fields Forever.

Available by mail order only from Heineken, this cassette was backed by newspaper advertisements in the British press and was only available for a short time before being quickly withdrawn due to objections by the Beatles.

The cassette, which features twelve tracks, includes the previously unreleased stereo version of Yes It Is. Amongst the remaining tracks is the original single version of Love Me Do together with a further ten tracks from various points in the Beatles' career. Despite the claims on the inlay card, the version of This Boy included is not 'a previously unreleased stereo version', but the reprocessed stereo version previously available on Love Songs and other compilations. The 'unreleased stereo version', at present, remains unreleased, however, the stereo version as released on singles in Australia and Canada in 1976 was included on the 1988 album Past Masters — Volumes One and Two.

Its short-lived and limited availability makes this cassette now a much sought-after collector's item.

Side One
Love Me Do   2:22
Twist And Shout (Medley–
   Russell)   2:32
She Loves You   2:18
This Boy   2:11
Eight Days A Week   2:43
All My Loving   2:04

Side Two
Ticket To Ride   3:03
Yes It Is   2:40
Ob-La-Di, Ob-La-Da   3:10
Lucy In The Sky With
   Diamonds   3:25
And I Love Her   2:27
Strawberry Fields Forever   4:05

All Lennon–McCartney songs except where stated.

UK Release : 7 March 1988
Parlophone BPM 1
US Release : 7 March 1988
Capitol : C129 90043
Intl CD No : CDP 7 90043 2
Producer : George Martin
Running Time : 42:30

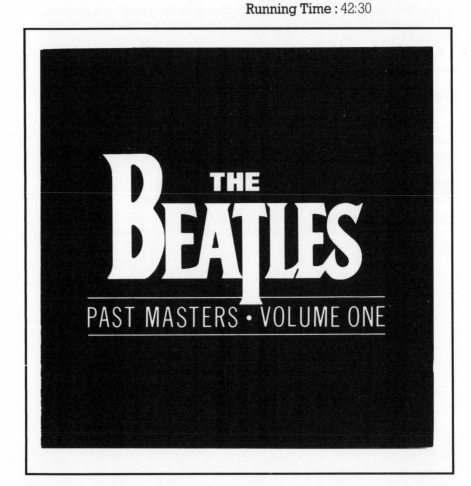

SIDE ONE : Love Me Do; From Me To You; Thank You Girl; She Loves You; I'll Get You; I Want To Hold Your Hand; This Boy; Komm, Gib Mir Deine Hand; Sie Liebt Dich.

SIDE TWO : Long Tall Sally; I Call Your Name; Slow Down; Matchbox; I Feel Fine; She's A Woman; Bad Boy; Yes It Is; I'm Down.

Following the world-wide release by EMI of the Beatles' original studio albums on compact disc, they have, in this and the accompanying volume, collected together the remaining studio material not included on those albums. Twenty-five of the thirty-three tracks on these two albums were originally issued on singles in Britain. A further two, Komm, Gib Mir Deine Hand and Sie Liebt Dich were originally issued as a single in Germany in 1964. Four others : Long Tall Sally, I Call Your Name, Slow Down and Matchbox, originate from the 1964 Long Tall Sally E.P.; while Bad Boy was issued as part of the 1966 album A Collection Of Beatles Oldies and Across The Universe was originally included on the charity album No One's Gonna Change Our World issued in 1969.

This first album covers the early days from Love Me Do through to the heady days of the Beatlemania years of 1964–5, and contains the material which wasn't destined for British albums at the time. Amongst the contents of this album (Volume One) is the original version of Love Me Do (with Ringo on drums) together with both the A and B-sides of a further four singles (From Me To You, She Loves You, I Want To Hold Your Hand and I Feel Fine, together with their respective B-sides of Thank You Girl, I'll Get You, This Boy and She's A Woman). Other tracks on this album are Komm, Gib Mir Deine Hand and Sie Liebt Dich (the German-language versions of I Want To Hold Your Hand and She Loves You) which were originally issued in Germany as a single in 1964. Long Tall Sally and I Call Your Name were originally part of the 1964 American album The Beatles Second — these, together with Slow Down and Matchbox, were later issued in Britain as the Long Tall Sally E.P. Bad Boy originates from the 1965 American album Beatles VI (later to be included on the 1966 British album A Collection Of Beatles Oldies). Finally are included Yes It Is and I'm Down, which were originally the B-sides of Ticket To Ride and Help! respectively (both of which are included on the Help! album), and are the only B-sides on this album not accompanied by their respective A-sides.

As previously mentioned, this album contains the original version of Love Me Do with Ringo on drums, and is the first of a number of tracks included here which originally were quite rare. The version of This Boy is the true stereo version originally only available on singles issued in Australia (Parlophone A8103) and Canada (Capitol 72144), and it makes its first appearance on an album here. She's A Woman, again in stereo, originates from the 1967 Australian album Greatest Hits Volume 2 (Parlophone PCSO 7534). Yes It Is, in its stereo form, was issued in Britain in 1986 as part of the Only The Beatles . . . cassette (Parlophone SMMC 151). Finally, I'm Down, in its stereo form, was originally issued as part of the Japanese Help! E.P. (Odeon EAS 30006). With the exception of I'm Down, these stereo versions have been given their first international release on this album.

In collecting together these tracks for these two albums, EMI have finally produced compilations which will be extremely welcome amongst Beatles' fans world-wide. Having these, together with the rest of the Beatles' collection, available on compact disc is virtually like having your own personal copy of the Beatles' studio master tapes.

These albums are worthy additions to any Beatles' record collection and, in the case of the compact disc collection, are absolutely essential as they finally 'tidy up' the studio material not included on the original albums.

SIDE ONE

Love Me Do (Lennon–McCartney)   2:22

Recorded : 4 September 1962, EMI Studios, Abbey Road, London

John Lennon : Harmonica and Lead Vocal
Paul McCartney : Bass Guitar and Lead Vocal
George Harrison : Acoustic Guitar and Harmony Vocal
Ringo Starr : Drums

This is the original version featuring Ringo on drums and not the version included on the Please Please Me album (which features session drummer Andy White). This version comes from the Beatles' first official recording session with EMI which took place on 4 September 1962 some three months after George Martin had first given them a recording test on 6 June 1962 (during which time Ringo had replaced Pete Best on drums).

The recording (completed in approximately fifteen takes) is dominated by John's harmonica. The main lead vocals are a duet from John and Paul, with John singing solo at various times. The lyrics are rather sparse but with the dominant harmonica and John's asthmatic-sounding Liverpudlian vocals it is still an excellent first effort from four (at the time) very nervous Beatles.

It is this version which was issued as a single (together with P.S. I Love You) on 5 October 1962. It entered the charts the following week and eventually achieved a highest position of No. 17. In 1982 it was reissued to celebrate its twentieth anniversary : on that occasion it reached No. 4.

From Me To You (Lennon–McCartney)   1:55

Recorded : 5 March 1963, EMI Studios, Abbey Road, London

John Lennon : Rhythm Guitar, Harmonica and Lead Vocal
Paul McCartney : Bass Guitar and Lead Vocal
George Harrison : Lead Guitar and Harmony Vocal
Ringo Starr : Drums

With this, the follow-up single to Please Please Me and the Beatles' second No. 1, they began to prove that they had both musical and song-writing ability. According to some charts Please Please Me only reached No. 2, and From Me To You was their first No. 1 single. If it was, it began a string of eleven consecutive No. 1 singles — a record that has never been equalled to date. Like so many of the Beatles' early recordings the lead vocal is shared by John and Paul with George joining in here and there and on chorus. The recording also makes very effective use of John's harmonica.

This song was reputed to have been written on 28 February 1963 after John and Paul had read the letters column From You To Us in the *New Musical Express* during a coach journey from York to Shrewsbury while they were on tour (as the support act!) with Helen Shapiro.

During the early sixties the Beatles had their own BBC radio show, some episodes of which were entitled From Us To You which featured a reworded recording of From Me To You.

Thank You Girl (Lennon–McCartney) 2:01

Recorded : 5 and 13 March 1963, EMI Studios, Abbey Road, London

John Lennon : Acoustic Guitar, Harmonica and Lead Vocal
Paul McCartney : Bass Guitar and Lead Vocal
George Harrison : Lead Guitar
Ringo Starr : Drums

This exciting track dates back to April 1963 when it was originally released as the B-side of the Beatles' third Parlophone single From Me To You. It has a predominant harmonica from John, and the usual John and Paul lead vocal duet featured on most of their 1963 singles. The recording was completed in thirteen takes on 5 March 1963 and some additional edit sections were recorded on 13 March 1963.

She Loves You (Lennon–McCartney) 2:18

Recorded : 1 July 1963, EMI Studios, Abbey Road, London

John Lennon : Rhythm Guitar and Lead Vocal
Paul McCartney : Bass Guitar and Lead Vocal
George Harrison : Lead Guitar and Harmony Vocal
Ringo Starr : Drums

This is the A-side of the Beatles' fourth single, issued on Parlophone in Britain on 23 August 1963, featuring the usual lead vocal duet from John and Paul. The song includes the now-famous catchy chorus line of 'yeah, yeah, yeah' and the equally famous 'oooo' which was previously used in I Saw Her Standing There on the Please Please Me album. If Love Me Do, Please Please Me and From Me To You had not convinced people that the Beatles had staying-power, the catchy chorus line and excitement generated by She Loves You must surely have done so.

I'll Get You (Lennon–McCartney) 2:04

Recorded : 1 July 1963, EMI Studios, Abbey Road, London

John Lennon : Rhythm Guitar, Harmonica and Lead Vocal
Paul McCartney : Bass Guitar and Harmony Vocal
George Harrison : Lead Guitar and Harmony Vocal
Ringo Starr : Drums

Originally considered as an A-side for the follow-up to From Me To You, this was released in 1963 as the B-side to She Loves You. The song is reminiscent of She Loves You with the opening 'Oh yeah' and the duet by John and Paul on lead vocals. John's overdubbed harmonica is prominent at the beginning and ending but is mixed back during the rest of the track. The take details of this, and She Loves You, are unknown. This is due to the studio master having been erased shortly after the session, which also accounts for the lack of stereo versions of both these tracks.

I Want To Hold Your Hand (Lennon–McCartney) 2:24

Recorded: 17 October 1963, EMI Studios, Abbey Road, London

John Lennon: Rhythm Guitar and Lead Vocal
Paul McCartney: Bass Guitar and Lead Vocal
George Harrison: Lead Guitar and Harmony Vocal
Ringo Starr: Drums

This record, as a single, sold over 15 million copies world-wide. In fact, prior to its release in Britain on 29 November 1963, there were advance orders approaching one million copies. Needless to say, upon its release in Britain it entered the charts at No. 1, where it remained for six weeks. This was the record which in 1964 gave birth to Beatlemania in America, where it sold nearly five million copies and opened up the American market for other British artists.

The recording opens with John's rhythm guitar, a sound which builds up to an intense pitch and then virtually explodes as John and Paul begin their lead vocal duet. For the chorus line John and Paul are joined by George and all three add excited hand-clapping to make this one of their most powerful early recordings.

Recorded in seventeen takes on 17 October 1963, this was the Beatles' first four-track recording, which enabled George Martin to, amongst other things, produce a rather better stereo image than the previous two-track recordings of earlier sessions.

This Boy (Lennon–McCartney) 2:11

Recorded: 17 October 1963, EMI Studios, Abbey Road, London

John Lennon: Acoustic Guitar and Lead Vocal
Paul McCartney: Bass Guitar and Harmony Vocal
George Harrison: Lead Guitar and Harmony Vocal
Ringo Starr: Drums

This track was originally released in 1963 as the B-side to the Beatles' multi-million seller I Want To Hold Your Hand. This Boy was recorded at the same 17 October 1963 session as I Want To Hold Your Hand, and also went to seventeen takes before the fifteenth was finally chosen for release.

The song is dominated by a close three-part harmony from John, Paul and George, with an extremely powerful solo vocal from John. For the film *A Hard Day's Night*, George Martin produced an orchestral version of this which was retitled Ringo's Theme and used in the film as the soundtrack to a section featuring Ringo, who, amongst other things, is seen walking along the banks of the River Thames.

Komm, Gib Mir Deine Hand (Lennon–McCartney–Nicolas–Hellmer) 2:24

Recorded : (Instrumental Track) 17 October 1963, EMI Studios, Abbey Road, London
(Vocal Track) 29 January 1964, Pathé Marconi Studios, Paris, France

John Lennon : Rhythm Guitar and Lead Vocal
Paul McCartney : Bass Guitar and Lead Vocal
George Harrison : Lead Guitar
Ringo Starr : Drums

The German-language versions of I Want To Hold Your Hand and She Loves You were not recorded, as many thought, as a tribute to the Beatles' early days in Hamburg, but in answer to a request from EMI in Germany, who wanted authentic versions for the German market. The Beatles were far from enthusiastic about the idea but George Martin eventually persuaded them to record the tracks in the EMI studios in Paris, where they were at the time. The two recordings were subsequently released in Germany as a double A-sided single on 5 March 1964 (Odeon 22671). The German lyrics of both songs were written by two German songwriters, one of whom was present at the recording session to ensure that the songs were sung with the correct accent.

For this version of the song the Beatles used the original backing track as used for the English version and, in eleven takes, added the new German vocals plus hand-claps.

Sie Liebt Dich (Lennon–McCartney–Nicolas–Montague) 2:18

Recorded : 29 January 1964, Pathé Marconi Studios, Paris, France

John Lennon : Rhythm Guitar and Lead Vocal
Paul McCartney : Bass Guitar and Lead Vocal
George Harrison : Lead Guitar and Harmony Vocal
Ringo Starr : Drums

This German-language version of She Loves You shares the same basic history as Komm, Gib Mir Deine Hand. But unlike Komm, Gib Mir Deine Hand, which used the backing track from I Want To Hold Your Hand, Sie Liebt Dich is a brand-new recording. The Beatles, unable to use the backing track to She Loves You for Sie Leibt Dich, due to the original studio master having been erased, had to make a completely new recording.

SIDE TWO

Long Tall Sally (Johnson–Penniman–Blackwell)   1:58

Recorded : 1 March 1964, EMI Studios, Abbey Road, London

John Lennon : Rhythm Guitar
Paul McCartney : Bass Guitar and Solo Vocal
George Harrison : Lead Guitar
Ringo Starr : Drums
George Martin : Piano

This Little Richard song, originally released as part of the American album The Beatles Second on 10 April 1964 and then in Britain on 19 June 1964 as the title track of an E.P., provides Paul with a perfect vehicle for his voice. Here, his solo vocal sounds just as enthusiastic and spontaneous as John's does on the classic Twist And Shout. In fact, like Twist And Shout, this was recorded in one take. The Beatles had used both songs for years during their live performances, which invariably opened with Twist And Shout and closed with Long Tall Sally — a format they were to continue with for their later, larger-scale concert performances.

I Call Your Name (Lennon–McCartney)   2:02

Recorded : 1 March 1964, EMI Studios, Abbey Road, London

John Lennon : Rhythm Guitar and Solo Vocal
Paul McCartney : Bass Guitar
George Harrison : Lead Guitar
Ringo Starr : Drums

This was originally written for Billy J. Kramer and The Dakotas, who recorded and issued it as the B-side to another Lennon–McCartney composition, Bad To Me. When John (who wrote it) discovered it had been buried on a B-side he decided that the Beatles should also record and issue it. So with John on lead vocals the Beatles recorded the song (which has a similar feel, both musically and vocally, to John's later You Can't Do That) in seven takes (the released version being an edit of takes 5 and 7) during the same session that produced Long Tall Sally. Like Long Tall Sally, this was issued as part of the American album The Beatles Second on 10 April 1964, and then in Britain on 19 June 1964 as part of the Long Tall Sally E.P.

Slow Down (Williams)   2:54

Recorded : 1 and 4 June 1964, EMI Studios, Abbey Road, London

John Lennon : Rhythm Guitar and Solo Vocal
Paul McCartney : Bass Guitar
George Harrison : Lead Guitar
Ringo Starr : Drums
George Martin : Piano

Released as part of the Long Tall Sally E.P. on 19 June 1964, this track, partially recorded during six takes on 1 June and completed on 4 June, which features John on lead vocal, is an extremely enthusiastic rendition of this little-known Larry Williams song. It is the first of three Williams songs which the Beatles recorded and released.

Matchbox (Perkins)   1:37

Recorded : 1 June 1964, EMI Studios, Abbey Road, London

John Lennon : Rhythm Guitar
Paul McCartney : Bass Guitar
George Harrison : Lead Guitar
Ringo Starr : Drums and Solo Vocal
George Martin : Piano

This was recorded in five takes during the same session as Slow Down and released as part of the Long Tall Sally E.P. Ringo gives a rousing rendition of this 1957 Carl Perkins song which was recorded with Perkins present (although not participating) during the session.

I Feel Fine (Lennon–McCartney)   2:19

Recorded : 18 October 1964, EMI Studios, Abbey Road, London

John Lennon : Rhythm Guitar, Lead Guitar and Lead Vocal
Paul McCartney : Bass Guitar and Backing Vocal
George Harrison : Lead Guitar and Backing Vocal
Ringo Starr : Drums

With advance orders of three quarters of a million copies, this was issued as a single on 27 November 1964 as the follow-up to A Hard Day's Night. It was the Beatles' eighth single and sixth consecutive No. 1. The recording, which was completed in nine takes, opens with a single note of feedback, which then goes into the riff around which the song is constructed. This was the first time that feedback had been used on a record, and it gave ideas to many musicians like Jimi Hendrix, who later used feedback as a musical note and not just as a noise. Theories at the time about the sound at the beginning of the record included the idea of an amplified humming bee. In fact the Beatles did not use any pre-recorded sound effects until 1966, two years later. The lead vocal is from John, with Paul and George joining him on the chorus. Paul and George also sing a wordless vocal backing.

She's A Woman (Lennon–McCartney)   2:57

Recorded : 8 October 1964, EMI Studios, Abbey Road, London

John Lennon : Rhythm Guitar
Paul McCartney : Bass Guitar, Piano and Solo Vocal
George Harrison : Lead Guitar
Ringo Starr : Drums and Percussion

This great chunk of syncopated rock and roll, written and sung by Paul in his best rock and roll style, was recorded in seven takes and originally issued as the B-side of I Feel Fine on 27 November 1964.

Bad Boy (Williams) 2:17

Recorded : 10–11 May 1965, EMI Studios, Abbey Road, London

John Lennon : Rhythm Guitar, Hammond Organ and Solo Vocal
Paul McCartney : Bass Guitar and Electric Piano
George Harrison : Lead Guitar
Ringo Starr : Drums and Tambourine

This was originally issued as part of the American album Beatles VI on 14 June 1965 and later included on the British album A Collection Of Beatles Oldies released on 9 December 1966. The recording, which was completed in four takes, features a solo vocal from John and a very enthusiastic backing from the rest of the Beatles. This and another Larry Williams song, Dizzy Miss Lizzy (recorded during the same session), were the last two songs (leaving aside the rather short rendition of Maggie Mae on Let It Be) issued by the Beatles during their collective career that they did not write themselves.

Yes It Is (Lennon–McCartney) 2:40

Recorded : 16 February 1965, EMI Studios, Abbey Road, London

John Lennon : Acoustic Guitar and Lead Vocal
Paul McCartney : Bass Guitar and Backing Vocal
George Harrison : Lead Guitar and Backing Vocal
Ringo Starr : Drums

The B-side to Ticket To Ride (included on the Help! album) released on 9 April 1965 was this beautiful ballad, which was recorded in fourteen takes on 16 February 1965 and written by John. The song is very reminiscent of his earlier This Boy and features a similar three-part harmony from John, Paul and George, with John singing solo in parts. The whining guitar in the backing is played by George who achieved the effect with a volume/tone control pedal with which he had been experimenting at the time.

I'm Down (Lennon–McCartney) 2:30

Recorded : 14 June 1965, EMI Studios, Abbey Road, London

John Lennon : Rhythm Guitar, Hammond Organ and Backing Vocal
Paul McCartney : Bass Guitar and Lead Vocal
George Harrison : Lead Guitar and Backing Vocal
Ringo Starr : Drums and Bongos

This is the Beatles at their rock and roll best! This superb McCartney-written track, similar in style to Little Richard's Long Tall Sally, was originally issued on 23 July 1965 as the B-side of Help! (included on the album of the same name). The recording, completed in seven takes, rattles along at an incredible pace with Paul shouting out the lyrics in true Little Richard style while John hammers away at the Hammond organ. Unbelievably, this recording was made during the same session that produced Yesterday.

UK Release : 7 March 1988
Parlophone BPM 2
US Release : 7 March 1988
Capitol : C12P 90044
Intl CD No : CDP 7 90044 2
Producer : George Martin
Running Time : 51:03

THE BEATLES

PAST MASTERS · VOLUME TWO

SIDE ONE : Day Tripper; We Can Work It Out; Paperback Writer; Rain; Lady Madonna; The Inner Light; Hey Jude; Revolution.

SIDE TWO : Get Back; Don't Let Me Down; The Ballad Of John And Yoko; Old Brown Shoe; Across The Universe; Let It Be; You Know My Name (Look Up The Number).

With the release of the Rubber Soul album in late 1965, together with the We Can Work It Out/Day Tripper single, the Beatles were slowly moving away from the three-minute pop single towards a more progressive (though still highly commercial) form of music which was to culminate in 1967 with the release of the Sgt. Pepper's Lonely Hearts Club Band album.

In 1966, prior to the release of Sgt. Pepper's, the Beatles were beginning to experiment in the studio with sound effects, backwards-running tapes and other such studio wizardry. Examples of their early experimentation in this field can be found on the Revolver album. One further example from the same period, Rain (though not included on Revolver) is included on this album. It features one of John Lennon's weirdest vocal performances, when, just near the end, he can be heard singing backwards.

By 1967 the Beatles (with more than a little help from George Martin), had virtually perfected the use of studio effects, a lot of which were used to great effect on both the Sgt. Pepper's album and the Magical Mystery Tour E.P.s. During 1967 the Beatles issued three singles : Penny Lane/Strawberry Fields Forever, All You Need Is Love/Baby, You're A Rich Man and Hello Goodbye/I Am The Walrus. These, together with the tracks from the Magical Mystery Tour E.P.s, were issued as an album in America and have subsequently been issued as a compact disc and are not included on this album.

In 1968, after the psychedelia of Sgt. Pepper's, the Beatles returned to rock and roll with Lady Madonna, which they followed up with their most popular single, Hey Jude, on the newly founded Apple label. Hey Jude was a record amongst records — as the longest single to have been issued up to that date, it clocks in at an amazing 7 minutes 11 seconds and despite its running time remains one of pop music's all-time classics.

During 1969 the Beatles issued two singles which were not included on albums at the time. The first, Get Back/Don't Let Me Down, was originally to have been two tracks from the Get Back album which the Beatles attempted to record during January 1969 at Apple Studios in Savile Row. The album was eventually abandoned, but the single was released on 11 April 1969.

After their brief stay at Apple the Beatles returned to Abbey Road to record their second single of 1969, the Ballad Of John And Yoko/Old Brown Shoe. The A-side was recorded by John and Paul during an eight and a half hour session on 14 April 1969 and Old Brown Shoe, which features all four Beatles, was recorded two days later. Both titles were issued as a single on 30 May 1969.

Following the release of the Abbey Road album, EMI issued a charity album entitled No One's Gonna Change Our World (Regal Starline SRS 5013) in December 1969. This album featured Across The Universe, a track which the Beatles had recorded virtually two years earlier in February 1968. That version, which over the years has become known as the 'Wildlife Version', is the only track included here not to have originated from a single.

1970 saw the release of the Beatles' final single and album Let It Be. Virtually the entire album had been taken from the Get Back sessions of January 1969 and remixed by Phil Spector. The single (though still from the same sessions) differs from the album version quite considerably, and is George Martin's original mix, issued on 6 March 1970.

Aside from the tracks already mentioned, this second album also contains : Paperback Writer (which together with Rain was issued as a single in June 1966); The Inner Light, the B-side to the March 1968 single Lady Madonna; Revolution, which was the flipside of the Beatles' first Apple single Hey Jude in August 1968; and, finally, You Know My Name (Look Up The Number), the B-side to their final single Let It Be in March 1970.

SIDE ONE

Day Tripper (Lennon–McCartney)   2:37

Recorded : 16 October 1965, EMI Studios, Abbey Road, London

John Lennon : Rhythm Guitar, Tambourine and Lead Vocal
Paul McCartney : Bass Guitar and Lead Vocal
George Harrison : Lead Guitar and Harmony Vocal
Ringo Starr : Drums

This track was issued together with We Can Work It Out as a double A-sided single on 3 December 1965; the same day also saw the release of the Rubber Soul album. It was written mainly by John with Paul contributing some of the lyrics. The lyrics are reminiscent of the earlier Ticket To Ride (and the title is similar). It was recorded in three takes on 16 October 1965, and features a lead vocal duet between John and Paul with George joining them for the harmony sections. Upon its release it entered the British charts at No. 1 where it stayed for five weeks, selling over one million copies before the end of the month.

We Can Work It Out (Lennon–McCartney)   2:10

Recorded : 20 and 29 October 1965, EMI Studios, Abbey Road, London

John Lennon : Harmonium and Harmony Vocal
Paul McCartney : Bass Guitar and Lead Vocal
George Harrison : Acoustic Guitar and Tambourine
Ringo Starr : Drums

This could be classified as the Beatles' first ever peace song. It predated All You Need Is Love by two years and Give Peace A Chance by four years. Released as the follow-up to Help! in 1965 this is the Beatles' eleventh Parlophone single and their ninth No. 1. By 1965 the Beatles had progressed from the 'beat group' sound of some of their early 1963–4 singles to a more technically and musically proficient group of musicians. Lead vocal on this is by Paul, with John joining in for the chorus and also playing harmonium. At various times the recording lapses into a slow waltz but then picks up again for the verses. John later used the same style for the instrumental break in the middle of Being For The Benefit Of Mr. Kite on Sgt. Pepper's Lonely Hearts Club Band. Paul's optimistic main lyrics are countered by John's realism with the verse beginning 'Life is very short . . .'. John did a similar thing with Paul's Getting Better on Sgt. Pepper's. The main part of the track was recorded in two takes on 20 October and completed with an overdub on 29 October.

Paperback Writer (Lennon–McCartney) 2:25

Recorded: 13 and 14 April 1966, EMI Studios, Abbey Road, London

John Lennon: Rhythm Guitar and Backing Vocal
Paul McCartney: Bass Guitar and Lead Vocal
George Harrison: Lead Guitar and Backing Vocal
Ringo Starr: Drums

This track was recorded in two takes (with one overdub) during the sessions for Revolver, and was issued as a single on 10 June 1966, some two months prior to that album. The song, written mainly by Paul, with John contributing some of the lyrics, was inspired by John Lennon's two books *In His Own Write* and *Spaniard In The Works*, and tells of Paul's wish to become a writer too. It begins with an a cappella introduction, followed by one of the best instrumental backings on any Beatles' record. The guitar sound on this record could be regarded as a foretaste of heavy metal. The lead vocal comes from Paul, who also joins John and George for the three-part harmony backing vocals, which are a combination of the title, together with a section of the French song *Frère Jacques*.

Rain (Lennon–McCartney) 2:59

Recorded: 14 and 16 April 1966, EMI Studios, Abbey Road, London

John Lennon: Rhythm Guitar and Lead Vocal
Paul McCartney: Bass Guitar and Backing Vocal
George Harrison: Lead Guitar and Backing Vocal
Ringo Starr: Drums and Tambourine

Previously issued as the B-side to Paperback Writer, this track features a stronger heavy guitar sound than the A-side, making the latter sound (in comparison) rather tame. The sound was to influence artists such as The Who, Cream and Jimi Hendrix. The guitars attack from the beginning; Ringo's superb drumbeat accentuates the heaviness of the sound and John's laconic sententious lead vocal grinds out of the left-hand channel. At the end of this recording one line of John's vocal is played backwards: 'Rain, when the rain comes they run and hide their heads' (note the substitution of 'when' for 'if', which is used in the main recording). Apparently, John took a copy of the master tape home and accidentally played it backwards, liked it, and included it on the final record. After this experiment, backwards-playing tapes were also included on (amongst others) I'm Only Sleeping and Tomorrow Never Knows on the Revolver album. The instrumental track to this, which was played fast, was recorded on 14 April 1966 and then remixed with the tape running on slow/vari-speed. The vocal track was added two days later on 16 April 1966 and, after eight takes, the seventh was chosen for the released stereo version.

Lady Madonna (Lennon–McCartney)   2:17

Recorded : 3 and 6 February 1968, EMI Studios, Abbey Road, London

John Lennon : Rhythm Guitar and Backing Vocal
Paul McCartney : Bass Guitar, Piano and Lead Vocal
George Harrison : Lead Guitar and Backing Vocal
Ringo Starr : Drums and Backing Vocal
Ronnie Scott : Tenor Saxophone
Harry Klein : Baritone Saxophone
Bill Povey : Tenor Saxophone
Bill Jackman : Baritone Saxophone

This was the last single issued by the Beatles on the Parlophone label in 1968, before the dream of Apple became a reality later that year. It was written and sung by Paul, who also plays piano in true rock and roll style, showing the influence of (amongst others) Little Richard and Jerry Lee Lewis. The song is rather like a rock version of his earlier Eleanor Rigby with loneliness again as the main theme. It was recorded in five takes on 3 February 1968 and completed with the saxophone backing played by Ronnie Scott, Harry Klein, Bill Povey and Bill Jackman three days later. The saxophone segment in the middle (according to various reports) was apparently originally some fifteen to twenty seconds longer, but was then edited. The vocal backing, by all four Beatles, was reputed to have been achieved by them singing with their hands cupped around their mouths.

The Inner Light (Harrison)   2:36

Recorded : (Instrumental Track) 12 January 1968, EMI Studios, Bombay, India
   (Vocal Track) 6 and 8 February 1968, EMI Studios, Abbey Road,
   London

John Lennon : Backing Vocal
Paul McCartney : Backing Vocal
George Harrison : Lead Vocal
Ringo Starr : Not Present
Session Musicians : All Instruments

Issued originally in 1968 as the B-side of Lady Madonna, this was George's first song to be released on a Beatles' single. It is the last of three Beatles' tracks by George Harrison featuring almost entirely Indian instrumentation. The previous two were Love You To, included on Revolver, and Within You, Without You, featured on Sgt. Pepper's Lonely Hearts Club Band. The instrumental track was recorded in five takes on 12 January 1968 at EMI Studios in Bombay, India, with some of India's virtuoso musicians, during the recording of George's Wonderwall album. The vocal track (including a brief backing from John and Paul) was overdubbed nearly a month later on 6 and 8 February 1968 at Abbey Road. Extracts from a Japanese poem by Roshi, translated into English by R. H. Bluth, formed the basis of George's lyrics for this interesting, and introspective, song.

Hey Jude (Lennon–McCartney) 7:11

Recorded : 31 July and 1 August 1968, Trident Studios, Wardour Street, London

John Lennon : Acoustic Guitar and Backing Vocal
Paul McCartney : Piano and Lead Vocal
George Harrison : Lead Guitar and Backing Vocal
Ringo Starr : Drums
Session Musicians : 36-Piece Orchestra

The A-side of the first single issued by the Beatles on their own Apple label, on 30 August 1968. It was the longest single issued to that date, totalling with its B-side Revolution, 10 minutes 33 seconds. Written by Paul, the song had started out as Hey Jules, about John's son Julian. The Beatles first attempted to record this at Abbey Road on 29 July 1968 but moved to Trident Studios in Soho where they recorded the song in four takes on 31 July (finally selecting take 1 for further overdubbing on 1 August). Paul sings lead vocal and accompanies himself on piano with backing vocals from John and George. The song starts simply, the main part lasting 3 minutes 11 seconds, but builds up until it finally explodes into a four-minute fade-out — the longest on a Beatles' record. The fade consists of all four Beatles plus a 36-piece orchestra (rather than the hundred which Paul had originally envisaged) playing and singing along to a one-line chorus of 'na, na-na-na-na-na, na'.

Revolution (Lennon–McCartney) 3:22

Recorded : 10–12 July 1968, EMI Studios, Abbey Road, London

John Lennon : Lead Guitar and Solo Vocal
Paul McCartney : Bass Guitar
George Harrison : Lead Guitar
Ringo Starr : Drums
Nicky Hopkins : Electric Piano

Previously issued as the B-side to the Beatles' first Apple single Hey Jude on 30 August 1968, this Lennon-written anti-war song (written by John in India) was recorded in sixteen takes between 10 and 12 July 1968 and features session man Nicky Hopkins on piano. The sound of a distorted guitar, played by John, is heard at the beginning of the record, to which Ringo then adds an electronically compressed drumbeat, giving the recording a solid 'heavy' sound. John's lead vocals (although recorded several times and rejected because he was dissatisfied with the result) were eventually completed after he had, as an experiment, lain on his back on the floor of the studio and sung them once more, finally achieving the sound he had originally wanted.

SIDE TWO

Get Back (Lennon–McCartney)   3:11

Recorded : 28 January 1969, Apple Studios, Savile Row, London

John Lennon : Lead Guitar and Harmony Vocal
Paul McCartney : Bass Guitar and Lead Vocal
George Harrison : Rhythm Guitar
Ringo Starr : Drums
Billy Preston : Organ

After the technical wizardry of the previous couple of years the Beatles decided to 'Get Back' to the simplicity of earlier years and make an album featuring straight performances : no orchestras, no tricks and no overdubs.

After numerous (unnumbered) recording takes which had begun some five days earlier, the Beatles finally selected this take (which was recorded live without any overdubs on 28 January 1969), for release as a surprise single on 11 April 1969. Copies of the single were sent to Radio 1 (without any prior announcement of its impending release) for broadcast on Easter Sunday 6 April 1969 (DJs Alan Freeman and John Peel duly obliging). After hearing the broadcast, the Beatles hurriedly remixed the record the following day and it was in the shops by the Friday of that week. The following Tuesday, 15 April 1969, the Beatles took out a quarter-page advert in the *Daily Mirror* to announce the release of the Get Back/Don't Let Me Down single, which described it as 'the Beatles as nature intended'. It then went on to describe the single as '. . . the first Beatles record which is as live as can be in this electronic age'.

The song, which was originally the title track of an album, features a lead vocal from Paul (who also wrote it) with harmonies in places from John.

The Beatles themselves had also decided to 'Get Back' to the basic three guitars and drums line-up of their first recordings. No studio trickery, no overdubs, just the Beatles, but with one addition — Billy Preston, who was brought in to supply the organ (for which he was to receive a gold disc). Preston can also be heard playing both on the following track and on the Let It Be album. The rather different version of this as featured on the Let It Be album was recorded on 27 January 1969.

Don't Let Me Down (Lennon–McCartney)   3:34

Recorded : 28 January 1969, Apple Studios, Savile Row, London

John Lennon : Lead Guitar and Lead Vocal
Paul McCartney : Bass Guitar and Harmony Vocal
George Harrison : Rhythm Guitar
Ringo Starr : Drums
Billy Preston : Organ

Previously issued as the B-side to the Get Back single on 11 April 1969, this recording, made within minutes of Get Back on 28 January 1969, features an extremely raw lead vocal from John, with harmony vocals from Paul. The Beatles are once again joined by Billy Preston who, whilst adding to the backing, also has a solo in the middle. The lyrics to this powerful blues-influenced song, written by John with Yoko in mind, are minimal, with John simply repeating the title over and over.

The Ballad Of John And Yoko (Lennon–McCartney) 2:58

Recorded : 14 April 1969, EMI Studios, Abbey Road, London

John Lennon : Acoustic Guitar, Lead Guitar, Percussion and Lead Vocal
Paul McCartney : Bass Guitar, Drums, Piano, Maracas and Harmony Vocal
George Harrison : Not Present
Ringo Starr : Not Present

This was released as a single on 20 May 1969 while Get Back was still at No. 1. It was recorded in eleven takes (take 10 being the released version) on 14 April 1969 (incidentally three days after the release of Get Back) at Abbey Road during an eight and a half hour session at which John and Paul played all the instruments heard. John is on lead vocal, acoustic and lead guitars and percussion, and Paul plays bass guitar, drums, piano and maracas together with supplying a harmony vocal in places. The song tells the story of John and Yoko's wedding in Gibraltar the previous month and their subsequent week-long bed-in for peace at the Amsterdam Hilton.

Old Brown Shoe (Harrison) 3:16

Recorded : 16 and 18 April 1969, EMI Studios, Abbey Road, London

John Lennon : Rhythm Guitar and Backing Vocal
Paul McCartney : Bass Guitar, Piano and Backing Vocal
George Harrison : Lead Guitar, Hammond Organ and Lead Vocal
Ringo Starr : Drums

Originally issued as the B-side to the 1969 single The Ballad Of John And Yoko, this was the second George Harrison song used as the B-side of a Beatles' single. (The first was The Inner Light on the B-side of Lady Madonna in 1968.) It was recorded in four takes between 16 and 18 April 1969, a few days after the completion of The Ballad Of John And Yoko. This, unlike the A-side, actually features all four Beatles and is quite an up-tempo song from George, who during the previous two years had been writing either Indian mantras or slower, more doleful songs like While My Guitar Gently Weeps and Blue Jay Way.

Across The Universe (Lennon–McCartney) 3:41

Recorded : 4 and 8 February 1968, EMI Studios, Abbey Road, London

John Lennon : Acoustic Guitar, Lead Guitar, Organ and Lead/Backing Vocal
Paul McCartney : Piano and Harmony/Backing Vocal
George Harrison : Tamboura, Maracas and Backing Vocal
Ringo Starr : Tomtoms
Lizzie Bravo : Backing Vocal
Gayleen Pease : Backing Vocal

Recorded in eight takes on 4 and 8 February 1968 during the same period as Lady Madonna, this was considered as a possible rival for the March 1968 single, but Lady Madonna was chosen instead.

Shortly after being rejected in favour of Lady Madonna, this was given to the World Wildlife Fund who included it on the charity album No One's Gonna Change Our World which was released on 12 December 1969 (Regal Starline SRS 5013). A different mix of the recording (minus the sound effects and a considerable amount of the original backing) then appeared with an orchestral and choral backing some four months later on the Let It Be album.

The track begins with the sound of birds (added for the purposes of the charity album) which then 'flies' across the stereo. When it fades the track proper begins, featuring John singing lead vocal on his own song, with Paul harmonising in places. The backing vocals were added by two young women, Lizzie Bravo and Gayleen Pease, who (whilst waiting outside to see the Beatles) were invited into the studio by Paul to add the falsetto harmony to John's lead vocal.

The lyrics to this song are some of John's most imaginative, with his incessant chorus line 'Nothing's gonna change my world' accentuating their dreamy effect.

Let It Be (Lennon–McCartney) 3:50

Recorded : 31 January and 30 April 1969 and 4 January 1970, Apple Studios, Savile Row, London and EMI Studios, Abbey Road, London

John Lennon : Bass Guitar
Paul McCartney : Piano, Maracas and Lead/Harmony Vocal
George Harrison : Lead Guitar and Harmony Vocal
Ringo Starr : Drums
Billy Preston : Organ
Session Musicians : Brass and Cellos

From Love Me Do to Let It Be was a very long (and often) winding road for the Beatles who (after a collective career spanning more than fifteen years, which began in the clubs of Liverpool and Hamburg in the late 1950s and finally ended in disarray) bowed out with this, their final single.

Paul (sounding rather like a choirboy singing a hymn at a requiem mass) leads the Beatles through this song, which was originally recorded on 31 January 1969, during the ill-fated Get Back sessions.

This and the version included on the Let It Be album, are in effect, the same basic recording. They both originate from the same eight-track master tape which contains two lead guitar tracks (one each for the two versions). The lead guitar heard on this version was overdubbed by George, during what turned out to be the Beatles final recording session (at which John wasn't present) on 4 January 1970, and the lead guitar heard on the album version is the original, recorded during the Get Back Sessions.

Let It Be, together with You Know My Name (Look Up The Number), was issued as a single on 6 March 1970.

You Know My Name (Look Up The Number)
(Lennon–McCartney)   4:20

Recorded : 17 May, 7 and 8 June 1967 and 30 April 1969, EMI Studios, Abbey Road, London

John Lennon : Maracas and Lead Vocal
Paul McCartney : Piano, Bass Guitar and Lead Vocal
George Harrison : Vibraphone and Backing Vocal
Ringo Starr : Drums, Bongos and Lead Vocal
Mal Evans : Backing Vocal
Brian Jones : Alto Saxophone

This intriguing off-beat track began life on 17 May 1967 shortly after the Sgt. Pepper's album had been completed, when a section of the backing track was recorded. On 7 and 8 June 1967 further sections were recorded and these were then edited together on 9 June the same year to form a final master track. Following that, it was abandoned. On 30 April 1969, John and Paul resurrected it and added the vocals and the sound effects, together with Mal Evans, but again it was shelved. On 26 November 1969 John edited the track down from its original six minutes to its current length of just under four and a half minutes and planned to issue it, together with another unreleased Beatles track, What's The New Mary Jane as a single under the banner of The Plastic Ono Band. At the last minute, despite being given the catalogue number Apple 1002 and a release date of 5 December 1969, it was withdrawn without explanation.

The track then finally emerged on 6 March 1970 when it was issued as the B-side of the Let It Be single. One of the interesting points concerning that release is that the catalogue number of Apple 1002 is stamped in the run-off groove.

The lyrics to this Lennon-conceived track are basically a repetition of the title, with various additional comments and sound effects thrown in for good measure. The jazz piano is supplied by Paul McCartney and the saxophone solo by Brian Jones of the Rolling Stones.

As this track (despite being originally planned as a Plastic Ono Band release) is the B-side to the Beatles' final single (and also the last track on this album) it is interesting to note that, right at the end of the track, the final comment is 'Goodbye'.

THE CHRISTMAS ALBUMS

UK Release : 18 December 1970
Apple LYN 2154 (*Fan Club Only*)
Intl CD No : To be released
Producers : George Martin and
The Beatles
Running Time : 43:58

SIDE ONE : The Beatles Christmas Record; Another Beatles Christmas Record; The Beatles Third Christmas Record; The Beatles Fourth Christmas Record.

SIDE TWO : Christmas Time Is Here Again!; The Beatles 1968 Christmas Record; The Beatles Seventh Christmas Record.

US Release : 18 December 1970
Apple SBC 100 (*Fan Club Only*)
Intl CD No : To be released
Producers : George Martin and The
The Beatles
Running Time : 43:58

SIDE ONE : The Beatles Christmas Record; Another Beatles Christmas Record; The Beatles Third Christmas Record; The Beatles Fourth Christmas Record.

SIDE TWO : Christmas Time Is Here Again!; The Beatles 1968 Christmas Record; The Beatles Seventh Christmas Record.

In the summer of 1963, with the popularity of the Beatles steadily growing and the fan club membership rapidly expanding, the volume of letters and enquiries became more difficult for the fan club secretaries, Fred Kelly and Bettina Rose, to handle and still maintain individual contact with the members.

With the membership standing at 25,000, Tony Barrow, the then PR and Publicity Manager of NEMS Enterprises (who also supervised the Beatles' Fan Club and ensured that all members got their money's worth and were kept up to date about the Beatles), came up with the idea of a Christmas record containing a personal message from the Beatles to their most devoted fans.

The first record, scripted by Tony Barrow, and originally intended as a one-off, was sent out during the first week of December 1963 to an unsuspecting 28,000 fan club members. The response was so great that the following year (by which time the fan club membership had more than doubled, to over 65,000, and Beatlemania was well and truly under way) the Beatles, having taken it for granted that Barrow's original idea was to be an annual event, recorded a further special message, a situation which was to continue until 1969.

Interest in these special fan club records became so great that each year the British music papers would review the records as though they had gone on general sale (which, unfortunately for a lot of non-fan-club members, they didn't). Radio stations would also beg for preview copies and play them with equal enthusiasm.

The idea of the 'Merry Christmas, and thank you' style of message on the first record continued through to the 1965 record. In 1966 the Beatles (always innovators) decided to be a bit different. That year their record, entitled Pantomime : Everywhere It's Christmas, contained just that — a pantomime! The record centres around the idea that everywhere it's Christmas (at the end of every year) and it contains three new songs : the title track plus Orowanyna and Please Don't Bring Your Banjo Back. For the 1967 record the Beatles continued in their 'Goonish' style of humour, this time centring the situation around a visit to BBC Broadcasting House, and again the record contains songs unavailable elsewhere.

In 1968 the enthusiastic banter of the earlier records and the lunacy of the 1966 and 1967 recordings had all but disappeared, to be replaced by a growing feeling of animosity between the Beatles. For both the 1968 and 1969 Christmas records the Beatles recorded their contributions separately and entrusted the job of producing a finished record to Kenny Everett, who edited the separate pieces together.

With no new material for Christmas 1970, the fan club compiled the previous seven Christmas records into an album entitled From Then To You which was sent to every member of the fan club as that year's Christmas record. In America, where the singles hadn't been issued, the album was retitled The Beatles Christmas Album. The American version also features a far superior sleeve, similar in style to the sleeve of the A Hard Day's Night album. This, unlike the British sleeve, which uses the cover of the 1963 Christmas record, shows each of the Beatles in various stages of their career, with four group photographs also taken at various times throughout the sixties.

The original flexi-disc singles (which were made by Lyntone Recordings), together with both pressings of the album (which contain all of those seven flexi-discs), contain a whole host of songs unavailable on any other Beatles record, and which are now extremely valuable collector's items.

The Beatles Christmas Record 5:00

Recorded : 17 October 1963, EMI Studios, Abbey Road, London

John Lennon : Talking and Singing
Paul McCartney : Talking and Singing
George Harrison : Talking and Singing
Ringo Starr : Talking and Singing

This record was recorded in a single afternoon session after the Beatles had completed I Want To Hold Your Hand and This Boy (which became their biggest-selling single and was to break all records world-wide, and also help establish Beatlemania in America).

Originally they worked from a script written for them by Tony Barrow, but this was quickly abandoned as both the recording and ad-libbing progressed.

The finished recording, produced by George Martin, was then released/sent out to members of the fan club on 6 December 1963 (Lyntone LYN 492).

The track opens with John singing the first of many reworded versions of Good King Wenceslas; he then launches into his scripted speech (which he very quickly abandons) with 'Hello, this is John speaking with his voice.' He goes on to say what a good year it's been and mentions topping the bill at the London Palladium and also being invited to perform at the Royal Variety Show (at which point he starts to whistle God Save The Queen, which the rest of the Beatles quickly join in). He continues with his very laboured speech and finishes off with a further reworded version of Good King Wenceslas.

Paul, who follows, comments that the Beatles much prefer making records to performing live and also mentions that they have been recording all day before starting to record this. (Having been performing live for at least five years by this point in their career, Paul's comments are perfectly understandable.) John then launches into a further version of Good King Wenceslas, this time in German!

Following that little bout of lunacy Ringo comes next and, prompted by Paul, wishes everyone a merry Christmas and then begins to sing Good King Wenceslas, in jazz. George, who follows, thanks the fan club secretaries (including the non-existent Ann Collingham) and finishes off with his version of Good King Wenceslas. The track comes to a close with a reworded version of Rudolph the Red-Nosed Reindeer ('Rudolph the Red-Nosed Ringo, Had a very shiny nose, When everybody picked it . . .') and finally ends with all four Beatles saying 'Merry Christmas everybody'.

Another Beatles Christmas Record 4:05

Recorded : 26 October 1964, EMI Studios, Abbey Road, London

John Lennon : Piano, Lead Vocal and Talking
Paul McCartney : Harmony Vocal and Talking
George Harrison : Harmony Vocal and Talking
Ringo Starr : Harmony Vocal and Talking

This recording, originally released on 18 December 1964 (Lyntone LYN 757), opens with a wildly out-of-tune Jingle Bells and continues with four very much more confident-sounding Beatles using the script as a basis for their lunacy. Paul starts it off by thanking people for buying all the records and adds, 'We hope you've enjoyed listening to the records as much as we've enjoyed melting them.'

John, having managed to get away with bad language on the *Around The Beatles* TV special earlier in the year, gets away with it again when he comments that 'It's been a busy year Beatles Peedles' ('Peedle' is Hamburg slang for the male organ), and then thanks everyone for buying his book *In His Own Write*.

Next is George, who thanks everyone for going to see the film *A Hard Day's Night* and mentions that the next film (*Help!*) will be in colour. Ringo then thanks the fans for just being fans and mentions the touring of 1964 and the amazing airport receptions.

Following their individual messages John starts playing the piano and begins to sing the first of the many songs featured on this album which are unavailable elsewhere, Can You Wash Your Father's Shirts. He is immediately joined by the remaining Beatles to perform this rather short, though still highly enjoyable song. The track finishes with all four Beatles wishing everyone a happy Christmas.

The Beatles Third Christmas Record   6:26

Recorded : 8 November 1965, EMI Studios, Abbey Road, London

John Lennon : Acoustic Guitar, Solo Vocal, Harmony Vocal and Talking
Paul McCartney : Harmony Vocal and Talking
George Harrison : Harmony Vocal and Talking
Ringo Starr : Tambourine, Harmony Vocal and Talking

Originally released on 17 December 1965 (Lyntone LYN 948), this, like the 1963 record, was recorded in a single afternoon session. With this recording a certain change in their attitude begins to show. After the constant touring, Beatlemania, two films and constant media attention, they were obviously getting a bit fed up with it all.

The photograph on the front cover of the single was taken by Robert Whitaker during the filming of the Granada TV special *The Music Of Lennon And McCartney* at the beginning of November.

This track opens with all four Beatles singing Yesterday which eventually goes out of tune. Following that there are various 'thank you' messages plus the odd cynical comment such as, 'Well Ringo, what have we done this year?' asks Paul.

'We've done a lot of things this year, Paul' replies Ringo, 'Well we've been away ... like last year.'

John then launches into a medley of lunatic songs, including an upbeat version of Auld Lang Syne. Paul is next and makes a few comments before John begins to sing The Four Tops' record It's The Same Old Song, which is brought to an abrupt end by George shouting 'Copyright Johnny'.

Paul then says 'Ey, er, alright what are we gonna do what's out of copyright?'

'Ow about We'll Gather Lilacs In An Old Brown Shoe?' suggests John.

Ringo then says 'Let's play a request for all the boys in BEAORE' (meaning BAOR). John and Ringo then go into a send-up of Two Way Family Favourites before John kicks off with a reworded/anti-war version of Auld Lang Syne ('Should old acquaintance be forgot, and never brought to hand, down in Vietnam and old penance too, and look at all those bodies floatin''), showing his thoughts on the war that was currently being fought in Vietnam. His thoughts in other directions are also made very obvious when, slightly later, he says, 'It's an all-white policy in this group.'

The record continues with various comments and John performs a further lunatic song before all four Beatles return to their reworded version of Yesterday. The record finishes with the group reverting to a Liverpool 'scouse' accent and John saying, 'This is Johnny Rhythm just sayin' good night to yez all and god bless yez.'

The Beatles Fourth Christmas Record
Pantomime : Everywhere It's Christmas   6:40

Recorded : 25 November 1966, Dick James Music, New Oxford Street, London

John Lennon : Harmony Vocal and Talking
Paul McCartney : Piano, Lead Vocal, Harmony Vocal and Talking
George Harrison : Harmony Vocal and Talking
Ringo Starr : Harmony Vocal and Talking
Mal Evans : Talking

The 1966 and 1967 records are undoubtedly the highlights of the seven Christmas singles sent to members of the Beatles' fan club. During this, and the 1967 record, they move away from the 'Merry Christmas and thank you for buying our records' style message of the previous three records and perform a pantomime instead. Scripted by the Beatles, under the strong influence of John Lennon (and possibly various illegal substances as well!), they set out to prove that, indeed, Everywhere It's Christmas (at the end of every year).

For this recording, which was originally released on 16 December 1966 (Lyntone LYN 1145) and features a front cover painting by Paul McCartney, the Beatles used a rather unusual setting away from Abbey Road — the recording studio in the offices of Dick James Music (where both John and Paul had recorded a number of demos of their songs). Unlike the previous records, which were recorded at the end of other sessions, the Beatles actually set up a special session specifically to record this. It contains three new songs which, unlike the various throw-away songs of the earlier records, were specially written. The first, Everywhere It's Christmas, opens the recording and features Paul on lead vocal and piano with John, George and Ringo throwing in odd comments and providing the harmony vocals. As it fades the second song, Orowanyna, performed by a small Corsican Choir (the Beatles), begins (and so does the 'Goonish' lunacy).

This time the lunacy includes such things as two elderly Scotsmen (John and George) high in the Swiss Alps munching on a rare cheese, and a loyal toast to the Queen on board HMS Tremendous (the Yellow Submarine?). The recording also includes a short sketch featuring John and George as Podgy The Bear and Jasper and a visit to Felpin Mansions where Paul (later joined by the remaining three Beatles) performs the third specially written song, Please Don't Bring Your Banjo Back. After a short message from Mal Evans the track finishes with a reprise of Everywhere It's Christmas.

SIDE TWO

Christmas Time Is Here Again! (Lennon–McCartney–Harrison–Starkey)   6:10

Recorded : 28 November 1967, EMI Studios, Abbey Road, London

John Lennon : Timpani, Harmony Vocal and Talking
Paul McCartney : Bass Guitar, Piano, Lead Vocal and Talking
George Harrison : Acoustic Guitar, Harmony Vocal and Talking
Ringo Starr : Drums and Talking
George Martin : Organ and Talking
Mal Evans : Talking
Victor Spinetti : Tap Dancing and Talking

Originally released on 15 December 1967 (Lyntone LYN 1360), this recording, which features much of the studio trickery which the Beatles had been experimenting with during 1966 and 1967, is based around a visit to BBC Broadcasting House and features, amongst other things, Ringo and Victor Spinetti tap dancing! This was the last Christmas record which the Beatles recorded together as a group and is also the last of these special recordings to be produced by George Martin. The front cover, similar in style to the Sgt. Pepper's sleeve, was designed by John and Ringo, and the painting on the back was by Julian Lennon. As with the Magical Mystery Tour album and E.P.s, the label of the single mentions the existence of the then mysterious Apple.

Like the 1966 record, this recording features songs specially written for the occasion. The title track, Christmas Time Is Here Again (the only new song featured on these special records to have actually been copyrighted), crops up at various times throughout, whilst Get One Of These For Your Trousers appears twice and Plenty Of Jam Jars (credited to The Ravellers) appears once.

The recording begins with the title song before developing into yet more 'Goonish' lunacy, which includes a couple of auditions, an interview with a typically evasive politician and a quiz show. Sections of these are then mixed in with one of the later appearances of Christmas Time Is Here Again to create a more musical version of the idea which John was to use some six months later to create Revolution 9.

Mal Evans again makes a brief appearance, as does George Martin, when just near the end he says, 'They'd like to thank you for a wonderful year.'

The recording ends with George Martin playing Auld Lang Syne on an organ while John (in his best Scottish accent) recites a poem, *When Christmas Time Is Over*.

The Beatles 1968 Christmas Record   7:55

Recorded : Autumn 1968 (Locations vary)

John Lennon : Talking
Paul McCartney : Acoustic Guitar, Solo Vocal and Talking
George Harrison : Talking
Ringo Starr : Talking
Yoko Ono : Talking
Mal Evans : Talking
Tiny Tim : Ukelele, Solo Vocal and Talking

This is the first of two Christmas records compiled from recordings made by each individual Beatle. Due to a number of factors, the growing animosity between the Beatles was such that they recorded their individual sections separately : John at his home in Weybridge, Surrey; Paul at his home in St John's Wood, London; George in California, USA while he was recording side two of his second solo album Electronic Sound (UK : Zapple 02; US : Zapple ST 3358); and Ringo at his home in Ascot, Berkshire. The individual recordings were then given to Kenny Everett who edited the different sections together and is credited on the sleeve of the single as producer. The recording was released on 29 December 1968 (Lyntone LYN 1743/4). The painting on the front cover was by Julian Lennon.

The track starts off with an introduction from Ringo which is quickly followed by the intro of Ob-La-Di, Ob-La-Da. Paul's sole contribution to the record is a new song, Happy Christmas, Happy New Year, which is heard twice. On the first version he accompanies himself with an acoustic guitar. This is followed by a speeded-up recording of Helter Skelter. John then makes his first appearance, reading the first of two poems, *Jock and Yono*, about how he and Yoko 'battled on against overwhelming oddities, including some of their beast friends'. George, with Mal Evans, comes next and they both wish everyone a happy Christmas. Ringo makes his second appearance with a little bit of lunacy while Yer Blues plays in the background. Paul then returns with a further short rendition of his earlier song and is quickly followed by John reading the second of his two poems *Once Upon A Pool Table*. Finally George introduces Tiny Tim who, with a little bit of encouragement from George, performs Nowhere Man the way that only Tiny Tim could!

The Beatles Seventh Christmas Record   7:42

Recorded : Autumn 1969 (Locations vary)

John Lennon : Acoustic Guitar, Solo Vocal and Talking
Paul McCartney : Acoustic Guitar, Electric Guitar, Solo Vocal and Talking
George Harrison : Talking
Ringo Starr : Acoustic Guitar, Solo Vocal and Talking
Yoko Ono : Piano, Harmony Vocal and Talking

Like the 1968 Christmas record, this was compiled by Kenny Everett (who is credited on the sleeve of the single under his real name of Maurice Cole) from recordings made by each of the four Beatles. It could be described as a John and Yoko Christmas record, since the contributions by the remaining three

Beatles are negligible. The longest contribution comes from Ringo who appears three times during the recording, once singing Good Evening To You Gentlemen, backed by an acoustic guitar, later to plug the film *Magic Christian* and finally at the end where he is heard laughing. Paul appears only once with a new song This Is To Wish You A Merry Merry Christmas and George's sole contribution lasts just over four seconds.

The photograph used for the front cover of the single was taken by Ringo and the drawing on the back was by Ringo's son Zak. The single was originally released on 19 December 1969 (Lyntone LYN 1970/1).

John and Yoko, who start the track off by discussing their thoughts on Christmas, recorded their section at Tittenhurst Park, Ascot, Berks. George's contribution, recorded at Apple in Savile Row, London, is a brief happy Christmas, the only time that George appears. Next comes Ringo performing Good Evening To You Gentlemen (which was recorded at his home in Weybridge, Surrey). This is quickly followed by a section of The End from Abbey Road which continues playing as John and Yoko make their second appearance, this time discussing the wall around Tittenhurst Park! Paul (who recorded his section at his home in St John's Wood, London) comes next and performs two versions of his new song, This Is To Wish You A Merry Merry Christmas, with a brief Christmas message in between.

John and Yoko reappear and discuss the coming decade of the 1970s, during which John sings Good King Wenceslas. John and Yoko then perform two versions of a rather avant-garde Christmas song with John playing an acoustic guitar. Ringo then makes a brief reappearance to plug the film *Magic Christian* before a return to John and Yoko who discuss Christmas presents. The track ends with a cathedral choir singing Noël, with Ringo making a final reappearance, laughing.

APPENDICES

50 The Alternative Versions

This chapter deals with a subject which has long been popular with Beatles' fans, the alternative versions of recordings issued by the Beatles which are available. There are a considerable number of these, the earliest example being Love Me Do, where the original single and the version included on the Please Please Me album are two entirely, and noticeably, different recordings. It is possible to obtain *seven* different edits of I Am The Walrus, four each of I'm Only Sleeping and Penny Lane, and at least two edits of a further 60 songs, as this chapter will reveal.

For ease of reference the British and American releases have been used as a basic guide even though some, or most, of the recordings mentioned here are available elsewhere in the world. Collected together from these records are details of some 63 songs involving between them a staggering 139 different recordings and versions. Of these 107 are available in both Britain and America, whilst seventeen are only available in Britain and a further thirteen are only available in America. There is also one version of I Am The Walrus which is currently only available on a German single, and a different stereo mix of I Want To Hold Your Hand which is, at present, only available on an Australian single. Neither of these two recordings is currently available in either Britain or America.

For each song, all known versions have been listed together with details of timings, differences and where each recording can be found. If the same recording is available on more than one record then, in the main, details of its first appearance are given. Not included as separate versions are recordings that feature a premature fade-out, as do several of the mono versions, for example, A Hard Day's Night, which on the mono version of the album, is a few seconds shorter than the stereo version. To include all of these would not do justice to those recordings that have differences which are considerably more noticeable. One exception to this is Hey Jude, which, as included on the American 20 Greatest Hits album, is considerably shorter than the normal version. Also not included are those 'Alternative Versions' created mainly by Capitol Records in America, who for reasons of their own saw fit to either edit in or edit out (in most cases badly) whole sections of recordings. The worst cases of sections being edited in are on A Hard Day's Night, where the final vocal section has been so badly edited in on the cassette version (United Artists K-9006) that it is an embarrassment to listen to. Also on the eight-track version of Sgt. Pepper's (8XT 2653) the last verse of the Sgt. Pepper's reprise has been repeated via such a bad edit that it sounds as though it were done by a drunken amateur. As for sections being edited out, the favourite target by Capitol seems to have been the 'White Album'. On the open reel versions of this album (Capitol L-101/102) there are whole sections missing from Don't Pass Me By, Glass Onion, Helter Skelter and Revolution 9, plus small sections missing from many of the other tracks.

Other odd or bad edits from around the world include the version of Devil In Her Heart as included on the Mexican album The Beatles Volume 3 (Capitol SLEM 045) : on this extremely bad edit a whole chunk of the coda has been so badly edited out that on first listening it sounds as though the record jumps. The same situation occurs with the Brazilian release of Penny Lane, only in this case if affects more than one record. For reasons known only to EMI Brazil the words 'in summer' have been edited out of nearly every release of this recording in Brazil. Similarly, when A Day in the Life was issued as a single world-wide in 1978, each country prepared its own master for the single, which has resulted in numerous edits, some of which have some *very* strange beginnings.

Finally, there is also included a list of Beatles' recordings that are (at present) only available in their mono form.

ACROSS THE UNIVERSE
Version 1   3:41
As included on the album Past Masters — Volume Two (Parlophone BPM 2)
Version 2   3:51
As included on the album Let It Be (Apple PCS 7096)

Although both versions of this track originate from the same recording, the first has the sound of birds at the beginning and backing vocals from Paul and two girls — Lizzie Bravo and Gayleen Pease — who were invited into the recording session. It is slightly faster than version 2, which has a solo vocal from John and an orchestral backing.

ALL MY LOVING
Version 1   2:04
As included on the album With The Beatles (Parlophone PCS 3045)
Version 2   2:07
As included on the eight-album set The Beatles Box (Parlophone/World Records SM 701–708)

Version 2 includes five taps of a hi-hat just prior to the beginning of the recording. These are missing from version 1.

ALL YOU NEED IS LOVE
Version 1   3:57
As available on the single (Parlophone R5620)
Version 2   3:47
As included on the album Yellow Submarine (Apple PCS 7070)

Although both these recordings were made on the same day and may appear to sound the same, they are entirely different. Version 1 is, at present, only available in mono. Version 2, in stereo, is not simply a stereo mix of version 1 : it is an entirely different recording. There are slight but significant differences between the lead vocals and also certain sections of the backing. Version 2 is also ten seconds shorter than version 1.

AND I LOVE HER
Version 1   2:27
As included on the American version of the album A Hard Day's Night (United Artists UAS 6366)
Version 2   2:27
As included on the British version of the album A Hard Day's Night (Parlophone PCS 3058)
Version 3   2:36
As included on the eight-album set The Beatles Box (Parlophone/World Records SM 701–708)

The three versions of this originate from the same recording and are simply different stages of that recording. Version 1 features Paul's lead vocal, mostly on its own, with only the chorus double-tracked; version 2 features Paul's lead vocal double-tracked, and then triple-tracked for the chorus. Version 3 has the same double-tracked lead vocals as version 2, but also has the guitar riff at the ending repeated six times, rather than four as on versions 1 and 2. There is also reputed to be a version of this song which features the ending riff repeated only twice — whether this actually exists or not has yet to be confirmed.

BABY, YOU'RE A RICH MAN
Version 1   3:03
As available on the single (Parlophone R5620)
Version 2   3:00
As included on the eight-album set The Beatles Box (Parlophone/World Records SM 701–708)

Although both versions of this originate from the same four-track master tape, the mono version (version 1) has an entirely different feel to it. This is due to the fact that it features 'tape spin', a studio trick which involves tape-delay fed back on itself, causing a gradual stuttering crescendo. In 1971, after a request for a stereo version, George Martin, assisted by Geoff Emerick, attempted to create a stereo version which also featured 'tape spin'. After spending nearly half an hour attempting to duplicate this effect, Martin abandoned it and did a straightforward stereo mix of what was on the original one-inch master, thereby creating version 2.

BACK IN THE USSR
Version 1   2:45
As included on the mono version of the double album The Beatles (Apple PMC 7067–8)
Version 2   2:45
As included on the stereo version of the double album The Beatles (Apple PCS 7067–8)

The sound effects as heard on both versions of this are in different places and the stereo recording includes some screams and shouts during the instrumental break, which are not heard on the mono version. Right at the end of the track, a final drumbeat can be heard on the mono version which is missing from the stereo recording.

BLACKBIRD
Version 1   2:20
As included on the mono version of the double album The Beatles (Apple PMC 7067–8)
Version 2   2:20
As included on the stereo version of the double album The Beatles (Apple PCS 7067–8)

Like a number of tracks on the 'White Album' there are slight, almost unnoticeable differences between the mono and stereo mixings. With this track the 'bird' sounds included are different on both tracks and are also in slightly different places.

BLUE JAY WAY
Version 1 3:50
As included on the mono version of the double E.P. Magical Mystery Tour (Parlophone MMT 1)
Version 2 3:50
As included on the stereo version of the double E.P. Magical Mystery Tour (Parlophone SMMT 1)

Both versions of this are essentially the same, but at various points the stereo recording includes backwards tapes which are not heard on the mono version. The multiple echo on the cello near the end is also missing from the mono version, as is the final organ note.

DAY TRIPPER
Version 1 2:37
As included on the stereo version of the album Past Masters — Volume Two, (Parlophone BPM 2)
Version 2 2:37
As included on the double album The Beatles 1962–1966 (Apple PCSP 717)

Although both recordings are basically the same, version 1 has the guitar intro double-tracked, with each track on a separate channel, and the vocals have had echo added. Version 2 has the guitar intro single-tracked on the left-hand channel only, and there is no echo on the vocals.

DON'T PASS ME BY
Version 1 3:45
As included on the mono version of the double album The Beatles (Apple PMC 7067–8)
Version 2 3:52
As included on the stereo version of the double album The Beatles (Apple PCS 7067–8)

With the exception of the violin at the end these two recordings are the same. Version 1 is slightly faster than version 2, due to the fact that it has been speeded up somewhat, making it seven seconds shorter than version 2 — this has the effect of transposing Ringo's voice into a higher key and giving the track a bouncier feel.

FLYING
Version 1 2:16
As included on the mono version of the double E.P. Magical Mystery Tour (Parlophone MMT 1)
Version 2 2:16
As included on the stereo version of the double E.P. Magical Mystery Tour (Parlophone SMMT 1)

The mono version of this includes some extra bass guitar and piano at the beginning which are not heard on the stereo recording. The final section of the vocal track included on the stereo version is absent from the mono. The sound effects at the end also appear earlier on the mono version.

THE FOOL ON THE HILL
Version 1 3:00
As included on the mono version of the double E.P. Magical Mystery Tour
(Parlophone MMT 1)
Version 2 3:00
As included on the stereo version of the double E.P. Magical Mystery Tour
(Parlophone SMMT 1)
 The stereo version includes some extra flute passages which are absent
from the mono recording, as are parts of the vocal track just near the end.

FROM ME TO YOU
Version 1 1:55
As included on the album Past Masters — Volume One (Parlophone BPM 1)
Version 2 1:55
As included on the double album The Beatles 1962–1966 (Apple PCSP 717)
 Version 1 (mono) includes a harmonica during the intro which is missing
from version 2 (stereo).

GET BACK
Version 1 3:11
As included on the album Past Masters — Volume Two (Parlophone BPM 2)
Version 2 3:09
As included on the album Let It Be (Apple PCS 7096)
 The differences between these two recordings are immediately noticeable.
Version 2 has a spoken intro not included on version 1. The endings are also
entirely different : whilst version 1 includes an extra verse and a fade, version
2 just stops and we hear John Lennon's classic statement 'I'd like to say "thank
you" on behalf of the group and ourselves and I hope we passed the audition.'

GOOD DAY SUNSHINE
Version 1 2:08
As included on the mono version of the album Revolver
(Parlophone PMC 7009)
Version 2 2:08
As included on the stereo version of the album Revolver
(Parlophone PCS 7009)
 On first listening the mono version appears to be exactly the same as the
stereo mix, which is almost true, except that the mono version includes extra
drum beats during the fade which are missing from the stereo version.

GOOD MORNING, GOOD MORNING
Version 1 2:35
As included on the mono version of the album Sgt. Pepper's Lonely Hearts
Club Band (Parlophone PMC 7027)
Version 2 2:35
As included on the stereo version of the album Sgt. Pepper's Lonely Hearts
Club Band (Parlophone PCS 7027)
 The basic track is the same for both versions, but on the mono version the
sound effects begin slightly earlier than on the stereo version.

GOT TO GET YOU INTO MY LIFE
Version 1   2:39
As included on the mono version of the album Revolver
(Parlophone PMC 7009)
Version 2   2:31
As included on the stereo version of the album Revolver
(Parlophone PCS 7009)

A lot of people are under the mistaken impression that the vocal track differs on both versions and that the closing lines during the fade are different. Although this is partially true, the mono and stereo versions are in fact exactly the same. The reason why the lyrics at the end appear to sound different is not because there are two separate lead vocals but because the mono version features an extra line of lyrics due to a longer fade-out.

HELP!
Version 1   2:16
As included on the mono version of the album Help! (Parlophone PMC 1255)
Version 2   2:16
As included on the stereo version of the album Help! (Parlophone PCS 3071)

Although these recordings may sound the same, they actually have a different lead vocal. Halfway through the first verse of version 1 the lyrics are 'And now these days . . .', whereas on version 2, the lyrics are 'But now these days . . .'. They are two entirely different recordings.

HELTER SKELTER
Version 1   3:38
As included on the mono version of the double album The Beatles (Apple PMC 7067–8)
Version 2   4:30
As included on the stereo version of the double album The Beatles (Apple PCS 7067–8)

Although the mono and stereo versions are, in effect, the same recording, they are mixed and edited differently. The fade-out of the mono version has several notes missing and the drumming is different. When it fades it does not reappear, as does the stereo version, and it thereby misses Ringo's statement 'I've got blisters on my fingers' — words sometimes credited erroneously to John.

HEY JUDE
Version 1   7:11
As included on the album Past Masters — Volume Two (Parlophone BPM 2)
Version 2   5:05
As included on the American album 20 Greatest Hits (Capitol SV 12245)

Version 2, although nearly two minutes shorter than version 1, is still the same recording but with an early fade-out. John Lennon's profanity, which is heard 5 minutes 40 seconds into the recording, is missing from the shorter version.

HONEY PIE
Version 1   2:42
As included on the mono version of the double album The Beatles (Apple PMC 7067–8)

Version 2   2:42

As included on the stereo version of the double album The Beatles (Apple PCS 7067–8)

Version 1 includes an extra guitar phrase at the end of the instrumental break which is missing from version 2.

I AM THE WALRUS

There are seven versions of this song, all slightly different edits of the same recording. This should have made them all slightly different lengths but because each one is slowed down or speeded up slightly they are all exactly the same timing.

Version 1   4:35

As included on the mono version of the double E.P. Magical Mystery Tour (Parlophone MMT 1)

The organ intro here is repeated four times as opposed to six on some other versions. Between the lyrics 'I'm crying' and 'Sitting on a cornflake' the drum track cuts out. Later when John repeats 'I'm crying' four times just before 'Yellow matter custard' the drum track again disappears between the first and second 'I'm crying'.

Version 2   4:35

As available on the American single (Capitol 2056)

Again the organ intro is repeated four times, then between the lyrics 'I'm crying' and 'Sitting on a cornflake' only the hi-hat and snare drum disappears, the remaining drum track still present. Then, as with version 1, during the four repeats of 'I'm crying', just before 'Yellow matter custard' the drum track again cuts out. Following the four repeats of 'I'm crying' there are some extra beats not heard on version 1.

Version 3   4:35

As included on the album Magical Mystery Tour (Parlophone PCTC 255)

This version also has the organ intro repeated four times. Then between the lyrics 'I'm crying' and 'Sitting on a cornflake', the main drum track cuts out leaving only the hi-hat and the snare drum. Finally, during the four repeats of 'I'm crying' the entire drum track cuts out.

Version 4   4:35

As available on the German single (Odeon 1 C 006–04 477)

This is virtually the same as version 3 except here the organ intro is repeated six times.

Version 5   4:35

As included on the stereo version of the double E.P. Magical Mystery Tour (Parlophone SMMT 1)

The organ intro here is repeated six times and the drum track is present throughout.

Version 6   4:35

As included on the eight-album set The Beatles Box (Parlophone/World Records SM 701–708)

This sixth version includes both the organ intro repeated six times and the few extra beats in the middle of the recording. It is the full version edited from versions 2 and 5.

Version 7   4:35

As included on the stereo version of the compact disc Magical Mystery Tour (Parlophone CDP 7 48062 2)

This is basically the same as version 5, but on some of the early copies the 'radio noises' heard just before the track changes from stereo to electronic stereo have been repeated.

I CALL YOUR NAME
Version 1   2:05
As included on the E.P. Long Tall Sally (Parlophone GEP 8913)
Version 2   2:05
As included on the stereo version of the American album The Beatles Second (Capitol ST 2080)
Version 3   2:05
As included on the stereo version of the album Past Masters — Volume One (Parlophone BPM 1)

   Although in effect the same recording, on version 1 the backing cowbell starts at the beginning of the recording, while on version 2 it does not start until half-way through the opening line and on version 3 it does not start until after the opening line.

I DON'T WANT TO SPOIL THE PARTY
Version 1   2:33
As included on the mono version of the album Beatles For Sale (Parlophone PMC 1240)
Version 2   2:33
As included on the stereo version of the album Beatles For Sale (Parlophone PCS 3062)

   There are two 'whoops' just before the instrumental break on the stereo version which are absent from the mono version.

I FEEL FINE
Version 1   2:20
As available on the single (Parlophone R5200)
Version 2   2:17
As included on the stereo version of the album Past Masters — Volume One (Parlophone BPM 1)
Version 3   2:19
As included on the double album The Beatles 1962–1966 (Apple PCSP 717)

   Version 1 has an entirely different lead vocal from versions 2 and 3. The latter two are basically the same recording except for two seconds of mysterious whispering on version 3, just before the beginning of the track.

I SHOULD HAVE KNOWN BETTER
Version 1   2:16
As included on the stereo version of the album A Hard Day's Night (Parlophone PCS 3058)
Version 2   2:16
As included on the American version of the album Reel Music (Capitol SV 12199)

   These recordings differ only in the harmonica intro. On version 1, this cuts out briefly, whereas on version 2 it is complete.

I WANT TO HOLD YOUR HAND
Version 1   2:24
As included on the stereo version of the album Past Masters — Volume One (Parlophone BPM 1)

Version 2   2:24
As included on the Australian single (Parlophone A-8103)
    Although both versions of this are actually the same recording, version 2 is remixed and has the vocals, which are in the centre of the stereo on version 1, mixed on to the right-hand channel. It also has the rhythm guitar which on version 1 is on the right-hand channel, mixed in to the centre.

I WILL
Version 1   1:46
As included on the mono version of the double album The Beatles (Apple PMC 7067–8)
Version 2   1:46
As included on the stereo version of the double album The Beatles (Apple PCS 7067–8)
    The bass guitar, which starts at the beginning of the stereo version, doesn't start until after the first verse on the mono version.

IF I FELL
Version 1   2:18
As included on the mono version of the album A Hard Day's Night (Parlophone PMC 1230)
Version 2   2:18
As included on the stereo version of the album A Hard Day's Night (Parlophone PCS 3058)
    The mono version single-tracks John's lead vocal intro, whereas the stereo version double-tracks it. Both feature a duet between John and Paul.
    On the stereo version, when they reach, for the second time, 'And I would be sad if our new love, was in vain' Paul's voice gives out on the word 'vain'. On the mono version, Paul sings the complete line, although on 'vain' his voice sounds strained.

I'LL CRY INSTEAD
Version 1   1:44
As included on the British album A Hard Day's Night (Parlophone PCS 3058)
Version 2   2:06
As included on the American album A Hard Day's Night (United Artists UAS 6366)
    Both versions originate from the same recording. Version 2 includes a repeat of the first verse just before the final verse; this is missing from version 1.

I'M LOOKING THROUGH YOU
Version 1   2:20
As included on the British album Rubber Soul (Parlophone PCS 3075)
Version 2   2:27
As included on the American album Rubber Soul (Capitol ST 2442)
    Although these are from the same basic recording, version 2 has two false starts which are not included on version 1.

I'M ONLY SLEEPING
Version 1   2:58
As included on the mono version of the British album Revolver (Parlophone PMC 7009)
Version 2   2:58
As included on the mono version of the American album Yesterday ... And Today (Capitol T 2553)
Version 3   2:58
As included on the stereo version of the British album Revolver (Parlophone PCS 7009)
Version 4   2:58
As included on the stereo version of the American album Yesterday ... And Today (Capitol ST 2553)

Versions 1 and 2, in mono, include backwards guitar during the third verse which is missing from versions 3 and 4. On version 2, moreover, there is a lot more backwards guitar during the third verse than there is on version 1. The backwards guitar at the end of version 2 starts a lot later than on any of the other versions.

Versions 3 and 4, which are both in stereo, appear to sound the same, but actually have the backwards guitar in slightly different places. During the second verse the backwards guitar starts earlier on version 4, and there is also more of it than on version 3. Then at the beginning of the instrumental break on version 4, where, on all the other versions, the backwards guitar starts immediately after John Lennon stops singing, it starts one beat later.

IT'S ONLY LOVE
Version 1   1:53
As included on the stereo version of the album Help! (Parlophone PCS 3071)
Version 2   1:53
As included on the stereo version of the compact disc Help! (Parlophone CDP 7 46439 2)

When EMI finally got round to releasing the Beatles' albums on compact disc, George Martin was called upon to prepare the digital masters for release. With the first four albums he cleaned up the mono versions and these were subsequently released world-wide on compact disc in 1987. With the Help! and Rubber Soul albums Martin returned to the original four-track master tapes and cleaned and remixed them. In doing so he also 'repaired' a fault on the stereo version of It's Only Love. On the original album version, part of the vocal track cuts out during the first chorus — this is now complete on the compact disc version.

KOMM, GIB MIR DEINE HAND
Version 1   2:24
As included on the British album The Beatles Rarities (Parlophone PCM 1001)
Version 2   2:24
As included on the American album Something New (Capitol ST 2018)
Although both recordings are virtually the same, version 2 has various screams and shouts over the musical intro which are missing from version 1.

LET IT BE
Version 1   3:50
As included on the album Past Masters — Volume Two (Parlophone BPM 2)

Version 2 4:01
As included on the album Let It Be (Apple PCS 7096)
    Both recordings originate from the same eight-track master tape. Version 2 is actually the original recording (complete with a sloppy lead guitar solo from George), whilst version 1 features a re-recorded, and far superior, guitar solo.

LOVE ME DO
Version 1 2:22
As included on the album Past Masters — Volume One (Parlophone BPM 1)
Version 2 2:19
As included on the album Please Please Me (Parlophone PCS 3042)
    Version 1 has Ringo on drums, while version 2 features Andy White (a session musician) on drums with Ringo on tambourine. The original version, besides not featuring a tambourine, is also slightly slower and in a different key; there is also hand-clapping during the harmonica solo. (For the history behind these two recordings see the Please Please Me album.)

MAGICAL MYSTERY TOUR
Version 1 2:48
As included on the mono version of the double E.P. Magical Mystery Tour (Parlophone MMT 1)
Version 2 2:48
As included on the stereo version of the double E.P. Magical Mystery Tour (Parlophone SMMT 1)
    On the mono version the sustained trumpet notes end three beats before the sustained 'now' at the end of the line 'The Magical Mystery Tour is hoping to take you away, hoping to take you away, now'. On the stereo version the sustained trumpet notes continue to the end of the sustained 'now'.

MONEY
Version 1 2:47
As included on the mono version of the album With The Beatles (Parlophone PMC 1206)
Version 2 2:47
As included on the stereo version of the album With The Beatles (Parlophone PCS 3045)
    These are two different recordings. The first, in mono, is slightly slower and has Ringo tapping his drumsticks together in time with the piano intro. John's lead vocal is also given more echo than on the stereo version, which does not include the drumstick tapping.

NO REPLY
Version 1 2:15
As included on the mono version of the album Beatles For Sale (Parlophone PMC 1240)
Version 2 2:15
As included on the stereo version of the album Beatles For Sale (Parlophone PCS 3062)
    On version 2 the first two lines of the second verse are single-tracked,

whereas on version 1 they are double-tracked. At the end of the same verse the words 'in my place' have backing vocals on all three words on version 2 but on version 1 only on the word 'place'.

NORWEGIAN WOOD (THIS BIRD HAS FLOWN)
Version 1   2:00
As included on the mono version of the album Rubber Soul (Parlophone PMC 1267)
Version 2   2:00
As included on the stereo version of the album Rubber Soul (Parlophone PCS 3075)

On the mono version someone coughs just after the line 'She told me to sit anywhere.' This has been left off the stereo version.

OB-LA-DI, OB-LA-DA
Version 1   3:10
As included on the mono version of the double album The Beatles (Apple PMC 7067–8)
Version 2   3:10
As included on the stereo version of the double album The Beatles (Apple PCS 7067–8)

Version 2 includes hand-clapping during the piano intro which is missing from version 1.

PAPERBACK WRITER
Version 1   2:25
As available on the single (Parlophone R5452)
Version 2   2:25
As included on the album Past Masters — Volume Two (Parlophone BPM 2)
Version 3   2:25
As included on the album Hey Jude (Parlophone PCS 7184)

Version 1, in mono, includes four taps during the multiple-echo sections which, together with some other minor extraneous noises, are missing from both stereo versions. Versions 2 and 3, although both in stereo, are different mixings. Version 3 is the stereo reverse of version 2; also, the backing vocals are mixed further forward than on version 2.

PENNY LANE
Version 1   3:00
As available on promotional copies of the American single (Capitol 5810)

This version is a much sought-after collector's item as it features seven extra notes played on a piccolo trumpet over the ending. It was distributed to radio stations in both the USA and Canada in this form, but when it reached the stores these seven notes had been left off.
Version 2   3:00
As available on the single (Parlophone R5570)

This record is as version 1, but minus the extra notes played over the ending.
Version 3   3:00
As included on the double album The Beatles 1966–1970 (Apple PCSP 718)

This version, which is in stereo, features a low trumpet after the line 'He likes to keep his fire engine clean, it's a clean machine.' This is missing from versions 1 and 2.

Version 4   3:00

As included on the eight-album set The Beatles Box (Parlophone/World Records SM 701–708)

This version, also in stereo, is version 3 with the seven extra notes from version 1 edited on to the ending.

PIGGIES

Version 1   2:04

As included on the mono version of the double album The Beatles (Apple PCS 7067–8)

Version 2   2:04

As included on the stereo version of the double album The Beatles (Apple PCS 7067–8)

The main recording is the same on both versions; the differences between the two versions are the grunts and their absence or presence at various points throughout the recording.

On the mono version, after the line 'Life is getting worse', there are three grunts; on the stereo version there are four. After the line 'Living piggy lives', there are two grunts on the stereo version but none on the mono version. Then after 'Clutching forks and knives', there is one grunt on the mono version which is missing from the stereo version. Finally, the grunts at the end are different : on the mono version there are about twelve and on the stereo version there are about eight.

PLEASE PLEASE ME

Version 1   2:00

As included on the mono version of the album Please Please Me (Parlophone PMC 1202)

Version 2   2:00

As included on the stereo version of the album Please Please Me (Parlophone PCS 3042)

At first listening, the mono and stereo recordings of this song appear to be identical. However, there is a slight difference in both the vocal and the lyrics between versions, particularly on the stereo recording when, half-way through the song, John fluffs the lyrics slightly. On the mono version, the lyrics are sung without fault. In addition, on the stereo version, the harmonica at the end is out of sequence with the rest of the backing, whereas on the mono version it is in sequence.

REVOLUTION

Version 1   3:22

As available on the single (Apple R5722)

Version 2   3:22

As included on the album Past Masters — Volume Two (Parlophone BPM 2)

The guide beat at the beginning of version 2 (which is stereo), is missing from version 1 (which is mono).

SEXY SADIE
Version 1   3:15
As included on the mono version of the double album The Beatles (Apple PMC 7067–8)
Version 2   3:15
As included on the stereo version of the double album The Beatles (Apple PCS 7067–8)

   On the mono version, there is one tambourine tap during the piano intro and on the stereo version there are two taps. While the bass guitar starts right at the beginning of the vocals on the stereo version it fades in half-way through the first line on the mono version.

SGT. PEPPER'S LONELY HEARTS CLUB BAND
Version 1   1:59
As included on the mono version of the album Sgt. Pepper's Lonely Hearts Club Band (Parlophone PMC 7027)
Version 2   1:59
As included on the stereo version of the album Sgt. Pepper's Lonely Hearts Club Band (Parlophone PCS 7027)

   The main difference between the two versions of this are the sound effects. On the last line of the song there are two whistles between 'lonely' and 'band' on the stereo version but only one on the mono. At the end, as 'Billy Shears' is sung, the audience-screams start simultaneously on the mono version but two beats earlier on the stereo version.

SGT. PEPPER'S LONELY HEARTS CLUB BAND (REPRISE)
Version 1   1:20
As included on the mono version of the album Sgt. Pepper's Lonely Hearts Club Band (Parlophone PMC 7027)
Version 2   1:20
As included on the stereo version of the album Sgt. Pepper's Lonely Hearts Club Band (Parlophone PCS 7027)

   The mono version of this track features a fourteen-tap introduction (along with an indecipherable comment from John) just before Paul says 'One, two, three, four'. The stereo version has only a ten-tap introduction and John's background comment is missing. The crowd sounds during the drumbeat sections of the opening are also different; and the mono version includes laughter from the crowd which is absent from the stereo track.

SHE'S A WOMAN
Version 1   2:57
As included on the album Past Masters — Volume One (Parlophone BPM 1)
Version 2   3:00
As included on the E.P. The Beatles (Parlophone SGE 1)

   Version 2 includes a 'One, two, three, four' count-in from Paul which is missing from version 1.

SLOW DOWN
Version 1   2:54
As included on the E.P. Long Tall Sally (Parlophone GEP 8913)

Version 2   2:54
As included on the stereo version of the album Past Masters — Volume One (Parlophone BPM 1)

These two versions have different vocals. The stereo version also includes John shouting 'ow' just before the last few bars of the track are played.

STRAWBERRY FIELDS FOREVER
Version 1   4:05
As available on the single (Parlophone R5570)
Version 2   4:05
As included on the album Magical Mystery Tour (Parlophone PCTC 255)
Version 3   4:05
As included on the double album The Beatles 1967–1970 (Apple PCSP 718)

During the two harpsichord sections on version 1 there are eight notes, but on versions 2 and 3 there are nine. Neither is there fade-out/in on version 1.

Versions 2 and 3, both in stereo, are different mixings. On version 2, when the orchestra joins in, it starts on the left-hand channel and immediately drifts across to the right. On version 3 it starts and remains on the right. On version 2, the slight instrumental breaks after the line 'Strawberry Fields Forever', remain in the centre, but on version 3 these instrumental breaks drift from right to left across the stereo.

At the point where version 3 fades out completely, version 2 only fades slightly; when version 3 fades back in, the 'horn' sound drifts from right to left, unlike version 2, where it goes from right to centre and back to right. Also, version 3 has a dominant snare drum on the fade-in which is missing from version 2.

TAXMAN
Version 1   2:36
As included on the mono version of the album Revolver (Parlophone PMC 7009)
Version 2   2:36
As included on the stereo version of the album Revolver (Parlophone PCS 7009)

On the mono version the cowbell starts after the line 'Should five per cent appear too small'. On the stereo version it doesn't start until after ''Cos I'm the taxman'. The entry point of the tambourine is also marginally different on both versions. On the stereo version it starts before the word 'cent', whereas on the mono version it starts after it.

TELL ME WHY
Version 1   2:06
As included on the mono version of the album A Hard Day's Night (Parlophone PMC 1230)
Version 2   2:06
As included on the stereo version of the album A Hard Day's Night (Parlophone PCS 3058)

However similar these two recordings may sound, they are entirely different. Aside from the fact that they are both played in a different key, John's lead vocal on the mono version is single-tracked, whereas the stereo version has it double-tracked.

THANK YOU GIRL
Version 1   2:01
As included on the album Past Masters — Volume One (Parlophone BPM 1)
Version 2   2:01
As included on the stereo version of the American album The Beatles Second
(Capitol ST 2080)

    Although both versions are from the same basic recording, version 2
includes the harmonica played twice during the track and also over the last
few bars; all of which is missing from version 1.

TOMORROW NEVER KNOWS
Version 1   2:59
As included on the mono version of the album Revolver (Parlophone PMC
7009)
Version 2   3:00
As included on the stereo version of the album Revolver (Parlophone PCS
7009)

    On the stereo version there is a gradual fade-in at the beginning, but on the
mono version the fade-in is sudden. This accounts for the one-second
difference in the timing. The tape loops and sound effects are different on the
two versions and are also in different places.

WE CAN WORK IT OUT
Version 1   2:10
As included on the stereo version of the album Past Masters — Volume Two
(Parlophone BPM 2)
Version 2   2:10
As included on the American album Yesterday ... And Today (Capitol ST
2553)

    These are two slightly different mixings of the same track. Version 1 has the
stereo split between the two channels without anything mixed into the centre,
whereas version 2 has sections of the organ mixed into the centre.

WHAT GOES ON
Version 1   2:44
As included on the mono version of the album Rubber Soul (Parlophone PMC
1267)
Version 2   2:44
As included on the stereo version of the album Rubber Soul (Parlophone PCS
3075)

    The lead guitar that can be heard over the ending of version 2 is absent
from version 1.

WHEN I GET HOME
Version 1   2:14
As included on the British version of the album A Hard Day's Night
(Parlophone PCS 3058)
Version 2   2:14
As included on the mono version of the American album Something New
(Capitol T 2018)

Version 2 features an entirely different lead vocal to version 1. On the line 'I'll love her more, till I walk out that door', the word 'till' comes in half a beat earlier than on version 1.

WHILE MY GUITAR GENTLY WEEPS
Version 1   4:46
As included on the mono version of the double album The Beatles (Apple PMC 7067–8)
Version 2   4:46
As included on the stereo version of the double album The Beatles (Apple PCS 7067–8)

At the end of the mono version the 'Yeah, yeah, yeah', which can be heard on the stereo version, is missing.

WHY DON'T WE DO IT IN THE ROAD?
Version 1   1:42
As included on the mono version of the double album The Beatles (Apple PMC 7067–8)
Version 2   1:42
As included on the stereo version of the double album The Beatles (Apple PCS 7067–8)

Included in the intro of the stereo version, along with the drumbeat, is hand-clapping absent from the mono version.

YELLOW SUBMARINE
Version 1   2:40
As included on the mono version of the album Revolver (Parlophone PMC 7009)
Version 2   2:40
As included on the stereo version of the album Revolver (Parlophone PCS 7009)

At the beginning of version 1, together with the lyrics 'In the town . . .', is an extra guitar passage not heard on version 2. On version 1, in the middle of the song, just after Ringo sings 'As we live a life of ease', John repeats 'A life of ease', which is also missing from version 2.

YOUR MOTHER SHOULD KNOW
Version 1   2:33
As included on the mono version of the double E.P. Magical Mystery Tour (Parlophone MMT 1)
Version 2   2:33
As included on the stereo version of the double E.P. Magical Mystery Tour (Parlophone SMMT 1)

The drum track is phased on the mono version, but not on the stereo version.

THE MONO RECORDINGS

As this chapter deals with Beatles' recordings that have alternative versions, it is the best place to mention the six recordings that are available only in mono; at the time of writing there are no stereo alternatives of these tracks available anywhere in the world.

Love Me Do, P.S. I Love You, She Loves You and I'll Get You were all recorded on two-track and then reduced to mono : the original tapes were then wiped.

Only A Northern Song and You Know My Name (Look Up The Number) were reduced to mono from master tapes that still exist; these have yet to be mixed into stereo.

51 The Unreleased Tracks

One fascinating aspect of the Beatles' recording career is the material recorded under various circumstances but never released.

Unfortunately, over the years much of this material has found its way into the hands of bootleggers who have produced illegal records. It is surprising that this has been allowed to continue as the Beatles and their record and publishing companies would benefit if the material was officially issued. Many fans and collectors, moreover, would prefer to buy these unreleased tracks as officially issued records rather than as inferior-quality bootlegs.

The material that remains unreleased falls into a minimum of nine different categories : auditions, demonstration recordings, radio broadcasts, television broadcasts, live recordings, interviews, recording session 'warm-ups', the 'Let It Be' sessions and actual unreleased tracks — plus the counterfeit records, which are described first.

BOGUS BEATLES

Before listing the unreleased tracks it is important to dispel some rumours and myths which have become associated with the Beatles over the years. A few records were thought by many to be unreleased Beatles tracks slipped out on other record labels. The following five records are quite definitely *not* the Beatles.

Have You Heard The Word/Futting Around — Fut (Beacon)

Legend has it that during the late 1960s, after the Beatles had finished Abbey Road, and effectively ended their recording career, John Lennon joined the Bee Gees to record this track. Some people thought it featured all four Beatles and the Bee Gees : another theory was that it was the Beatles' last recording. It has appeared on a surprising number of bootlegs, although it is not the Beatles. It isn't exactly the Bee Gees either, but actually Maurice Gibb of the Bee Gees together with Steve Kipner of Tin Tin (a group discovered by the Bee Gees in the late sixties).

L.S. Bumble Bee/Bee Side — Peter Cooke and Dudley Moore (Decca)

Issued early in 1967, this recording has appeared on many Beatles' bootlegs. It is a send-up of psychedelia which has a vocal sounding slightly like John Lennon. It is in fact Dudley Moore with backing by Peter Cooke.

We Are The Moles Parts I And II — The Moles (Parlophone)

Although released on the Parlophone label, this is not the Beatles under another name. Mystery surrounded the release of the record in 1968 : the master tapes were deposited in a left-luggage locker in a London railway station, and the key, with a mysterious letter, was sent to a leading British music paper, stating that the record was to be issued on the Parlophone label; it also stated that if the record reached the top ten, the identity of the group would be revealed.

Many people assumed that the record was by the Beatles, but even so it sold poorly. A few years later The Moles were revealed as Simon Dupree and the Big Sound (later Gentle Giant), who also recorded for the Parlophone label at the time. Again, the recording has appeared on a few Beatles bootlegs and some people still believe it to be the Beatles.

People Say/I'm Walking — John and Paul (London)
Issued in 1965 at the height of the Beatles' fame, this has appeared on a number of Beatles bootlegs and has been incorrectly identified as a duet by John Lennon and Paul McCartney. It is not, of course, but although it doesn't even sound like Lennon and McCartney, rumours continue and so does its inclusion on Beatles' bootlegs.

Ram You Hard — John Lennon and The Bleechers (Punch)
This reggae record, issued in early 1970, may well feature a John Lennon, but it is not *the* John Lennon.

The following pages describe the *real* Beatles' unreleased tracks.

AUDITIONS
During 1962, when the Beatles were trying to secure a recording contract, they had auditions with both Decca and EMI. All were recorded, and amongst the recordings are some fifteen titles which the Beatles never originally intended for release. Although they are really quite good it was thought highly unlikely that they would ever find their way on to official records.

Fortunately, twelve of these recordings have now, after twenty years, been issued (see The Decca Sessions 1.1.62 album). Amongst the titles recorded are Beatles versions of their own Hello Little Girl, Like Dreamers Do and Love Of The Loved (which are not included on The Decca Sessions 1.1.62), plus versions of other people's material such as Take Good Care Of My Baby, Besame Mucho, Memphis Tennessee and Three Cool Cats (which are included on the Decca Sessions 1.1.62), along with a further eight songs which they had included in their early stage performances.

DEMONSTRATION RECORDINGS
These consist of songs written by Lennon and McCartney and 'given away' to other artists, but demonstrated on record by John Lennon, Paul McCartney or the Beatles so that the artist involved could hear how the song sounded. A number of these were recorded at the offices of Dick James and are quite literally just basic run-throughs of the songs. Others were recorded at Abbey Road and are of a higher quality, both technically and musically.

With the exception of I'm The Greatest, written after the split-up, the tracks included by other artists on the album The Songs Lennon And McCartney Gave Away were recorded originally in one form or another by the Beatles.

RADIO BROADCASTS
Between 1962 and 1965 the Beatles appeared on many BBC radio shows for which they recorded material specifically for broadcast. In addition to alternative versions of material that they did release, there were also 44 tracks recorded for broadcast but never issued. Amongst these are the Beatles' own version of the Lennon–McCartney song I'll Be On My Way, together with many rock and roll songs.

The following is a complete list of the unreleased songs which the Beatles recorded for the BBC : Beautiful Dreamer; Besame Mucho; Carol; Clarebella; A Crimble Mudley (a medley of Love Me Do; Please Please Me; From Me To You; She Loves You; I Want To Hold Your Hand and Rudolph, The Red Nosed Reindeer); Crying, Waiting, Hoping; Don't Ever Change; Dream Baby; From Us To You; Glad All Over; Happy Birthday Saturday Club; Hippy Hippy Shake; The Honeymoon Song; I Forgot To Remember To Forget; I Got A Woman; I Got To Find My Baby; I Just Don't Understand; I'll Be On My Way; I'm Gonna Sit Right Down and Cry (Over You); (I'm) Talking About You; Johnny B. Goode; Keep Your Hands Off My Baby; Lend Me Your Comb; Lonesome Tears In My Eyes; Lucille; Memphis, Tennessee; Nothin' Shakin' (But The Leaves On The Trees); Ooh! My Soul; A Picture Of You; Pop Go The Beatles; A Shot Of Rhythm And Blues; Side By Side; So How Come (No One Loves Me); Soldier Of Love (Lay Down Your Arms); Some Other Guy; Sure To Fall; Sweet Little Sixteen; That's Alright Mama; Tie Me Kangaroo Down Sport (with Rolf Harris); To Know Her Is Love Her; Too Much Monkey Business and Youngblood.

Although both Sheila and Three Cool Cats were also recorded, they were never broadcast.

TELEVISION BROADCASTS

During the 1960s the Beatles appeared in countless television broadcasts world-wide. During some of their broadcasts on British television they performed a number of songs which have never appeared on record. The first of these was Some Other Guy which was filmed and recorded at the Cavern Club, Liverpool, on 22 August 1962 and was first broadcast by Granada Television during their *People and Places* current affairs programme on 17 October 1962, twelve days after the release of Love Me Do. Next came After You've Gone, which was performed with Terry Hall, Patsy Ann Noble, The Raindrops and The Bert Hayes Octet at the end of the BBC children's television show *Pops And Lenny* on 16 May 1963. On 4 November 1963 the Beatles appeared on *The Royal Variety Command Performance* and joined in with the rest of the cast to sing the final song of the show, God Save The Queen. The show was recorded and broadcast on 10 November 1963.

During 1964, the Beatles appeared on ATV's *The Morecambe and Wise Show* and joined Eric Morecambe and Ernie Wise in a rendition of On Moonlight Bay.

On 6 May 1964 ATV broadcast a Beatles 'special' called *Around The Beatles*; during this show the Beatles mimed to recordings made earlier, on 19 April 1964. Amongst the songs was their version of the Isley Brothers' song Shout! which came complete with some very graphic expletives from John Lennon. How they got away with the language is anyone's guess! During the same show the Beatles also performed a medley of their first five Parlophone singles Love Me Do; Please Please Me; From Me To You; She Loves You and I Want To Hold Your Hand.

Finally, during 1965 the Beatles were filmed on Blackpool beach singing I Do Like To Be Beside The Seaside for the ATV show *Blackpool Night Out*.

LIVE RECORDINGS

Besides the recording of Some Other Guy, which Granada Television made at the Cavern Club in Liverpool, there are at least two other tapes of the Beatles performing live at The Cavern which are known to exist. The first was made, and is still owned, by Mike McCartney. Unfortunately the contents of this tape are, at present, unknown. The second tape was recorded by a Beatles' fan during July 1962 and contains (amongst others) : Hey! Baby; Hippy Hippy Shake and If You Gotta Make A Fool Of Somebody. This second tape was bought by Paul McCartney when it was sold at Sotheby's in August 1985 for £2,100.

The Star Club Tapes also contain one further track that has yet to be issued : John's rendition of My Girl Is Red Hot. Given the general condition of the recordings on the tape, this must be of extremely poor quality for it not to have been issued.

Although numerous tapes of concerts exist, they only contain 'live' versions of issued material and are therefore not really relevant to this chapter.

INTERVIEWS
During various interviews one or more of the Beatles would occasionally burst into song (a situation which led to the existence of various 'unreleased tracks'). There is, for example, a recording of John singing (very badly) Those Were The Days which he launched into during an interview in 1968.

There is also a recording of the Beatles performing a totally off-the-cuff song (All Together On The Wireless Machine) during the first airing of the Magical Mystery Tour tracks on BBC Radio One on 2 December 1967.

One the most famous of the 'unreleased tracks' recorded during an interview is Cottonfields, sung during an interview with Kenny Everett on 18 July 1968, during a break in the White Album sessions at Abbey Road. The song, together with the interview, has finally been released as part of an interview album (UK : Interviews II; US : The Golden Beatles — see the following chapter, The Non-Album Tracks, for full details).

Other 'unreleased tracks' which are now available include Waltzing Matilda, a recording of which was sent to an Australian DJ prior to the Beatles' tour there in 1964. This, together with a second version and a short rendition of Tie Me Kangaroo Down, Sport, has, like Cottonfields, actually been released (again, see the following chapter, The Non-Album Tracks, for details).

RECORDING SESSION 'WARM-UPS'
There are a number of songs which the Beatles used to 'warm up' their recording sessions. Over the years these have found their way on to innumerable Beatles' bootlegs, invariably described as 'working versions' of songs. The truth is that these short tracks were never considered by the Beatles to be serious recordings, nor did they intend to record full versions for release. They are simply recordings of the Beatles messing about in the studio, relaxing and getting ready to record, by singing anything that came to mind — like Ba Ba Black Sheep, Tea For Two and The Third Man Theme.

These 'warm-up' recordings last from thirty to ninety seconds and a good example is Maggie Mae on Let It Be.

THE 'LET IT BE' SESSIONS
During the month-long fiasco of January 1969, which was eventually to become known as Let It Be, the Beatles, whilst recording the ill-fated (and still unreleased) Get Back album, also filmed the event for a television documentary (see the Let It Be album). In total, some 96 hours of sound film was shot, of which only 90 minutes was eventually used.

The 94½ hours of film that remains unissued (together with the studio tapes) contains an enormous amount of unreleased material, including Beatles' versions of many songs which John, Paul and George were later to re-record for solo release. These include : Gimme Some Truth and Jealous Guy (later re-recorded by John for his 1971 album Imagine); Teddy Boy, Hot As Sun and Junk (re-recorded by Paul and included on his McCartney album); and The Back Seat Of My Car (again re-recorded by Paul and released in 1971 on his solo album Ram). George's songs later re-recorded by him include All Things Must Pass, Isn't It A Pity and Not Guilty. Other songs recorded but never released include Shakin' In The Sixties — a Lennon-written rocker, dedicated to Dick James, who ran the Beatles' music publishers, Northern Songs. In addition there is a whole host of rock and roll, country and western and late fifties and early sixties songs.

One semi-released (and copyrighted) song to emerge from these sessions, and featured in the film, is Suzy Parker, a McCartney-written song. Whether it was ever considered for release on record is open to speculation but, should it ever be, the film soundtrack would have to be used as no known stereo master of the track exists.

ACTUAL UNRELEASED TRACKS

The total number of unreleased tracks recorded is open to debate, but judging by the amount of bootlegs available one would think that the rejection rate by the Beatles was 50 per cent. What constitutes an unreleased track, however? Is it, as the bootleggers would have us believe, every single cough, splutter and twang of a guitar string ever committed to tape? Or is it, in all good sense, a finished recording that the Beatles once considered as a possible release?

To answer the first question is relatively easy. Amongst the master tapes are numerous 'unreleased tracks' recorded by the Beatles, but most of them fall into one of the above categories, and were never even considered for release.

In answer to the second question, there are a small number of 'finished' tracks which were recorded, but for various reasons were not released. Amongst these are : How Do You Do It? (recorded as a possible follow-up to Love Me Do); Leave My Kitten Alone (recorded during the sessions for the Help! album); Not Guilty (recorded during the White Album sessions); and the most famous unreleased Beatles' track of all — What's The New Mary Jane (also recorded during the White Album sessions). The latter track was always going to be the next Beatles' single, but never was.

Early in 1985 EMI planned to issue an album of unreleased tracks entitled Sessions which was to contain the following tracks : Come And Get It; Leave My Kitten Alone; Not Guilty; I'm Looking Through You; What's The New Mary Jane; How Do You Do It; Besame Mucho; One After 909; If You Got Troubles; That Means A Lot; While My Guitar Gently Weeps; Mailman Bring Me No More Blues and Christmas Time Is Here Again. This, together with a single featuring Leave My Kitten Alone and an alternative unreleased version of Ob-La-Di, Ob-La-Da, was scrapped and returned to the vaults due to objections by the Beatles.

The following list of 200 titles lists every track generally assumed to have been recorded by the Beatles (in one form or another) but not released. Also included in the listing (at the beginning) are eight titles which were recorded before the Beatles recorded for either Polydor or EMI Records.

Two of the eight titles, That'll Be The Day and In Spite Of All The Danger, were recorded by The Quarrymen (John Lennon's first group) at Kensington Recording Studio, Liverpool, in 1958. The line-up for these recordings is believed to have been : John Lennon — rhythm guitar and lead vocal; Paul McCartney — bass guitar and harmony vocal; George Harrison — lead guitar and harmony vocal; Colin Hanton — drums; and John Lowe — piano. There is only one known copy (a 78 r.p.m. single) of these recordings in existence, the master tapes having been destroyed.

A further three originate from a tape recorded in May 1960 in Paul McCartney's home in Liverpool, and together with John, Paul and George, also feature Stuart Sutcliffe. Although the tape contains nearly an hour and a half of various rehearsals of a number of songs there are only three songs — Hallelujah, I Love Her So, I'll Follow The Sun and One After 909 — which could really be described as full recordings.

The remaining three titles — Fever, September Song and Summertime — were recorded by the Beatles backing Lu Walters, bass guitarist and sometime vocalist with another Liverpool group, Rory Storme and The Hurricanes, in September 1960, in Akustic Studios, Hamburg, West Germany. The recordings also featured another member of The Hurricanes who was later to become a Beatle — Ringo Starr. Ringo had sat in on drums because Pete Best, then the Beatles' drummer, was nowhere to be found at the time the recording was due to take place. According to legend there were only four copies of these recordings made as one-sided 78 r.p.m. records, but over the years they have apparently been lost.

All songs are unpublished individual Beatle or Lennon and McCartney compositions except where stated.

The Quarrymen (Recorded in Liverpool, 1958)
That'll Be The Day (Allison–Petty–Holly)
In Spite Of All The Danger

The Beatles (Recorded in Liverpool, May 1960)
Hallelujah, I Love Her So (Charles)
I'll Follow The Sun
One After 909

The Beatles With Lu Walters (Recorded in Hamburg, September 1960)
Fever (Davenport–Cooley)
September Song (Weill–Anderson)
Summertime (Gershwin–Gershwin)

The Beatles (Recorded in London, January 1962)
Hello Little Girl
Like Dreamers Do
Love Of The Loved

The Beatles (Recorded in Liverpool, Manchester and London 1962–70)
After You've Gone (Creamer–Layton) (*with Terry Hall, Patsy Ann Noble, The Raindrops and The Bert Hayes Octet*)

Ain't That A Shame (Domino–Bartholomew)
All Along The Watchtower (Dylan)
All Shook Up (Blackwell–Presley)

All Things Must Pass
All Together On The Wireless
    Machine

Ba Ba Black Sheep (Trad.)
Baby, I Don't Care (Leiber–Stoller)
Back Seat Of My Car, The
Bad To Me
Beautiful Dreamer (Foster)
Be Bop A Lula (Vincent–Davis)
Be My Baby (Greenwich–Barry–
    Spector)
Blowin' In The Wind (Dylan)
Blue Suede Shoes (Perkins)
Bye Bye Love (Bryant–Bryant)

Carol (Berry)
Catcall
Clarebella (Pingatore)
C'mon Everybody (Cochran–
    Capehart)
Come And Get It
Commonwealth Song
Cottonfields (Ledbetter)
Crimble Mudley, A

Da Doo Ron Ron (Greenwich–
    Barry–Spector)
Digging My Potatoes (Trad.)
Don't Be Cruel (Blackwell–Presley)
Don't Ever Change (Goffin–King)
Don't Let The Sun Catch You Crying
    (Marsden)
Dream Baby (Walker)

Early In The Morning (Darin–
    Harris)
Etcetera
Every Night

Fool Like Me (Clements–Maddox)
From A Window
From Us To You

Gimme Some Truth
Glad All Over (Schroeder–Tepper–
    Bennett)
God Save The Queen (Trad.) (From
    the 1963 *Royal Variety Command
    Performance*)
Going Up The Country (Wilson)
Goodbye
Good Rockin' Tonight (Brown)

Great Balls Of Fire (Hammer–
    Blackwell)

Happy Birthday Saturday Club
    (Hill–Hill, Arr. Lennon)
Hare Krishna Mantra (Trad.)
Heather
Hey! Baby (Cobb–Channel)
Hi-Heel Sneakers (Higgenbotham)
Hi Ho Silver
Hippy Hippy Shake (Romero)
Hitch Hike (Gaye–Paul–Stevenson)
Home (Clarkson–Clarkson–
    Steeden)
Honeymoon Song, The
    (Theodorakis–Sansom)
Hot As Sun
House Of The Rising Sun (Trad.)
How Do You Do It? (Murray)

I Do Like To Be Beside The Seaside
    (Glover–Kind)
I Don't Want To See You Again
I Forgot To Remember To Forget
    (Kesler–Feathers)
I Got A Woman (Charles–Richards)
I Got To Find My Baby (Berry)
I Just Don't Understand (Wilkin–
    Westberry)
I Shall Be Released (Dylan)
I Threw It All Away (Dylan)
If You Gotta Make A Fool Of
    Somebody (Clark)
If You've Got Trouble
I'll Be On My Way
I'll Build A Stairway To Paradise
    (Gershwin–Da Silva–Francis)
I'll Keep You Satisfied
I'm Gonna Sit Right Down And Cry
    (Over You) (Thomas–Biggs)
I'm In Love
Isn't It A Pity
It's For You
It's So Easy (Allison–Petty–Holly)

Jealous Guy
Jessie's Dream
Johnny B. Goode (Berry)
Junk

Kansas City (Leiber–Stoller)
Keep Your Hands Off My Baby
    (Goffin–King)

Lawdy Miss Clawdy (Price)
Leave My Kitten Alone (McDougal–
Turner)
Lend Me Your Comb (Twomey–
Wise–Wiseman)
Little Queenie (Berry)
Lonesome Tears In My Eyes
(Burnette–Burnette–Burlinson–
Mortimer)
Look At Me (Allison–Petty–Holly)
Los Paranois
Lucille (Collins–Penniman)

Mailman Bring Me No More Blues
(Roberts–Katz–Clayton)
Mama, You've Been On My Mind
(Dylan)
Maybe I'm Amazed
Maybellene (Berry–Fratto–Freed)
Michael Row The Boat Ashore
(Trad.)
Midnight Special (Trad.)
Miss Ann (Penniman)
Moonglow (Hudson–De Lange–Mills)
Move It (Samwell)
My Girl Is Red Hot
My Kind Of Girl (Bricusse)

Nobody I Know
Not Fade Away (Allison–Petty–
Holly)
Not Guilty
Nothing' Shakin' (But The Leaves On
The Trees) (Colacrai–Fontaine–
Lampert–Cleveland)

Oh Carol (Greenfield–Sedaka)
On Moonlight Bay (Madden–
Wenrich) (*With Morecambe and
Wise*)
One And One Is Two
Ooh! My Soul (Penniman)

Peggy Sue (Allison–Petty–Holly)
Peggy Sue Got Married (Allison–
Petty–Holly)
Penina
Picture Of You, A (Beveridge–
Oakman)
Piece Of My Heart (Berns–
Ragavoy)
Pop Go The Beatles (Trad., Arr.
Patrick)

Portrait Of My Love (Ornadel–
Newell)

Ramrod (Casey)
Raunchy (Justis–Manker)
Ready Teddy (Marascalco–
Blackwell)
Red Sails In The Sunset (Williams–
Kennedy)
Reelin' And Rockin' (Berry)
Reminiscing (Curtis)
Right String But The Wrong Yo-Yo,
The (Perryman)
Rip It Up (Blackwell–Marascalco)
Rock Island Line, The (Trad.)
Rocker

Save The Last Dance For Me
(Pomus–Shuman)
Send Me Some Lovin' (Price–
Marascalco)
Shake Rattle And Roll (Calhoun)
Shakin' In The Sixties
Sheila (Roe)
Shimmy Shake (South–Land)
Shirley's Wild Accordion
Short Fat Fanny (Williams)
Shot Of Rhythm And Blues, A
(Thompson)
Shout! (O'Kelly–Isley–Isley)
Side By Side (Woods) (*With The
Karl Denver Trio*)
Singing The Blues (Endsley)
So How Come (No One Loves Me)
(Bryant–Bryant)
Soldier Of Love (Lay Down Your
Arms) (Cason–Moon)
Some Other Guy (Leiber–Stoller–
Barrett)
Somethin' Else (Cochran)
Spiritual Regeneration (*Recorded at
Rishikesh, India, 1967–8*)
Stand By Me (King–Leiber–Stoller–
Jones)
Step Inside Love
Suicide
Suzy Parker
Suzy's Parlour
Sweet Little Sixteen (Berry)

Talking About You (I'm) (Berry)
Tea For Two (Youmans–Caesar–
Harbach)

52 The Non-Album Tracks

This chapter deals with those Beatles' recordings which, although generally available, are not, in the main, available on Beatles' albums. The recordings discussed here originate from three different sources : videograms, singles and interview albums.

Four of the tracks discussed are at present only available on the soundtracks of videograms. The first, That'll Be The Day, although originating from a record made by The Quarrymen in 1958, is currently only available on the soundtrack of the videogram The Real Buddy Holly Story. Some Other Guy was filmed/recorded in the Cavern Club in Liverpool in 1962 and a section of it is included on the videogram The Compleat Beatles. Shout! and the Love Me Do Medley originate from the 1964 TV special *Around The Beatles*, sections of which were released in 1985 on the videogram The Beatles Live!

During the enormous number of television appearances which the Beatles made during their collective career they performed a number of songs (including some with other artists) which are not available on record. Four of those have previously been mentioned. Others, including I Do Like To Be Beside The Seaside, which they performed on Blackpool beach in 1965 (the film still being in existence), and On Moonlight Bay, which they performed with Eric Morecambe and Ernie Wise on *The Morecambe and Wise Show*, also in 1965, are at present not available. With the increasing use of the domestic video recorder, however, these, together with other pieces of rare film containing unreleased songs, will hopefully be made generally available in the not-too-distant future.

With the release by EMI of the Beatles' entire Parlophone/Apple catalogue on compact disc (including two albums containing those recordings which were originally released on singles and E.P.s), the only Beatles' Parlophone recording which is currently only available on a single is The Beatles' Movie Medley (see below).

Finally, Cottonfields and Waltzing Matilda (both recorded during interviews) were, after numerous appearances on bootlegs, finally issued during the 1980s on interview albums. These are just two of a number of songs recorded during interviews which, when included on bootleg records, were invariably described as 'working versions' by the bootleggers, when in fact they were off-the-cuff songs which were never considered as serious recordings by the Beatles.

The following is a complete list of songs which are currently available only on videograms, singles and interview albums.

That'll Be The Day (Allison–Petty–Holly)

Recorded : 1958, Kensington Recording Studios, Liverpool
Availability : Videogram The Real Buddy Holly Story

John Lennon : Rhythm Guitar and Lead Vocal
Paul McCartney : Bass Guitar and Backing Vocal
George Harrison : Lead Guitar and Backing Vocal
Colin Hanton : Drums
John Lowe : Piano

The videogram features two separate sections of the record totalling 1 minute 26 seconds together with an interview with Paul McCartney (during which he performs an acoustic version of Love Me Do plus a slower, more relaxed version of Words Of Love).

The record itself features a young, but still very gutsy-sounding, John Lennon on lead vocals with backing vocals from (presumably) Paul and George. Instrumentally, they sound extremely enthusiastic and capable. For a first recording the whole thing comes across extremely well.

Some Other Guy (Leiber–Stoller–Barrett)

Recorded : 22 August 1962, The Cavern Club, 10 Mathew St, Liverpool
Availability : Videogram The Compleat Beatles

John Lennon : Rhythm Guitar and Solo Vocal
Paul McCartney : Bass Guitar
George Harrison : Lead Guitar
Ringo Starr : Drums

Although recorded and filmed by Granada Television in August of 1962, this was not broadcast until 17 October that year (twelve days after the release of Love Me Do). The sound quality of the recording can be compared to The Star Club Tapes (recorded some four months later) but the real advantage of this film/recording is that it gives the rest of the world a chance to see what the Beatles looked and sounded like at The Cavern.

John handles this Richie Barrett song with a great deal of enthusiasm and power and is given an equally enthusiastic backing from Paul, George and Ringo.

Love Me Do Medley (Lennon–McCartney)

Recorded : 19 April 1964, IBC Studios, 35 Portland Place, London
Availability : Videogram The Beatles Live!

John Lennon : Rhythm Guitar, Harmonica and Lead Vocal
Paul McCartney : Bass Guitar and Lead Vocal
George Harrison : Lead Guitar and Harmony Vocal
Ringo Starr : Drums

This is the only medley of their own material that the Beatles ever purposely recorded; it predates the messy The Beatles' Movie Medley (which was compiled without the Beatles' permission) by eighteen years. It is not (as is the case with The Beatles' Movie Medley) sections of the versions previously issued, edited together, but a different recording entirely. The line-up and vocalists, however, remain the same. The medley includes : Love Me Do; Please Please Me; From Me To You; She Loves You and I Want To Hold Your Hand.

Shout! (O'Kelly–Isley–Isley)

Recorded : 19 April 1964, IBC Studios, 35 Portland Place, London
Availability : Videogram The Beatles Live!

John Lennon : Rhythm Guitar and Lead Vocal
Paul McCartney : Bass Guitar and Lead Vocal
George Harrison : Lead Guitar and Lead Vocal
Ringo Starr : Drums and Lead Vocal

Without a doubt the highlight of the show of The Beatles Live! was this rousing rendition of The Isley Brothers' 1959 classic; it was the only time the Beatles performed the song, either on stage or television, and what a dynamic performance it is! All four Beatles share lead vocals with the audience joining them on 'shout'. Paul kicks the whole thing off in his best rock and roll style, to be followed by George and then Ringo. To round off the foursome John begins his section and then alters the lyrics somewhat (i.e. 'Everyone f...in' shout now')! How they got away with that is anyone's guess.

The contents of the videogram, which include the rather unique Love Me Do Medley and Shout! (both unavailable on record), originate from the 1964 TV special *Around The Beatles*. This was filmed on 27 and 28 April 1964 at Wembley TV studios and first broadcast on 6 May 1964 (and eventually issued on 29 April 1985 by Dave Clark International through the video branch of EMI, Picture Music International).

The original TV special included other artists such as Cilla Black, P.J. Proby and Sounds Incorporated, but for reasons known only to Dave Clark (of the Dave Clark Five) these other artists were edited out, thereby reducing the running time of the film from its original 50 minutes to just eighteen. Clark also took the rather curious decision to retitle the film The Beatles Live! and issue it as a Ready Steady Go! special edition. The only connection between this and Ready Steady Go! is that they were both produced by the now-defunct Associated Rediffusion Television from whom Clark bought the rights.

The full contents of the videogram, which features brand-new studio recordings made some nine days prior to filming (to which the Beatles mime) are : Twist And Shout, Roll Over Beethoven, I Wanna Be Your Man, Long Tall Sally, Love Me Do Medley (including Love Me Do, Please Please Me, From Me To You, She Loves You and I Want To Hold Your Hand), Can't Buy Me Love and Shout!, plus All You Need Is Love, which wasn't written or recorded until three years later, played over the closing titles.

The Beatles' Movie Medley (Lennon–McCartney)   3:56

Recorded : Dates and locations vary
Availability : Single (UK : Parlophone R6055; US : Capitol B-5107)

John Lennon : Numerous Instruments and Lead Vocal on Six Sections
Paul McCartney : Numerous Instruments and Lead Vocal on One Section
George Harrison : Lead Guitar and Backing Vocal
Ringo Starr : Drums

Following the world-wide success of the 1981–2 Stars on 45 medley by the 'Beatles soundalike' Dutch group Starsound (a medley which contained some very believable John Lennon-like vocals), Capitol Records decided to put together their own Beatles medley (without the Beatles' consent) using the original Beatles' master tapes. The medley, which contains excerpts from Magical Mystery Tour, All You Need Is Love, You've Got To Hide Your Love Away, I Should Have Known Better, A Hard Day's Night, Ticket To Ride and Get Back, was then issued as a single on 30 March 1982 (Capitol B-5107).

All the excerpts were from tracks included on the then newly released Reel Music album (UK : Parlophone PCS 7218; US : Capitol SV 12199).

In Britain, EMI Records decided that the editing together of different Beatles' recordings was unacceptable and withheld release of the record (but still allocated it a catalogue number, just in case). Demand for the imported copies of the US record was so high that EMI conceded and eventually issued it on 25 May 1982 (Parlophone R6055).

Despite EMI's original reluctance to issue the record in Britain it entered the chart shortly after release, eventually reaching its highest position of No. 7.

Cottonfields (Ledbetter)

Recorded : 18 July 1968, EMI Studios, Abbey Road, London
Availability : Single (Italy Only) (Apple DPR 108)
Interview LP (UK : Interviews II; US : The Golden Beatles)

John Lennon : Acoustic Guitar and Solo Vocal
Paul McCartney : Elsewhere in the Studio
George Harrison : Elsewhere in the Studio
Ringo Starr : Elsewhere in the Studio

Recorded as part of an interview with Kenny Everett during the sessions for the White Album in 1968 and originally issued by Apple (together with sections of the interview) as part of a four-record set in Italy the same year. The entire interview, together with Cottonfields and a further nine similarly spontaneous songs were then issued on various interview albums world-wide during the late 1980s.

Throughout the interview John, accompanied by an acoustic guitar, launches into a number of improvised songs. Shortly after the interview opens (when he has already performed three spontaneous songs), John, tongue-in-cheek, launches into a perverted version of this Huddie Ledbetter classic. He is then further interviewed by that oddball of British television and radio, Kenny Everett. Between the offbeat humorous Lennon/Everett exchanges, the interview briefly touches on such subjects as John's return from India, at which point John breaks into a feigned foreign language, best described as gobbledygook. This is followed by Ringo's first song, Apple and Sgt. Pepper.

They are then joined by Paul who, together with John, performs an improvised song, Goodbye To Kenny Everett. John then comments on Tiny Tim (who was enjoying a brief spell of fame singing such songs as Tiptoe Through The Tulips in a falsetto vocal. He also appears on The Beatles Christmas Album singing Nowhere Man). John then launches into the next improvised song, Tiny Tim For President. Following this, various comments are made about Kenny Everett being dismissed from the BBC (due to a comment about the wife of the then British Transport Minister having passed her driving test).

Ringo, accompanied by drums, then proceeds to sing a further improvised song, Goodbye Kenny, which is followed by a further display of general lunacy. Kenny then asks the Beatles to sing Strawberry Fields Forever in a jazz tempo, and with Paul as lead vocalist, they perform a short a cappella version. The interview closes with Paul singing a falsetto version of Ringo's earlier Goodbye Kenny.

A complete list of the songs performed during the interview are as follows: Vague Idea; Somebody Stole My Girl; Goodbye Jingle (two versions); Cottonfields; The Kenny Everett Show; Goodbye to Kenny Everett; Tiny Tim For President; Goodbye Kenny; Strawberry Fields Forever and Goodbye Kenny (again!).

Waltzing Matilda (Trad.)

Recorded : February–March 1964 (other details not available)
Availability : Interview LP The Beatles Talk Downunder

John Lennon : Lead Vocal
Paul McCartney : Lead Vocal
George Harrison : Lead Vocal
Ringo Starr : Lead Vocal

This short, though entertaining, version of the traditional Australian song originates from a studio tape which was sent to Australian DJ Barry Ferber in March 1964. It is the opening (though uncredited) track of the Australian interview album The Beatles Talk Downunder.

During the various interviews included on this album, one or more of the Beatles occasionally bursts into song. During the interview recorded at the President Hotel in Hong Kong on 10 June 1964, John and George perform a further version of Waltzing Matilda plus a short rendition of Tie Me Kangaroo Down, Sport. Then during one of the later interviews recorded at the New City Hotel, Dunedin, New Zealand on 26 June 1964, Paul, when discussing songwriting, mentions that Ringo has written his first song, Don't Pass Me By. Paul then launches into a brief a cappella rendition of the song, which was to be recorded and eventually released by the Beatles some four years later.

DISCOGRAPHY

This discography is divided into four separate sections. First is a complete list of the international compact disc albums (CD singles from Love Me Do to Let It Be to be released internationally during 1988/9). This is followed by British, American and Australian discographies of all records released in those countries up to the end of December 1988. Where, as is the case in Britain, singles have been re-released and also released as picture discs (which have an RP prefix, denoting picture disc, instead of the normal R prefix), these have not been included. Though, in the case of 12-inch singles and cassette singles, these have. In the case of both the American and Australian discographies, again, only special editions of singles i.e. 12-inch singles are the only re-releases to be included. In all three countries, where an album has been re-released with a new catalogue number, these have been included with the minimum of information relating to the original release.

The International Compact Discs

POLYDOR

823 701–2 The Beatles First
Ain't She Sweet; Cry For A Shadow; When The Saints Go Marching In; Why; If You Love Me, Baby; (What'd I Say); Sweet Georgia Brown; (Let's Dance); (Ruby Baby); My Bonnie; Nobody's Child; (Ready Teddy); (Ya Ya); (Kansas City).

Titles in parentheses performed by Tony Sheridan and The Beat Brothers. All other songs performed by either the Beatles or the Beatles with Tony Sheridan.

VARIOUS LABELS

The Decca Tapes
Three Cool Cats; Memphis, Tennessee; Besame Mucho; The Sheik Of Araby; Till There Was You; Searchin'; Sure To Fall (In Love With You); Take Good Care Of My Baby; Money; To Know Her Is To Love Her; September In The Rain; Crying, Waiting, Hoping.

The Star Club Tapes
I'm Gonna Sit Right Down And Cry (Over You); I Saw Her Standing There; Roll Over Beethoven; Hippy Hippy Shake; Sweet Little Sixteen; Lend Me Your Comb; Your Feets Too Big; Twist And Shout; Mr. Moonlight; A Taste Of Honey; Besame Mucho; Reminiscing; Kansas City/Hey Hey Hey Hey; Where Have You Been All My Life; Till There Was You; Nothin' Shakin' (But The Leaves On The Trees); To Know Her Is To Love Her; Little Queenie; Falling In Love Again; Ask Me Why; Be Bop A Lula; Hallelujah, I Love Her So; Sheila; Red Sails In The Sunset; Everybody's Trying To Be My Baby; Matchbox; (I'm) Talking About You; Shimmy Shake; Long Tall Sally; I Remember You.

PARLOPHONE

CDP 7 46435 2 Please Please Me
I Saw Her Standing There; Misery; Anna (Go To Him); Chains; Boys; Ask Me Why; Please Please Me; Love Me Do; P.S. I Love You; Baby It's You; Do You Want To Know A Secret; A Taste Of Honey; There's A Place; Twist And Shout.

CDP 7 46436 2 With The Beatles
It Won't Be Long; All I've Got To Do; All My Loving; Don't Bother Me; Little Child; Till There Was You; Please Mister Postman; Roll Over Beethoven; Hold Me Tight; You Really Got A Hold On Me; I Wanna Be Your Man; Devil In Her Heart; Not A Second Time; Money.

CDP 46437 2 A Hard Day's Night
A Hard Day's Night; I Should Have Known Better; If I Fell; I'm Happy Just To Dance With You; And I Love Her; Tell Me Why; Can't Buy Me Love; Any Time At All; I'll Cry Instead; Things We Said Today; When I Get Home; You Can't Do That; I'll Be Back.

CDP 7 46438 2 Beatles For Sale
No Reply; I'm A Loser; Baby's In Black; Rock And Roll Music; I'll Follow The Sun; Mr. Moonlight; Kansas City/Hey Hey Hey Hey; Eight Days A Week; Words Of Love; Honey Don't; Every Little Thing; I Don't Want To Spoil The Party; What You're Doing; Everybody's Trying To Be My Baby.

CDP 7 46439 2 Help!
Help!; The Night Before; You've Got To Hide Your Love Away; I Need You; Another Girl; You're Going To Lose That Girl; Ticket To Ride; Act Naturally; It's Only Love;

You Like Me Too Much; Tell Me What You See; I've Just Seen A Face; Yesterday; Dizzy Miss Lizzy.

CDP 7 46440 2 Rubber Soul

Drive My Car; Norwegian Wood (This Bird Has Flown); You Won't See Me; Nowhere Man; Think For Yourself; The Word; Michelle; What Goes On; Girl; I'm Looking Through You; In My Life; Wait; If I Needed Someone; Run For Your Life.

CDP 7 46441 2 Revolver

Taxman; Eleanor Rigby; I'm Only Sleeping; Love You To; Here, There And Everywhere; Yellow Submarine; She Said, She Said; Good Day Sunshine; And Your Bird Can Sing; For No One; Dr. Robert; I Want To Tell You; Got To Get You Into My Life; Tomorrow Never Knows.

CDP 7 46442 2 Sgt. Pepper's Lonely Hearts Club Band

Sgt. Pepper's Lonely Hearts Club Band; With A Little Help From My Friends; Lucy In The Sky With Diamonds; Getting Better; Fixing A Hole; She's Leaving Home; Being For The Benefit Of Mr. Kite; Within You, Without You; When I'm Sixty Four; Lovely Rita; Good Morning, Good Morning; Sgt. Pepper's Lonely Hearts Club Band (Reprise); A Day In The Life.

CDS 7 46443 8 The Beatles (2 CDs)
Disc One

Back In The USSR; Dear Prudence; Glass Onion; Ob-La-Di, Ob-La-Da; Wild Honey Pie; The Continuing Story Of Bungalow Bill; While My Guitar Gently Weeps; Happiness Is A Warm Gun; Martha My Dear; I'm So Tired; Blackbird; Piggies; Rocky Racoon; Don't Pass Me By; Why Don't We Do It In The Road?; I Will; Julia.

Disc Two

Birthday; Yer Blues; Mother Nature's Son; Everybody's Got Something To Hide Except Me And My Monkey; Sexy Sadie; Helter Skelter; Long, Long, Long; Revolution 1; Honey Pie; Savoy Truffle; Cry Baby Cry; Revolution 9; Goodnight.

CDP 7 46445 2 Yellow Submarine

Yellow Submarine; Only A Northern Song; All Together Now; Hey Bulldog; It's All Too Much; All You Need Is Love; Plus incidental music by The George Martin Orchestra.

CDP 7 48062 2 Magical Mystery Tour

Magical Mystery Tour; The Fool On The Hill; Flying; Blue Jay Way; Your Mother Should Know; I Am The Walrus; Hello Goodbye; Strawberry Fields Forever; Penny Lane; Baby, You're A Rich Man; All You Need Is Love.

CDP 7 46446 2 Abbey Road

Come Together; Something; Maxwell's Silver Hammer; Oh! Darling; Octopus's Garden; I Want You (She's So Heavy); Here Comes The Sun; Because; You Never Give Me Your Money; Sun King; Mean Mr. Mustard; Polythene Pam; She Came In Through The Bathroom Window; Golden Slumbers; Carry That Weight; The End; Her Majesty.

CDP 7 46447 2 Let It Be

Two Of Us; Dig A Pony; Across The Universe; I Me Mine; Dig It; Let It Be; Maggie Mae; I've Got A Feeling; One After 909; The Long And Winding Road; For You Blue; Get Back.

CDP 7 90043 2 Past Masters — Volume One

Love Me Do; From Me To You; Thank You Girl; She Loves You; I'll Get You; I Want To Hold Your Hand; This Boy; Komm, Gib Mir Deine Hand; Sie Liebt Dich; Long Tall Sally; I Call Your Name; Slow

Down; Matchbox; I Feel Fine;
She's A Woman; Bad Boy; Yes It Is;
I'm Down.

CDP 7 90044 2 Past Masters —
Volume Two

Day Tripper; We Can Work It Out;
Paperback Writer; Rain; Lady
Madonna; The Inner Light; Hey
Jude; Revolution; Get Back; Don't
Let Me Down; The Ballad Of John
And Yoko; Old Brown Shoe;
Across The Universe; Let It Be;
You Know My Name (Look Up The
Number).

British Releases

PARLOPHONE–EMI/APPLE*
MUSIC FOR PLEASURE/FAME*****
UNITED ARTISTS††

Singles

R4949 Love Me Do/
P.S. I Love You [5 October 1962]
R4983 Please Please Me/
Ask Me Why [11 January 1963]
R5015 From Me To You/
Thank You Girl [12 April 1963]
R5055 She Loves You/
I'll Get You [28 August 1963]
R5084 I Want To Hold Your Hand/
This Boy [29 November 1963]
R5114 Can't Buy Me Love/
You Can't Do That [16 March
1964]
R5160 A Hard Day's Night/
Things We Said Today [10 July
1964]
R5200 I Feel Fine/
She's A Woman [23 November
1964]
R5265 Ticket To Ride/
Yes It Is [9 April 1965]
R5305 Help!/
I'm Down [19 July 1965]
R5389 We Can Work It Out/
Day Tripper [3 December 1965]
R5452 Paperback Writer/
Rain [30 May 1966]
R5489 Yellow Submarine/
Eleanor Rigby [5 August 1966]
R5570 Penny Lane/
Strawberry Fields Forever [17
February 1967]
R5620 All You Need Is Love/
Baby, You're A Rich Man [7 July
1967]
R5655 Hello Goodbye/
I Am The Walrus [24 November
1967]
R5675 Lady Madonna/
The Inner Light [15 March 1968]
R5722* Hey Jude/
Revolution [30 August 1968]

R5777* Get Back/
Don't Let Me Down [11 April 1969]
R5786* The Ballad Of John And
Yoko/
Old Brown Shoe [30 May 1969]
R5814* Something/
Come Together [6 October 1969]
R5833* Let It Be/You Know My
Name (Look Up The Number)
[6 March 1970]
R6013 Yesterday/
I Should Have Known Better [8
March 1976]
R6016 Back In The USSR/
Twist And Shout [25 June 1976]
R6022 Sgt. Pepper's Lonely Hearts
Club Band/With A Little Help
From My Friends/A Day In The
Life [30 September 1978]
R6055 The Beatles' Movie Medley/
I'm Happy Just To Dance With
You [25 May 1982]
12R4949 Love Me Do/
P.S. I Love You/Love Me Do
(*12-inch Single*) [1 November
1982]
**BCS 1 The Beatles' Singles
Collection (26 Singles)**
Love Me Do to The Beatles'
Movie Medley.
[4 December 1982]
12R5620 All You Need Is Love/
Baby, You're A Rich Man (*12-inch
Single*) [6 July 1987]
TC–R5620 All You Need Is Love
All You Need Is Love/
Baby, You're A Rich Man
(*Cassette Single*) [6 July 1987]
12R5722 Hey Jude/
Revolution (*12-inch Single*) [30
August 1988]

Extended Play

GEP 8882 Twist And Shout
Twist And Shout; A Taste Of Honey; Do You Want To Know A Secret; There's A Place. [12 July 1963]

GEP 8880 The Beatles Hits
From Me To You; Thank You Girl; Please Please Me; Love Me Do. [6 September 1963]

GEP 8883 The Beatles No. 1
I Saw Her Standing There; Misery; Anna (Go To Him); Chains. [1 November 1963]

GEP 8891 All My Loving
All My Loving; Ask Me Why; Money; P.S. I Love You. [7 February 1964]

GEP 8913 Long Tall Sally
Long Tall Sally; I Call Your Name; Slow Down; Matchbox. [19 June 1964]

GEP 8920 Extracts From The Film A Hard Day's Night
I Should Have Known Better; If I Fell; Tell Me Why; And I Love Her. [6 November 1964]

GEP 8924 Extracts From The Album A Hard Day's Night
Any Time At All; I'll Cry Instead; Things We Said Today; When I Get Home. [6 November 1964]

GEP 8931 Beatles For Sale
No Reply; I'm A Loser; Rock And Roll Music; Eight Days A Week. [6 April 1965]

GEP 8938 Beatles For Sale No. 2
I'll Follow The Sun; Baby's In Black; Words Of Love; I Don't Want To Spoil The Party. [4 June 1965]

GEP 8946 The Beatles Million Sellers
She Loves You; I Want To Hold Your Hand; Can't Buy Me Love; I Feel Fine. [6 December 1965]

GEP 8948 Yesterday
Yesterday; Act Naturally; You Like Me Too Much; It's Only Love. [4 March 1966]

GEP 8952 Nowhere Man
Nowhere Man; Drive My Car; Michelle; You Won't See Me. [8 July 1966]

MMT/SMMT 1 Magical Mystery Tour
Magical Mystery Tour; Your Mother Should Know; I Am The Walrus; The Fool On The Hill; Flying; Blue Jay Way. [8 December 1967]

BEP 14 The Beatles' E.P.s Collection
This 14-E.P. set contains all the above-listed 13 E.P.s plus the following free bonus E.P. which is not on sale separately.

SGE 1 The Beatles
The Inner Light; Baby, You're A Rich Man; She's A Woman; This Boy. [7 December 1981]

Long Play

PMC 1202 Please Please Me
PCS 3042
Side One
I Saw Her Standing There; Misery; Anna (Go To Him); Chains; Boys; Ask Me Why; Please Please Me.
Side Two
Love Me Do; P.S. I Love You; Baby It's You; Do You Want To Know A Secret; A Taste Of Honey; There's A Place; Twist And Shout. [22 March 1963]

PMC 1206 With The Beatles
PCS 3045
Side One
It Won't Be Long; All I've Got To Do; All My Loving; Don't Bother Me; Little Child; Till There Was You; Please Mister Postman.
Side Two
Roll Over Beethoven; Hold Me Tight; You Really Got A Hold On Me; I Wanna Be Your Man; Devil In Her Heart; Not A Second Time; Money. [22 November 1963]

PMC 1230 A Hard Day's Night
PCS 3058
Side One
A Hard Day's Night; I Should Have Known Better; If I Fell; I'm Happy Just To Dance With You; And I Love Her; Tell Me Why; Can't Buy Me Love.
Side Two
Any Time At All; I'll Cry Instead; Things We Said Today; When I Get Home; You Can't Do That; I'll Be Back. [10 July 1964]

PMC 1240 Beatles For Sale
PCS 3062
Side One
No Reply; I'm A Loser; Baby's In Black; Rock And Roll Music; I'll Follow The Sun; Mr. Moonlight; Kansas City/Hey Hey Hey Hey.
Side Two
Eight Days A Week; Words Of Love; Honey Don't; Every Little Thing; I Don't Want To Spoil The Party; What You're Doing; Everybody's Trying To Be My Baby. [4 December 1964]

PMC 1255 Help!
PCS 3071
Side One
Help!; The Night Before; You've Got To Hide Your Love Away; I Need You; Another Girl; You're Going To Lose That Girl; Ticket To Ride.
Side Two
Act Naturally; It's Only Love; You Like Me Too Much; Tell Me What You See; I've Just Seen A Face; Yesterday; Dizzy Miss Lizzy. [6 August 1965]

PMC 1267 Rubber Soul
PCS 3075
Side One
Drive My Car; Norwegian Wood (This Bird Has Flown); You Won't See Me; Nowhere Man; Think For Yourself; The Word; Michelle.
Side Two
What Goes On; Girl; I'm Looking Through You; In My Life; Wait; If I Needed Someone; Run For Your Life. [3 December 1965]

PMC/PCS 7009 Revolver
Side One
Taxman; Eleanor Rigby; I'm Only Sleeping; Love You To; Here, There And Everywhere; Yellow Submarine; She Said, She Said.
Side Two
Good Day Sunshine; And Your Bird Can Sing; For No One; Dr. Robert; I Want To Tell You; Got To Get You Into My Life; Tomorrow Never Knows. [5 August 1966]

PMC/PCS 7016 A Collection Of Beatles Oldies
Side One
She Loves You; From Me To You; We Can Work It Out; Help!; Michelle; Yesterday; I Feel Fine; Yellow Submarine.

Can't Buy Me Love; Bad Boy; Day Tripper; A Hard Day's Night; Ticket To Ride; Paperback Writer; Eleanor Rigby; I Want To Hold Your Hand. [10 December 1966]

PMC/PCS 7027 Sgt. Pepper's Lonely Hearts Club Band
Side One
Sgt. Pepper's Lonely Hearts Club Band; With A Little Help From My Friends; Lucy In The Sky With Diamonds; Getting Better; Fixing A Hole; She's Leaving Home; Being For The Benefit Of Mr. Kite.
Side Two
Within You, Without You; When I'm Sixty-Four; Lovely Rita; Good Morning, Good Morning; Sgt. Pepper's Lonely Hearts Club Band (Reprise); A Day In The Life. [1 June 1967]

PMC/PCS 7067/8* The Beatles (2 L.P.s)
Side One
Back In The USSR; Dear Prudence; Glass Onion; Ob-La-Di, Ob-La-Da; Wild Honey Pie; The Continuing Story Of Bungalow Bill; While My Guitar Gently Weeps; Happiness Is A Warm Gun.
Side Two
Martha My Dear; I'm So Tired; Blackbird; Piggies; Rocky Racoon; Don't Pass Me By; Why Don't We Do It In The Road?; I Will; Julia.
Side Three
Birthday; Yer Blues; Mother Nature's Son; Everybody's Got Something To Hide Except Me And My Monkey; Sexy Sadie; Helter Skelter; Long, Long, Long.
Side Four
Revolution 1; Honey Pie; Savoy Truffle; Cry Baby Cry; Revolution 9; Goodnight. [22 November 1968]

PMC/PCS 7070* Yellow Submarine
Side One
Yellow Submarine; Only A Northern Song; All Together Now; Hey Bulldog; It's All Too Much; All You Need Is Love.

Side Two
The George Martin Orchestra. [17 January 1969]

PCS 7088* Abbey Road
Side One
Come Together; Something; Maxwell's Silver Hammer; Oh! Darling; Octopus's Garden; I Want You (She's So Heavy)
Side Two
Here Comes The Sun; Because; You Never Give Me Your Money; Sun King; Mean Mr. Mustard; Polythene Pam; She Came In Through The Bathroom Window; Golden Slumbers; Carry That Weight; The End; Her Majesty. [26 September 1969]

PXS 1/PCS 7096* Let It Be
Side One
Two Of Us; Dig A Pony; Across The Universe; I Me Mine; Dig It; Let It Be; Maggie Mae.
Side Two
I've Got A Feeling; One After 909; The Long And Winding Road; For You Blue; Get Back. (PXS 1 includes *Get Back* book.) [8 May/6 November 1970]

PCSP 717* The Beatles 1962–1966 (2 L.P.s)
Side One
Love Me Do; Please Please Me; From Me To You; She Loves You; I Want To Hold Your Hand; All My Loving; Can't Buy Me Love.
Side Two
A Hard Day's Night; And I Love Her; Eight Days A Week; I Feel Fine; Ticket To Ride; Yesterday.
Side Three
Help!; You've Got To Hide Your Love Away; We Can Work It Out; Day Tripper; Drive My Car; Norwegian Wood (This Bird Has Flown).
Side Four
Nowhere Man; Michelle; In My Life; Girl; Paperback Writer; Eleanor Rigby; Yellow Submarine. [20 April 1973]

PCSP 718* The Beatles 1967–1970 (2 L.P.s)
Side One
Strawberry Fields Forever; Penny Lane; Sgt. Pepper's Lonely Hearts Club Band; With A Little Help From My Friends; Lucy In The Sky With Diamonds; A Day In The Life; All You Need Is Love.
Side Two
I Am The Walrus; Hello Goodbye; The Fool On The Hill; Magical Mystery Tour; Lady Madonna; Hey Jude; Revolution.
Side Three
Back In The U.S.S.R.; While My Guitar Gently Weeps; Ob-La-Di, Ob-La-Da; Get Back; Don't Let Me Down; The Ballad Of John And Yoko; Old Brown Shoe.
Side Four
Here Comes The Sun; Come Together; Something; Octopus's Garden; Let It Be; Across The Universe; The Long And Winding Road. [20 April 1973]

PCSP 719 Rock And Roll Music (2 L.P.s)
Side One
Twist And Shout; I Saw Her Standing There; You Can't Do That; I Wanna Be Your Man; I Call Your Name; Boys; Long Tall Sally.
Side Two
Rock And Roll Music; Slow Down; Kansas City/Hey Hey Hey Hey; Money; Bad Boy; Matchbox; Roll Over Beethoven.
Side Three
Dizzy Miss Lizzy; Any Time At All; Drive My Car; Everybody's Trying To Be My Baby; The Night Before; I'm Down; Revolution.
Side Four
Back In The USSR; Helter Skelter; Taxman; Got To Get You Into My Life; Hey Bulldog; Birthday; Get Back. [11 June 1976]

PCTC 255 Magical Mystery Tour
Side One
Magical Mystery Tour; The Fool On The Hill; Flying; Blue Jay Way; Your Mother Should Know; I Am The Walrus.
Side Two
Hello Goodbye; Strawberry Fields Forever; Penny Lane; Baby, You're A Rich Man; All You Need Is Love. [19 November 1976]

EMTV 4 The Beatles At The Hollywood Bowl
Side One
Twist And Shout; She's A Woman; Dizzy Miss Lizzy; Ticket To Ride; Can't Buy Me Love; Things We Said Today; Roll Over Beethoven.
Side Two
Boys; A Hard Day's Night; Help!; All My Loving; She Loves You; Long Tall Sally. [6 May 1977]

PCSP 721 Love Songs (2 L.P.s)
Side One
Yesterday; I'll Follow The Sun; I Need You; Girl; In My Life; Words Of Love; Here, There And Everywhere.
Side Two
Something; And I Love Her; If I Fell; I'll Be Back; Tell Me What You See; Yes It Is.
Side Three
Michelle; It's Only Love; You're Going To Lose That Girl; Every Little Thing; For No One; She's Leaving Home.
Side Four
The Long And Winding Road; This Boy; Norwegian Wood (This Bird Has Flown); You've Got To Hide Your Love Away; I Will; P.S. I Love You. [28 November 1977]

BC 13 The Beatles Collection (13 L.P.s)
Please Please Me; With The Beatles; A Hard Day's Night; Beatles For Sale; Help!; Rubber Soul; Revolver; Sgt. Pepper's Lonely Hearts Club Band; The Beatles; Yellow Submarine; Abbey Road; Let It Be; The Beatles Rarities. [2 November 1978]

PCS 7184 Hey Jude
Side One

Can't Buy Me Love; I Should Have Known Better; Paperback Writer; Rain; Lady Madonna; Revolution.

Side Two

Hey Jude; Old Brown Shoe; Don't Let Me Down; The Ballad Of John And Yoko. [21 May 1979]

PCM 1001 The Beatles Rarities
Side One

Across The Universe; Yes It is; This Boy; The Inner Light; I'll Get You; Thank You Girl; Komm, Gib Mir Deine Hand; You Know My Name (Look Up The Number); Sie Liebt Dich.

Side Two

Rain; She's A Woman; Matchbox; I Call Your Name; Bad Boy; Slow Down; I'm Down; Long Tall Sally. [29 October 1979]

PCS 7214 The Beatles Ballads
Side One

Yesterday; Norwegian Wood (This Bird Has Flown); Do You Want To Know A Secret; For No One; Michelle; Nowhere Man; You've Got To Hide Your Love Away; Across The Universe; All My Loving; Hey Jude.

Side Two

Something; The Fool On The Hill; Till There Was You; The Long And Winding Road; Here Comes The Sun; Blackbird; And I Love Her; She's Leaving Home; Here, There And Everywhere; Let It Be. [20 October 1980]

MFP 50506** Rock And Roll Music Volume 1

Record One of PCSP 719 Rock And Roll Music [27 October 1980]

MFP 50507** Rock And Roll Music Volume 2

Record Two of PCSP 719 Rock And Roll Music [27 October 1980]

SM 701–708 The Beatles Box (8 L.P.s)

SM 701 Record 1
Side One

Love Me Do; P.S. I Love You; I Saw Her Standing There; Please Please Me; Misery; Do You Want To Know A Secret; A Taste Of Honey; Twist And Shout.

Side Two

From Me To You; Thank You Girl; She Loves You; It Won't Be Long; Please Mister Postman; All My Loving; Roll Over Beethoven; Money.

SM 702 Record 2
Side One

I Want To Hold Your Hand; This Boy; Can't Buy Me Love; You Can't Do That; A Hard Day's Night; I Should Have Known Better; If I Fell; And I Love Her.

Side Two

Things We Said Today; I'll Be Back; Long Tall Sally; I Call Your Name; Matchbox; Slow Down; She's A Woman; I Feel Fine.

SM 703 Record 3
Side One

Eight Days A Week; No Reply; I'm A Loser; I'll Follow The Sun; Mr. Moonlight; Every Little Thing; I Don't Want To Spoil The Party; Kansas City/Hey Hey Hey Hey.

Side Two

Ticket To Ride; I'm Down; Help!; The Night Before; You've Got To Hide Your Love Away; I Need You; Another Girl; You're Going To Lose That Girl.

SM 704 Record 4
Side One

Yesterday; Act Naturally; Tell Me What You See; It's Only Love; You Like Me Too Much; I've Just Seen A Face; Day Tripper; We Can Work It Out.

Side Two

Michelle; Drive My Car; Norwegian Wood (This Bird Has

Flown); You Won't See Me;
Nowhere Man; Girl; I'm Looking
Through You; In My Life.

SM 705 Record 5
Side One
Paperback Writer; Rain; Here,
There And Everywhere; Taxman;
I'm Only Sleeping; Good Day
Sunshine; Yellow Submarine.
Side Two
Eleanor Rigby; And Your Bird Can
Sing; For No One; Dr. Robert; Got
To Get You Into My Life; Penny
Lane; Strawberry Fields Forever.

SM 706 Record 6
Side One
Sgt. Pepper's Lonely Hearts Club
Band; With A Little Help From My
Friends; Lucy In The Sky With
Diamonds; Fixing A Hole; She's
Leaving Home; Being For The
Benefit Of Mr. Kite; A Day In The
Life.
Side Two
When I'm Sixty-Four; Lovely Rita;
All You Need Is Love; Baby,
You're A Rich Man; Magical
Mystery Tour; Your Mother Should
Know; The Fool On The Hill; I Am
The Walrus.

SM 707 Record 7
Side One
Hello Goodbye; Lady Madonna;
Hey Jude; Revolution; Back In The
USSR; Ob-La-Di, Ob-La-Da; While
My Guitar Gently Weeps.
Side Two
The Continuing Story Of Bungalow
Bill; Happiness Is A Warm Gun;
Martha My Dear; I'm So Tired;
Piggies; Don't Pass Me By; Julia;
All Together Now.

SM 708 Record 8
Side One
Get Back; Don't Let Me Down; The
Ballad Of John And Yoko; Across
The Universe; For You Blue; Two
Of Us; The Long And Winding
Road; Let It Be.

Side Two
Come Together; Something;
Maxwell's Silver Hammer;
Octopus's Garden; Here Comes
The Sun; Because; Golden
Slumbers; Carry That Weight; The
End; Her Majesty.
[27 October 1980]

PCS 7218 Reel Music
Side One
A Hard Day's Night; I Should Have
Known Better; Can't Buy Me Love;
And I Love Her; Help!; You've Got
To Hide Your Love Away; Ticket
To Ride; Magical Mystery Tour.
Side Two
I Am The Walrus; Yellow
Submarine; All You Need Is Love;
Let It Be; Get Back; The Long And
Winding Road. [12 March 1982]

PCTC 260 20 Greatest Hits
Side One
Love Me Do; From Me To You;
She Loves You; I Want To Hold
Your Hand; Can't Buy Me Love; A
Hard Day's Night; I Feel Fine;
Ticket To Ride; Help!; Day
Tripper; We Can Work It Out.
Side Two
Paperback Writer; Yellow
Submarine; Eleanor Rigby; All You
Need Is Love; Hello Goodbye;
Lady Madonna; Hey Jude; Get
Back; The Ballad Of John And
Yoko. [18 October 1982]

FA 413081*** A Collection Of
Beatles Oldies
As PCS 7016 [31 October 1983]

CAV 1 Tribute To The Cavern
Side One : Various Artists.
Side Two
Love Me Do; I Saw Her Standing
There; Twist And Shout; She Loves
You; Money; I Want To Hold Your
Hand; Can't Buy Me Love; A Hard
Day's Night. [26 April 1984]

MFP 41–5676–1** The Beatles At The Hollywood Bowl
As EMTV 4 [3 September 1984]

SMMC 151 Only The Beatles ...
Side One
Love Me Do; Twist And Shout; She Loves You; This Boy; Eight Days A Week; All My Loving.
Side Two
Ticket To Ride; Yes It Is; Ob-La-Di, Ob-La-Da; Lucy In The Sky With Diamonds; And I Love Her; Strawberry Fields Forever.
(*Cassette Only*) [30 June 1986]

BPM 1 Past Masters — Volumes One and Two (2 L.P.s)
Side One
Love Me Do; From Me To You; Thank You Girl; She Loves You; I'll Get You; I Want To Hold Your Hand; This Boy; Komm, Gib Mir Deine Hand; Sie Liebt Dich.
Side Two
Long Tall Sally; I Call Your Name; Slow Down; Matchbox; I Feel Fine; She's A Woman; Bad Boy; Yes It Is; I'm Down.
Side Three
Day Tripper; We Can Work It Out; Paperback Writer; Rain; Lady Madonna; The Inner Light; Hey Jude; Revolution.
Side Four
Get Back; Don't Let Me Down; The Ballad Of John And Yoko; Old Brown Shoe; Across The Universe; Let It Be; You Know My Name (Look Up The Number).
[10 November 1988]

PARLOPHONE EXPORT RECORDS

Singles

DP 562 If I Fell/Ask Me Why
DP 563 Dizzy Miss Lizzy/Yesterday
DP 564 Michelle/Drive My Car
DP 570 Hey Jude/Revolution
BCSP 1 The Beatles' Singles
Collection
As BCS 1 but also includes Love
Me Do picture disc.

Long Play

CPCS 101 Something New
Side One
Cry Instead; Things We Said
Today; Any Time At All; When I
Get Home; Slow Down; Matchbox.
Side Two
Tell Me Why; And I Love Her; I'm
Happy Just To Dance With You; If I
Fell; Komm, Gib Mir Deine Hand.

CPCS 103 The Beatles' Second Album
Side One
Roll Over Beethoven; Thank You
Girl; You Really Got A Hold On
Me; Devil In Her Heart; Money;
You Can't Do that.
Side Two
Long Tall Sally; I Call Your Name;
Please Mister Postman; I'll Get
You; She Loves You.

CPCS 104 The Beatles VI
Side One
Kansas City/Hey Hey Hey Hey;
Eight Days A Week; You Like Me
Too Much; Bad Boy; I Don't Want
To Spoil The Party; Words Of
Love.
Side Two
What You're Doing; Yes It Is; Dizzy
Miss Lizzy; Tell Me What You See;
Every Little Thing.

CPCS 106 Hey Jude
As PCS 7184 but with Apple label
instead of Parlophone label.

PCS 7067–8 The Beatles (2 L.P.s)
As normal PCS 7067–8 release but
with Parlophone label instead of
Apple label.

NON-BEATLES RECORDS
(Containing Lennon–McCartney songs)

UP 1165†† Love In The Open Air/
Theme From The Family Way
The George Martin Orchestra [23
December 1966]

4* Thingumybob/
Yellow Submarine
John Fosters and Sons Ltd. Black
Dyke Mills Band [6 September
1968]

10* Goodbye/
(Sparrow)
Mary Hopkin [28 March 1969]

13* Give Peace A Chance/
(Remember Love)
The Plastic Ono Band [4 July 1969]

1001* Cold Turkey/
(Don't Worry Kyoko)
The Plastic Ono Bank [24 October
1969]

20* Come And Get It/
(Rock Of All Ages)
Badfinger [5 December 1969]

**NUT 18 The Songs Lennon And
McCartney Gave Away**
Side One
I'm The Greatest (Ringo Starr);
One And One Is Two (The
Strangers with Mike Shannon);
From A Window (Billy J. Kramer
and The Dakotas); Nobody I Know
(Peter and Gordon); Like
Dreamers Do (The Applejacks);
I'll Keep You Satisfied (Billy J.
Kramer and The Dakotas); Love Of
The Loved (Cilla Black); Woman
(Peter and Gordon); Tip Of My
Tongue (Tommy Quickly); I'm In
Love (The Fourmost).

Side Two

Hello Little Girl (The Fourmost);
That Means A Lot (P.J. Proby); It's
For You (Cilla Black); Penina
(Carlos Mendes); Step Inside Love
(Cilla Black); World Without Love
(Peter and Gordon); Bad To Me
(Billy J. Kramer and The Dakotas);
I Don't Want To See You Again
(Peter and Gordon); I'll Be On My
Way (Billy J. Kramer and The
Dakotas); Catcall (The Chris
Barber Band). [9 April 1979]

The Hamburg, Decca and Star Club Tapes

The records listed on this and the following page are only a selection of the ever-growing number of releases of the Hamburg, Decca and Star Club Tapes and is not meant as a full discography of these recordings. To list every single release would, in the main, only lead to confusion.

Because these recordings appear to be available to anyone who cares to set up a record label, releases in the future will no doubt become as prolific and diverse as the innumerable record companies who release them.

The Hamburg Tapes

POLYDOR RECORDS

Singles

NH 66–833 My Bonnie/
The Saints [5 January 1962]
NH 52–906 Sweet Georgia Brown/
Nobody's Child [31 January 1964]
NH 52–275 Why/
Cry For A Shadow [28 February 1964]
NH 52–317 Ain't She Sweet/
Take Out Some Insurance On Me, Baby [29 May 1964]

Extended Play

H 21–610 My Bonnie
My Bonnie; Why; Cry For A Shadow; The Saints. [12 July 1963]

Long Play

236–201 The Beatles First
Side One
Ain't She Sweet; Cry For A Shadow; (Let's Dance); My Bonnie; Take Out Some Insurance On Me, Baby; (What'd I Say).
Side Two
Sweet Georgia Brown; The Saints; (Ruby Baby); Why; Nobody's Child; (Ya Ya). [19 June 1964]

Titles in parentheses performed by Tony Sheridan and The Beat Brothers. All other songs performed by either the Beatles or the Beatles with Tony Sheridan.

The Decca Tapes

AFE RECORDS

Singles

AFS 1 Searchin'/Money/Till There Was You [8 October 1982]

Long Play

AFELP 1047 The Complete Silver Beatles
Side One
Three Cool Cats; Crying, Waiting, Hoping; Besame Mucho; Searchin'; The Sheik Of Araby; Money.
Side Two
To Know Her Is To Love Her; Take Good Care Of My Baby; Memphis, Tennessee; Sure To Fall (In Love With You); Till There Was You; September In The Rain.
[10 September 1982]

TOPLINE RECORDS

Long Play

TOP 181 The Decca Sessions 1.1.62
Side One
Three Cool Cats; Memphis, Tennessee; Besame Mucho; The Sheik Of Araby; Till There Was You; Searchin'.

Side Two
Sure To Fall (In Love With You); Take Good Care Of My Baby; Money; To Know Her Is To Love Her; September In The Rain; Crying, Waiting, Hoping. [19 October 1987]

The Star Club Tapes

LINGASONG RECORDS

Singles

NB 1 Falling In Love Again/ Twist And Shout [25 May 1977]

Long Play

LNL 1 The Beatles Live! At The Star Club In Hamburg, Germany; 1962. (2 L.P.s)
Side One
I Saw Her Standing There; Roll Over Beethoven; Hippy Hippy Shake; Sweet Little Sixteen; Lend Me Your Comb; Your Feets Too Big.
Side Two
Twist And Shout; Mr. Moonlight; A Taste Of Honey; Besame Mucho; Reminiscing; Kansas City/Hey, Hey, Hey, Hey.
Side Three
Nothin' Shakin' (But The Leaves On The Trees); To Know Her Is To Love Her; Little Queenie; Falling In Love Again; Ask Me Why; Be Bop A Lula; Hallelujah, I Love Her So.
Side Four
Red Sails In The Sunset; Everybody's Trying To Be My Baby; Matchbox; (I'm) Talking About You; Shimmy Shake; Long Tall Sally; I Remember You. [25 May 1977]

AFE RECORDS

Long Play

AFELD 1018 Historic Sessions (2 L.P.s)
Side One
I'm Gonna Sit Right Down And Cry (Over You); I Saw Her Standing There; Roll Over Beethoven; Hippy Hippy Shake; Sweet Little Sixteen; Lend Me Your Comb; Your Feets Too Big.
Side Two
Twist And Shout; Mr. Moonlight; A Taste Of Honey; Besame Mucho; Reminiscing; Kansas City/Hey Hey Hey Hey; Where Have You Been All My Life.
Side Three
Till There Was You; Nothin' Shakin' (But The Leaves On The Trees); To Know Her Is To Love Her; Little Queenie; Falling In Love Again; Ask Me Why; Be Bop A Lula; Hallelujah, I Love Her So.
Side Four
Sheila; Red Sails In The Sunset; Everybody's Trying To Be My Baby; Matchbox; (I'm) Talking About You; Shimmy Shake; Long Tall Sally; I Remember You. [25 September 1981]

American Releases

CAPITOL/CAPITOL STARLINE†
UNITED ARTISTS††/APPLE*

Singles

5112 I Want To Hold Your Hand/
I Saw Her Standing There
[13 January 1964]
5150 Can't Buy Me Love/
You Can't Do That [16 March 1964]
5222 A Hard Day's Night/
I Should Have Known Better
[13 July 1964]
5234 I'll Cry Instead/
I'm Happy Just To Dance With You
[20 July 1964]
5235 And I Love Her/
If I Fell [20 July 1964]
5255 Matchbox/
Slow Down [24 August 1964]
5327 I Feel Fine/
She's A Woman
[23 November 1964]
5371 Eight Days A Week/
I Don't Want To Spoil The Party
[15 February 1965]
5407 Ticket To Ride/
Yes It Is [19 April 1964]
5476 Help/
I'm Down [19 July 1965]
5498 Yesterday/
Act Naturally [13 September 1965]
6061† Twist And Shout/
There's A Place [11 October 1965]
6062† Love Me Do/
P.S. I Love You [11 October 1965]
6063 Please Please Me/
From Me To You [11 October 1965]
6064† Do You Want To Know A
Secret/
Thank You Girl [11 October 1965]
6065† Roll Over Beethoven/
Misery [11 October 1965]
6066† Boys/
Kansas City/Hey Hey Hey Hey
[11 October 1965]
5555 We Can Work It Out/
Day Tripper [6 December 1965]
5587 Nowhere Man/
What Goes On [21 February 1966]

5651 Paperback Writer/
Rain [30 May 1966]
5715 Yellow Submarine/
Eleanor Rigby [8 August 1966]
5810 Penny Lane/
Strawberry Fields Forever
[13 February 1967]
5964 All You Need Is Love/
Baby, You're A Rich Man
[17 July 1967]
2056 Hello Goodbye/
I Am The Walrus
[27 November 1967]
2138 Lady Madonna/
The Inner Light [18 March 1968]
2276* Hey Jude/
Revolution [26 August 1968]
2490* Get Back/
Don't Let Me Down [5 May 1969]
2531* The Ballad Of John And Yoko/
Old Brown Shoe [4 June 1969]
2654* Something/
Come Together [6 October 1969]
2764* Let It Be/
You Know My Name (Look Up The
Number) [11 March 1970]
2837* The Long And Winding Road/
For You Blue [11 May 1970]
4274 Got To Get You Into My Life/
Helter Skelter [31 May 1976]
4347 Ob-La-Di, Ob-La-Da/
Julia [8 November 1976]
4612 Sgt. Pepper's Lonely Hearts
Club Band/With A Little Help From
My Friends/A Day In The Life
[28 August 1978]
B5107 The Beatles' Movie Medley/
I'm Happy Just To Dance With You
[30 March 1982]
B5189 Love Me Do/
P.S. I Love You
[12 November 1982]

Extended Play

EAP 2121 Four By The Beatles
Roll Over Beethoven; All My Loving; This Boy; Please Mister Postman. [11 May 1964]

R5365 By The Beatles
Honey Don't; I'm A Loser; Mr. Moonlight; Everybody's Trying To Be My Baby. [1 February 1965]

Long Play

ST 2047 Meet The Beatles
Side One
I Want To Hold Your Hand; I Saw Her Standing There; This Boy; It Won't Be Long; All I've Got To Do; All My Loving.
Side Two
Don't Bother Me; Little Child; Till There Was You; Hold Me Tight; I Wanna Be Your Man; Not A Second Time. [20 January 1964]

ST 2080 The Beatles' Second Album
Side One
Roll Over Beethoven; Thank You Girl; You Really Got A Hold On Me; Devil In Her Heart; Money; You Can't Do That.
Side Two
Long Tall Sally; I Call Your Name; Please Mister Postman; I'll Get You; She Loves You.
[10 April 1964]

UAS 6366†† A Hard Day's Night
Side One
A Hard Day's Night; Tell Me Why; I'll Cry Instead; (I Should Have Known Better); I'm Happy Just To Dance With You; (And I Love Her).
Side Two
I Should Have Known Better; If I Fell; And I Love Her; (Ringo's Theme — This Boy); Can't Buy Me Love; (A Hard Day's Night).
[26 June 1964]

Titles in parentheses performed by The George Martin Orchestra.

ST 2018 Something New
Side One
I'll Cry Instead; Things We Said Today; Any Time At All; When I Get Home; Slow Down; Matchbox.
Side Two
Tell Me Why; And I Love Her; I'm Happy Just To Dance With You; If I Fell; Komm, Gib Mir Deine Hand.
[20 July 1964]

STBO 2222 The Beatles' Story (2 L.P.s)
Side One
On Stage With The Beatles; How Beatlemania Began; Beatlemania In Action; Man Behind The Beatles — Brian Epstein; John Lennon; Who's A Millionaire?
Side Two
Beatles Will Be Beatles; Man Behind The Music — George Martin; George Harrison.
Side Three
A Hard Day's Night — Their First Movie; Paul McCartney; Sneaky Haircuts And More About Paul.
Side Four
The Beatles Look At Life : 'Victims' Of Beatlemania; Beatle Medley; Ringo Starr; Liverpool And All The World! [23 November 1964]

ST 2228 Beatles 65
Side One
No Reply; I'm A Loser; Baby's In Black; Rock And Roll Music; I'll Follow The Sun; Mr. Moonlight.
Side Two
Honey Don't; I'll Be Back; She's A Woman; I Feel Fine; Everybody's Trying To Be My Baby.
[15 December 1964]

ST 2309 The Early Beatles
Side One
Love Me Do; Twist And Shout; Anna (Go To Him); Chains; Boys; Ask Me Why.
Side Two
Please Please Me; P.S. I Love You; Baby It's You; A Taste Of Honey; Do You Want To Know A Secret.
[22 March 1965]

ST 2358 Beatles VI
Side One
Kansas City/Hey Hey Hey Hey; Eight Days A Week; You Like Me Too Much; Bad Boy; I Don't Want To Spoil The Party; Words Of Love.
Side Two
What You're Doing; Yes It Is; Dizzy Miss Lizzy; Tell Me What You See; Every Little Thing. [14 June 1965]

SMAS 2386 Help!
Side One
(The James Bond Theme); Help!; The Night Before; (From Me To You Fantasy); You've Got To Hide Your Love Away; I Need You; (In The Tyrol).
Side Two
Another Girl; (Another Hard Day's Night); Ticket To Ride; (The Bitter End/You Can't Do That); You're Going To Lose That Girl; (The Chase). [13 August 1965]

Titles in parentheses performed by The George Martin Orchestra.

ST 2442 Rubber Soul
Side One
I've Just Seen A Face; Norwegian Wood (This Bird Has Flown); You Won't See Me; Think For Yourself; The Word; Michelle.
Side Two
It's Only Love; Girl; I'm Looking Through You; In My Life; Wait; Run For Your Life. [6 December 1966]

ST 2553 Yesterday ... And Today
Side One
Drive My Car; I'm Only Sleeping; Nowhere Man; Dr. Robert; Yesterday; Act Naturally.
Side Two
And Your Bird Can Sing; If I Needed Someone; We Can Work It Out; What Goes On; Day Tripper. [20 June 1965]

ST 2576 Revolver
Side One
Taxman; Eleanor Rigby; Love You To; Here, There and Everywhere; Yellow Submarine; She Said, She Said.
Side Two
Good Day Sunshine; For No One; I Want To Tell You; Got To Get You Into My Life; Tomorrow Never Knows. [5 August 1966]

SMAS 2653 Sgt. Pepper's Lonely Hearts Club Band
As British album [2 June 1967]

SMAL 2835 Magical Mystery Tour
As British album
[27 November 1967]

SWBO 101* The Beatles (2 L.P.s)
As British album
[25 November 1968]

SW 153* Yellow Submarine
As British album [13 January 1969]

SO 383* Abbey Road
As British album
[26 September 1969]

SW 385* Hey Jude
As British album
[26 February 1970]

AR 34001* Let It Be
As British album [18 May 1970]

SKBO 3403* The Beatles 1962–1966 (2 L.P.s)
As British album [2 April 1973]

SKBO 3404* The Beatles 1967–1970 (2 L.P.s)
As British album [2 April 1973]

SKBO 11537 Rock And Roll Music (2 L.P.s)
As British album [7 June 1976]

SMAS 11638 The Beatles At The Hollywood Bowl
As British album [2 May 1977]

SKBL 11711 Love Songs (2 L.P.s)
As British album [24 November 1977]

SW 11922 Let It Be
Reissue of AR 34001 [12 March 1979]

SHAL 12060 Rarities
Side One
Love Me Do; Misery; There's A Place; Sie Liebt Dich; And I Love Her; Help!; I'm Only Sleeping; I Am The Walrus.
Side Two
Penny Lane; Helter Skelter; Don't Pass Me By; The Inner Light; Across The Universe; You Know My Name (Look Up The Number); Sgt. Pepper Inner Groove.
[24 March 1980]

SN 16020 Rock And Roll Music — Volume 1
As British album [27 October 1980]

SN 16021 Rock And Roll Music — Volume 2
As British album [27 October 1980]

SW 11921 A Hard Day's Night
Reissue of UAS 6366
[17 August 1981]

SV 12199 Reel Music
As British album [12 March 1982]

SV 12245 20 Greatest Hits
Side One
She Loves You; Love Me Do; I Want To Hold Your Hand; Can't Buy Me Love; A Hard Day's Night; I Feel Fine; Eight Days A Week; Ticket To Ride; Help!; Yesterday; We Can Work It Out; Paperback Writer.

Side Two
Penny Lane; All You Need Is Love; Hello Goodbye; Hey Jude; Get Back; Come Together; Let It Be; The Long And Winding Road.
[18 October 1982]

CLJ 46435 Please Please Me
As British album [February 1987]

CLJ 46436 With The Beatles
As British album [February 1987]

CLJ 46437 A Hard Day's Night
As British album [February 1987]

CLJ 46438 Beatles For Sale
As British album [February 1987]

CLJ 46439 Help!
As British album [April 1987]

CLJ 46440 Rubber Soul
As British album [April 1987]

CLJ 46441 Revolver
As British album [April 1987]

SV C12P 90043 Past Masters — Volumes One and Two (2 L.P.s)
As British album [24 October 1988]

Prior to release by Capitol Records, some early Beatles EMI recordings were issued by the following labels:

VEEJAY RECORDS

Singles

VJ 498 Please Please Me/
    Ask Me Why [25 February 1963]
VJ 522 From Me To You/Thank You
    Girl [27 May 1963]
VJ 581 Please Please Me/
    From Me To You [30 January 1964]
VJ 587 Do You Want To Know A
Secret?/
    Thank You Girl [23 March 1964]

Extended Play

VJEP 1–903 The Beatles
    Misery; A Taste Of Honey; Ask Me
    Why; Anna (Go To Him).
    [23 March 1964]

Long Play

VJLP 1062 Introducing The Beatles
Side One
    I Saw Her Standing There; Misery;
    Anna (Go To Him); Chains; Boys;
    Love Me Do.
Side Two
    P.S. I Love You; Baby It's You; Do
    You Want To Know A Secret; A
    Taste Of Honey; There's A Place;
    Twist And Shout. [22 July 1963]

VJLP 1062 Introducing The Beatles
Side One
    I Saw Her Standing There; Misery;
    Anna (Go To Him); Chains; Boys;
    Ask Me Why.
Side Two
    Please Please Me; Baby It's You;
    Do You Want To Know A Secret; A
    Taste Of Honey; There's A Place;
    Twist And Shout. [27 January 1964]

SWAN RECORDS

Singles

4152 She Loves You/
    I'll Get You [16 September 1963]
4182 Sie Liebt Dich/
    I'll Get You [21 May 1964]

TOLLIE RECORDS

Singles

9001 Twist And Shout/
    There's A Place [2 March 1964]
9008 Love Me Do/
    P.S. I Love You [27 April 1964]

The Hamburg, Decca and Star Club Tapes

The records listed on this page are only a selection of the ever-growing number of releases of The Hamburg, Decca and Star Club Tapes and is not meant as a full discography of these recordings. To list every single release would, in the main, only lead to confusion.

Because these recordings appear to be available to anyone who cares to set up a record label, releases in the future will no doubt become as prolific and diverse as the innumerable record companies who release them.

The Hamburg Tapes

DECCA RECORDS

Singles

31382 My Bonnie/
   The Saints [23 April 1962]

MGM RECORDS

Singles

K13213 My Bonnie/
   The Saints [27 January 1964]
K13227 Why/
   Cry For A Shadow [27 March 1964]

ATCO RECORDS

Singles

6302 Sweet Georgia Brown/
   Take Out Some Insurance On Me,
   Baby [1 June 1964]
6308 Ain't She Sweet/
   Nobody's Child [6 July 1964]

POLYDOR RECORDS

Long Play

24–4504 The Beatles — Circa 1960 — In The Beginning
Side One
   Ain't She Sweet; Cry For A
   Shadow; (Let's Dance); My Bonnie;
   Take Out Some Insurance On Me,
   Baby; (What'd I Say).
Side Two
   Sweet Georgia Brown; The Saints;
   (Ruby Baby); Why; Nobody's
   Child; Ya Ya. [4 May 1970]

Titles in parentheses performed by Tony Sheridan and The Beat Brothers. All other songs performed by either the Beatles or the Beatles with Tony Sheridan.

The Decca Tapes

AFE RECORDS

Long Play

AR 2452 The Complete Silver Beatles
Side One
Three Cool Cats; Crying, Waiting, Hoping; Besame Mucho; Searchin'; The Sheik Of Araby; Money.

Side Two
To Know Her Is To Love Her; Take Good Care Of My Baby; Memphis, Tennessee; Sure To Fall (In Love With You); Till There Was You; September In The Rain. [10 September 1982]

The Star Club Tapes

LINGASONG RECORDS

Long Play

LS–2–7001 The Beatles Live! At The Star Club, Hamburg, Germany; 1962 (2 L.P.s)
Side One
I'm Gonna Sit Right Down And Cry (Over You); Roll Over Beethoven; Hippy Hippy Shake; Sweet Little Sixteen; Lend Me Your Comb; Your Feets Too Big.

Side Two
Where Have You Been All My Life; Mr. Moonlight; A Taste Of Honey; Besame Mucho; Till There Was You; Kansas City/Hey Hey Hey Hey.

Side Three
Hallelujah, I Love Her So; Nothin' Shakin' (But The Leaves On The Trees); To Know Her Is To Love Her; Little Queenie; Falling In Love Again; Be Bop A Lula.

Side Four
Red Sails In The Sunset; Everybody's Trying To Be My Baby; Matchbox; (I'm) Talking About You; Shimmy Shake; Long Tall Sally; I Remember You. [28 June 1977]

Australian Releases

PARLOPHONE/APPLE*   AXIS†

Singles

A8080 Please Please Me/
Ask Me Why [21 February 1963]
A8083 From Me To You/
Thank You Girl [9 May 1963]
A8093 She Loves You/
I'll Get You [29 August 1963]
A8103 I Want To Hold Your Hand/
This Boy [12 December 1963]
A8105 Love Me Do/
I Saw Her Standing There [16
January 1964]
A8107 Roll Over Beethoven/
Hold Me Tight [5 March 1964]
A8113 Can't Buy Me Love/
You Can't Do That [30 April 1964]
A8117 Komm, Gib Mir Deine Hand/
Sie Liebt Dich [25 June 1964]
A8123 A Hard Day's Night/
Things We Said Today [10 July 1964]
A8125 I Should Have Known Better/If
I Fell [20 August 1964]
A8133 I Feel Fine/
She's A Woman [27 November
1964]
A8143 Rock And Roll Music/
Honey Don't [11 March 1965]
A8153 Ticket To Ride/
Yes It Is [15 April 1965]
A8163 Help!/
I'm Down [23 July 1965]
A8173 Yesterday/
Act Naturally [14 October 1965]
A8183 We Can Work It Out/
Day Tripper [9 December 1965]
A8193 Nowhere Man/
Norwegian Wood (This Bird Has
Flown) [24 March 1966]
A8203 Paperback Writer/
Rain [16 June 1966]
A8213 Yellow Submarine/
Eleanor Rigby [25 August 1966]
A8243 Penny Lane/
Strawberry Fields Forever [16
March 1967]
A8263 All You Need Is Love/
Baby, You're A Rich Man [13 July
1967]

A8273 Hello Goodbye/
I Am The Walrus [7 December
1967]
A8293 Lady Madonna/
The Inner Light [29 March 1968]
A8493* Hey Jude/
Revolution [20 September 1968]
A8693* Ob-La-Di, Ob-La-Da/
While My Guitar Gently Weeps [20
February 1969]
A8763* Get Back/Don't Let Me Down
[9 May 1969]
A8793* The Ballad Of John And Yoko/
Old Brown Shoe [19 June 1969]
A8943* Something/
Come Together [19 October 1969]
A9083* Let It Be/
You Know My Name (Look Up The
Number) [13 March 1970]
A9163* The Long And Winding
Road/
For You Blue [11 June 1970]
A11115 Yesterday/
I Should Have Known Better [31
May 1976]
A11182 Got To Get You Into My Life/
Helter Skelter [July 1976]
A12000 Sgt. Pepper's Lonely Hearts
Club Band/With A Little Help From
My Friends/A Day In The Life [28
August 1978]
A689 The Beatles' Movie Medley/
I'm Happy Just To Dance With You
[8 April 1982]
AB34 The Beatles Singles Collection
A boxed set containing the above
34 singles. [October 1982]
ED48 Love Me Do/P.S. I Love You/
Love Me Do (*12-inch single*) [July
1983]

Extended Play

GEPO 8882 Twist And Shout
Twist And Shout; A Taste Of

Honey; Do You Want To Know A Secret; There's A Place. [28 September 1963]

GEPO 8880 The Beatles Hits
From Me To You; Thank You Girl; Please Please Me; Love Me Do. [6 February 1964]

GEPO 8883 The Beatles No. 1
I Saw Her Standing There; Misery; Anna (Go To Him); Chains. [19 March 1964]

GEPO 8891 All My Loving
All My Loving; Ask Me Why; Money; P.S. I Love You. [April 1964]

GEPO 70013 Requests
Long Tall Sally; I Call Your Name; Please Mister Postman; Boys. [18 June 1964]

GEPO 70014 More Requests
Slow Down; Matchbox; Till There Was You; I Wanna Be Your Man. [20 August 1964]

GEPO 70015 Further Requests
She Loves You; I Want To Hold Your Hand; Roll Over Beethoven; Can't Buy Me Love. [19 November 1964]

GEPO 8920 Extracts From The Film A Hard Day's Night
I Should Have Known Better; If I Fell; Tell Me Why; And I Love Her. [10 December 1964]

GEPO 70016 With The Beatles
Devil In Her Heart; Not A Second Time; It Won't Be Long; Don't Bother Me. [4 February 1965]

GEPO 8924 Extracts From The Album A Hard Day's Night
Any Time At All; I'll Cry Instead; Things We Said Today; When I Get Home. [4 March 1965]

GEPO 70019 Beatles For Sale
No Reply; I'm A Loser; Words Of Love; Eight Days A Week. [24 June 1965]

GEPO 70020 Beatles For Sale No. 2
I'll Follow The Sun; Baby's In Black; Kansas City/Hey Hey Hey Hey; I Don't Want To Spoil The Party. [2 September 1965]

GEPO 70026 Yesterday
Yesterday; It's Only Love; You Like Me Too Much; Dizzy Miss Lizzy. [5 May 1966]

GEPO 8952 Nowhere Man
Nowhere Man; Drive My Car; Michelle; You Won't See Me. [3 November 1966]

GEPO 70043 Help!
Help!; She's A Woman; Ticket To Ride; I Feel Fine. [16 November 1967]

GEPO 70044 Norwegian Wood
Paperback Writer; We Can Work It Out; Day Tripper; Norwegian Wood (This Bird Has Flown). [8 February 1968]

MMT/SMMT 1 Magical Mystery Tour
Magical Mystery Tour; Your Mother Should Know; I Am The Walrus; The Fool On The Hill; Flying; Blue Jay Way. [14 March 1968]

GEPO 70045 Penny Lane
Penny Lane; Eleanor Rigby; Strawberry Fields Forever; Yellow Submarine. [4 July 1968]

BEP 14 The Beatles E.P.s Collection
This 14-E.P. set contains all of the 13 E.P.s as originally issued in Britain, plus a free bonus E.P. which is only available as part of this collection. That E.P. is:
SGE 1 The Beatles
The Inner Light; Baby, You're A

Rich Man; She's A Woman; This Boy. [April 1982]

Long Play

PMCO 1202 Please Please Me
PCSO 3042
As British album [9 April 1963]

PMCO 1206 With The Beatles
PCSO 3405
As British album [13 April 1964]

PMCO 1230 A Hard Day's Night
PCSO 3058
As British album [3 September 1964]

PMCO 1240 Beatles For Sale
PCSO 3062
As British album [11 February 1965]

PMCO 1255 Help!
PCSO 3071
As British album [30 September 1965]

PMCO 1267 Rubber Soul
PCSO 3075
As British album [17 February 1966]

PMCO/PCSO 7533 The Beatles Greatest Hits — Volume 1
Side One
Please Please Me; From Me To You; She Loves You; I'll Get You; I Want To Hold Your Hand; Love Me Do; I Saw Her Standing There.
Side Two
Twist And Shout; Roll Over Beethoven; All My Loving; Hold Me Tight; Can't Buy Me Love; You Can't Do That; Long Tall Sally. [11 August 1966]

PMCO/PCSO 7009 Revolver
As British album [29 September 1966]

PMCO/PCSO 7534 The Beatles Greatest Hits — Volume 2
Side One
A Hard Day's Night; Boys; I Should Have Known Better; I Feel Fine; She's A Woman; Till There Was You; Rock And Roll Music.
Side Two
Anna (Go To Him); Ticket To Ride; Eight Days A Week; Help!; Yesterday; We Can Work It Out; Day Tripper. [16 February 1967]

PMCO/PCSO Sgt. Pepper's Lonely Hearts Club Band
As British album [28 July 1967]

PMCO/PCSO 7016 A Collection Of Beatles Oldies
As British album [16 May 1968]

PMCO/PCSO 7067–8* The Beatles (2 L.P.s)
As British album [4 December 1968]

PMCO/PCSO 7070* Yellow Submarine
As British album [23 January 1969]

PCSO 7088 Abbey Road
As British album [17 October 1969]

PCSO 7560 Hey Jude
As British album [23 March 1970]

PXS 1 Let It Be
Includes *Get Back* book. As British album [1 June 1970]

PCSO 7076 Let It Be
Minus *Get Back* book. As British album [December 1970]

TVSS 8 The Essential Beatles
Side One
Love Me Do; Boys; Long Tall Sally; Honey Don't; P.S. I Love You; Baby, You're A Rich Man; All My Loving; Yesterday; Penny Lane.
Side Two
Magical Mystery Tour; Norwegian Wood (This Bird Has Flown); With A Little Help From My Friends; All

You Need Is Love; Something; Ob-
La-Di, Ob-La-Da; Let It Be. [2
February 1972]

**PCSO 7171–8 The Beatles 1962–1966
(2 L.P.s)**
As British album [5 July 1973]

**PCSO 7181–2 The Beatles 1967–1970
(2 L.P.s)**
As British album [5 July 1973]

**PCSP 719 Rock And Roll Music
(2 L.P.s)**
As British album [15 June 1976]

**PCSO 7577 The Beatles At The
Hollywood Bowl**
As British album [5 May 1977]

PCSO 7580 Love Songs (2 L.P.s)
As British album [21 November
1977]

BC 13 The Beatles Collection (13 L.P.s)
As British album [29 November
1978]

PCSO 3077 Magical Mystery Tour
As British album [16 July 1979]

PCSO 7581 Rarities
As American album [19 May 1980]

PCMO 1001 The Beatles Rarities
As British album [December 1980]

R 91103–10 The Beatles Box (8 L.P.s)
As British album [March 1981]

PLAY 1005 The Beatles Ballads
As British album [3 April 1981]

PCSO 7584 A Hard Day's Night
As American album [July 1981]

**AXIS 6439† Rock And Roll Music
Volume 1**
As British album [10 August 1981]

**AXIS 6440† Rock And Roll Music
Volume 2**
As British album [10 August 1981]

PCSO 7218 Reel Music
As British album [May 1982]

PLAY 1024 The Number Ones
As British 20 Greatest Hits album
but also includes the following
three-track single:
A980 Love Me Do/I Feel Fine/
Rock And Roll Music [May 1983]

**BPM 1 Past Masters — Volumes
One and Two (2 L.P.s)**
As British album [24 October 1988]

INDEX

INDEX

This index of song and album titles indicates the main text listing and descriptions of songs and single records and/or as individual tracks on albums, with secondary references chiefly to descriptions of alternative recorded versions. Albums are identified by (LP) and are listed according to their main entries within the text.

All the known unreleased tracks are listed in alphabetical order on pages 262–270.

(Throughout, indexing of the definite and indefinite articles as the first word of a title has been avoided.)

308